The
Upside *of*
Uncertainty

The Upside *of* Uncertainty

A Guide to Finding Possibility in the Unknown

NATHAN FURR

SUSANNAH HARMON FURR

HARVARD BUSINESS REVIEW PRESS
BOSTON, MASSACHUSETTS

Printed in the United States of America

10 9 8 7 6 5 4 3 2 1

The web addresses referenced in this book were live and correct at the time of the book's publication but may be subject to change.

Library of Congress Cataloging-in-Publication Data

Names: Furr, Nathan R., author. | Furr, Susannah Harmon, author.
   Title: The upside of uncertainty : a guide to finding possibility in the
     unknown / Nathan Furr and Susannah Harmon Furr.
   Description: Boston, Massachusetts : Harvard Business School Publishing
     Corporation, [2022] | Includes index.
   Identifiers: LCCN 2021058565 (print) | LCCN 2021058566 (ebook) |
     ISBN 9781647823016 (hardcover) | ISBN 9781647823023 (epub)
   Subjects: LCSH: Uncertainty—Handbooks, manuals, etc. |
     Opportunity—Handbooks, manuals, etc. | Economics—Psychological
     aspects—Handbooks, manuals, etc. | Success in business—Handbooks,
     manuals, etc.
   Classification: LCC HB615 .F867 2022 (print) | LCC HB615 (ebook) |
     DDC 338/.04—dc23/eng/20220202
   LC record available at https://lccn.loc.gov/2021058565
   LC ebook record available at https://lccn.loc.gov/2021058566

ISBN: 978-1-64782-301-6
eISBN: 978-1-64782-302-3

The paper used in this publication meets the requirements of the American National Standard for Permanence of Paper for Publications and Documents in Libraries and Archives Z39.48-1992.

For all those who have inspired us

on our journey to the upside of uncertainty.

And for you reading this now.

Contents

Section Three
Do

Section Four
Sustain

What Is the Upside of Uncertainty?

Thank you for being curious about the upside of uncertainty. It's truly the first step to navigating the unknown well, so you're already on your way! Did you know that the neurotransmitter for curiosity is dopamine? Our brains are instinctively wired so that if we stay curious, we will keep learning and growing.

This book is the product of an intense shared curiosity about uncertainty and possibility, one that started thirty years ago when the two of us met as university freshman. Both researchers, writers, and entrepreneurs but in vastly different fields (Nathan—technology, strategy, fiction; Susannah—art history, fashion, mindfulness), we have built a life together that's fueled by a fascination with and belief in the human ability for *transilience*. From the Latin root for "leap across," it's an old word worth reviving, which means to abruptly change something from one state to another. Every brilliant insight, choice, act, and innovation comes only after a phase of uncertainty. And the uncertainty brought about by every mistake, setback, discouragement, and even disaster carries possibility within it.

Our first joint research and writing project, as nineteen-year-old students, was about zombies: brain-dead creatures being led around by hunger. This one is about the exact opposite: fully awake and conscious individuals taking responsibility for the possibility in their lives. Whether you are a manager or a creator, a team member or a team leader, a parent or a partner, leading a company or just getting started in your education or career, uncertainty is an unavoidable part of being human. But because uncertainty's downsides can be so intense, they often disguise or temporarily obstruct our view of what's possible. This book is about the upside of uncertainty—believing, finding, and living into the opportunity that attends every unknown.

We all come from different perspectives and circumstances. Some of us may have resources or situations that allow for bold choices and others do not; in addition, too many people suffer from very real unfairness and injustice in their daily lives. It is our hope that together with service-minded leaders, courageous individuals can work to eradicate unfairness and inequality, creating a growing tide of possibility for others. But in every situation and circumstance, when we believe in the upside of uncertainty, we increase our chances of finding it.

The Upside of Uncertainty offers a hopeful framework for making the leap across uncertainty even in the face of limitation and constraint. It's filled with tools and personal applications based on interviews, research, and personal experience, all aimed at helping you start moving now. We invite you to hold tight to your curiosity and dig right in.

Unlocking the Upside of Uncertainty

"We're always living in a state of uncertainty—two years ago, two years from now—therefore, part of our challenge as I see it is to make uncertainty . . . our home. This is where we're living, every day of our lives. . . . Let's rejoice in it, furnish it, close the door, rearrange the books, and say, Make this as beautiful as it can, given that forest fire, earthquake, or who knows what will be coming tomorrow—or tremendous beauty and love may be coming in the door tomorrow."

—Pico Iyer

Recall for a moment any big change you've experienced in your life, perhaps a new work project, career, geography, or relationship. What made it hard? What held you back? What tempted you not to make the change? The answer is *uncertainty*. Now consider that everything you really care about in your life came only after a period of uncertainty. Even now, behind every uncertainty you are facing—even the unwanted and unpromising varieties—insight, growth, and possibility are waiting in the wings. We are all wired to fear the downsides of uncertainty, but we forget that change, creation, transformation, and innovation rarely show up without some measure of it. In this book we invite you to consider that the only way to get to the possibilities you dream about is to navigate your way there through the treacherous realm of the unknown.

Consider the massive uncertainty in each of these real-life examples: a fashion executive jumping ship to become a baker, a young trainee raising her hand to tackle the company's thorniest problem, a banker abandoning his year-end bonus to create a startup in a rented garage, a goldsmith stress-running at 4 a.m. as his business fails and his wife battles cancer, a venture capitalist investing in a project that will lose every cent, a software engineer receiving a cease-and-desist letter about his new project from the almighty Apple, a couple teaching inmates how to code without access to the internet.

Every single one of these people had to face immense uncertainty to get to the possibility they were celebrated for later. Some of their names you might recognize, like Indra Nooyi or Jeff Bezos, but they weren't famous when facing the situations described above. And while many of the names you may not know yet, the common thread is that whether they chose the unknown or it was forced on them, they unlocked something beyond resilience: the upside of uncertainty. When we talk about uncertainty in this book, we are referring to anything unknown, any ambiguous state where you may not even know what to pay attention to, let alone all the ways it could play out. Uncertainty is broader than just risk, even though people often use them interchangeably. But risk usually involves taking only a small chance on knowable outcomes. Although people may say you have to "take a risk" when you face any uncertainty, they really mean you're stepping into uncharted territory.

When we talk about the upside of uncertainty, we don't mean to minimize the downsides. We feel them first and intensively, and too much uncertainty is a bad thing. But it was our hunch that everyone reading this would be familiar with the downsides: anxiety, stress, exhaustion, and confusion are states that have hindered all of us on our way to doing things we deeply care about. We also don't want to minimize the frustration and grief that uncertainty causes, especially when the unexpected blindsides us. We aren't claiming that it's possible to sidestep the loss and tragedy that some uncertainties bring. Nor are we encouraging naive forays into pursuits that might hurt yourself or others. But we do believe that even in despairing situations, there are new possibilities that can emerge and old hopes that can be salvaged when we learn to navigate the unknown.

Most importantly, by enduring uncertainty well, even when pushed to their limits, the individuals described above accessed a different kind of possibility. Unlike possibilities that arise out of sheer luck, like winning a lottery, or those that arise from efficiency, such as the time gained after buying a dishwasher, the most interesting kind of possibilities—the ones we daydream about, the ones we write about, the ones that we talk about late into the night and that make our hearts ache—are those we find only after facing uncertainty. Recall the achievements you are most proud of, the commitments you made that feel right, the leaps into the dark that changed the course of your life. They all involved uncertainty.

Uncertainty Is Increasing

Moreover, we are all being called to deal with uncertainty more frequently. According to the World Uncertainty Index, created by economists at Stanford and the International Monetary Fund to capture economic and policy uncertainty, uncertainty has been rising steadily over recent decades (see figure I-1). "There is ambiguity and paradox everywhere," observed Jostein Solheim, former CEO at Ben and Jerry's. "For people who like the linear route forward, life is getting harder and harder, in any field!"[1]

It's getting harder because there is *no* linear route forward in a world where up to 65 percent of elementary-school-age children may work in jobs that don't even exist yet.[2] Technology has only magnified the uncertainty, lowering the barriers to participate in many industries, increasing the pace of change. And while we learn many things in school, from mathematics and biology to personal finance, we do not learn how to prepare for and face uncertainty. Without the right tools, we fall into maladaptive traps such as threat rigidity, unproductive rumination, premature certainty, and misinvention. If you don't believe these traps are real, consider that in response to the Covid-19 pandemic, 110,000 people in California purchased guns.[3] And rising in the corporate ranks doesn't give you immunity. Executives at the top feel uncertainty more than ever, with CEO turnover doubling in the last decade.[4] One CTO recently lamented, "You find uncertainty on so many levels . . . in industry, boardroom, management, execution. . . . I thought as my career progressed I would feel more certain, but as your career progresses, uncertainty just increases."[5]

Uncertainty is here to stay. Learning to face the unknown well is critical to our ability to survive and thrive. Numerous studies across academic fields suggest that people comfortable with uncertainty are more creative and are more successful as entrepreneurs and more effective as leaders. We have heard many times and in many ways what serial entrepreneur

FIGURE I-1

World Uncertainty Index

GDP-weighted average of more than 140 countries

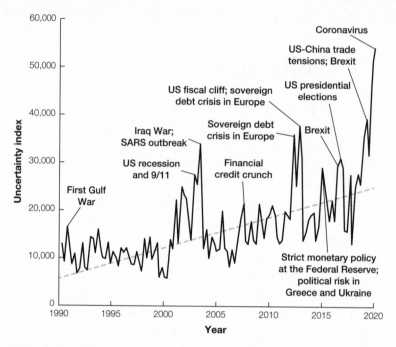

Note: This analysis captures only economic and political uncertainty. The World Uncertainty Index (WUI) calculates the GDP-weighted average of uncertainty in more than 140 countries. Specifically, the "WUI is computed by counting the percent of the word 'uncertain' (or its variant) in the Economist Intelligence Unit country reports. The WUI is then rescaled by multiplying by 1,000,000. A higher number means higher uncertainty and vice versa. For example, an index of 200 corresponds to the word uncertainty accounting for 0.02 percent of all words, which—given the EIU reports are on average about 10,000 words long—means about 2 words per report."

Source: Hites Ahir, Nicholas Bloom, and Davide Furceri, "The World Uncertainty Index," October 29, 2018, https://ssrn.com/abstract=3275033.

---

and CEO Sam Yagan stated so clearly: "The single biggest predictor of executive success is how you deal with ambiguity."[6] Likewise, strategy consulting firm McKinsey & Company argues that "what leaders need during a crisis is not a predefined response plan but behaviors and mindsets that will prevent them from overreacting to yesterday's developments and help them to look ahead."[7] But what few of these studies or reports make clear is how to develop this can-do approach to uncertainty.

We offer this book as a guide to help readers discover and hold on to the upside of uncertainty—all the possibilities that come to those who learn to ride its waves. If we can tolerate uncertainty, and even pursue scenarios in spite of it, we can develop an *uncertainty ability*—the skill to navigate unknowns both planned (such as starting a new venture or leaving a job) and unplanned (such as losing a job, experiencing a health crisis, or going through a relationship breakdown). The people we admire—the ones who do new and inventive things and those who respond nobly to tragedy—have our admiration precisely because they have developed a healthy relationship with uncertainty, increasing their *possibility quotient*, or the likelihood that they see and seize new opportunities.

The Tools for Uncertainty

Since new things are inherently unknown, the arenas of innovation and entrepreneurship are a fascinating spot to better understand if and how one can learn to navigate uncertainty. We started by interviewing pathbreakers in these fields and found that, even though they felt the anxiety that comes with uncertainty just like the rest of us, many of them had learned to meet uncertainty with greater courage, resilience, and skill. While each of us comes with differing capacities to handle uncertainty, and while neuroscience highlights that every skill is shaped by genes, environment, and learning, a significant part of this uncertainty ability appears to be learned.[8] Research in the domains of ambiguity tolerance, uncertainty avoidance, and resilience all underscore that we can learn to face uncertainty well.

In addition to our interviews, we reviewed historical case studies as well as the relevant academic literature in the fields of strategy, organizational behavior, psychology, neuroscience, and political science. Along the way, it became obvious that we needed to include examples of other groups of people who have developed remarkable uncertainty ability: artists, creatives, paramedics, change makers, and contrarians, among others. The practical framework that emerged from this project leverages the validated empirical research where possible but fills the many gaps with interviews and sometimes our own framework when the research frontier lags behind real life. Sprinkled throughout, we will share some of our personal experiences as individuals fascinated by uncertainty but unwilling to let the downsides have the last word. These include our decision to live abroad, our experience as spiritual nomads

FIGURE I-2

Uncertainty first-aid cross

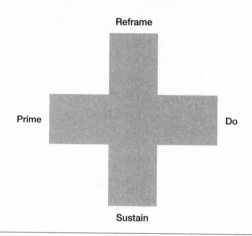

after what many call a "faith crisis," and our life as a married couple and parents unlearning toxic, archaic patterns in favor of more authentic and helpful partnerships with our children and each other.

There are four groups of tools that increase uncertainty ability, organized around an uncertainty first-aid cross to remind you that there is help available for facing the unknown (see figure I-2). *Reframe* tools enable and strengthen a perspective shift, motivating you to look creatively for all the possibilities and to believe in an upside that you can't see yet. *Prime* tools prepare you by encouraging projects that matter to you, taking into account your personal uncertainty landscape to enable satisfying outcomes when it's time to act. *Do* tools describe how to thoughtfully unlock the rewarding possibilities hidden in the uncertainties you face to promote a future you want to live in. *Sustain* tools give comfort and remind you why and how to keep going, or how to pivot when things don't go as planned.

We have chosen symbols that inspire and recall the main thrust for each set of tools (see figure I-3). The compass highlights how Reframe tools point to the steady "true north" upside of uncertainty when in the fog; the backpack reminds that Prime tools impact the quality of the uncertainty journey and where you end up; the sailboat symbolizes how Do tools are about taking advantage of when the wind blows to move forward with boldness, cleverness, and agility but also recognizing how

FIGURE I-3

Uncertainty first-aid cross icons

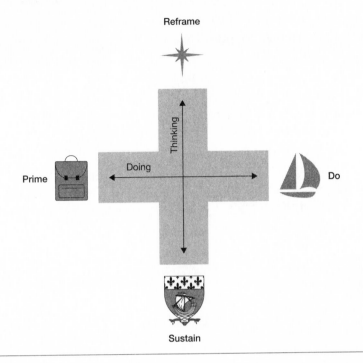

to adjust course when needed; and the emblem of Paris—a boat on the water, often paired with the motto "tossed but not sinking"—assures that Sustain tools will calm your fears, bolster your efforts, and reveal the possibilities. Thus, the north-south "thinking" axis is akin to the poles by which we navigate the world, and the east-west "doing" axis recalls the action required to travel across time zones.

The book is divided into four sections, each centering on one of the four arms of the uncertainty first-aid cross, with each tool given a short chapter followed by an activity to help you reflect on and practice what you've read. (For clarity, note that each chapter is named for its tool.) Applying the uncertainty tools is not meant to be a linear process, as they inform each other and even overlap. Instead, use what resonates for you in a given moment. We have tried to arrange the tools so they can be applied to maximum effect, which resulted in the Sustain tools being grouped according to three critical themes—*emotional hygiene*, *reality check*, and *magic*—to make them easier to remember in times of trouble.

The tools are for everyone, from leaders in organizations to creatives exploring new domains, from parents trying to raise children to adults trying to raise themselves. They are tools for all of us, no matter what role we may be playing, because at some point we may face an uncertainty we are tempted to hide or retreat from but are meant to pursue or engage with. We forget that, as legendary technologist Martin van den Brink argued, "Not doing things also has consequences; that's part of the uncertainty. Standing still is not a choice."[9] Uncertainty will happen to us even when we try to avoid it. To reach our highest potential and live our noblest values, we need to be willing to step into uncertainty. Our hope is that by reading this book, you will more readily find the upside of uncertainty. When you do, you will also find your own *transilience*—a transformation beyond resilience where you leap from the darkness of the unknown to the brilliance of change, growth, and infinite possibility.

Section One

Reframe

D iscovering the upside of uncertainty starts with undergoing a radical shift in perspective: Instead of fearing and avoiding the unknown, you recognize and embrace it as the origin of possibility. It's that simple. Every person, process, and product has passed through countless uncertainties before arriving at the current "known" iteration. Even if something wonderful seems to fall into our life (a fabulous career opportunity, a long-awaited pregnancy, a great new restaurant in our neighborhood, an inspiring political candidate, a mended relationship), either we are not seeing the uncertainty that preceded it or it's about to bring tons of uncertainty . . . and sometimes both are true. And whether these "certain" scenarios remain as they are or shift again into new possibilities is uncertain.

The value of changing how you see uncertainty, or *reframing* uncertainty, has strong roots in empirical research and in practice. There is even an entire business school in Denmark, Kaospilot (using the Danish word for "chaos"), dedicated to teaching students how to deal with uncertainty. During their program, students are given challenging tasks, like redesigning water delivery in the Sahara, but never with enough time, resources, or skills. The key, according to head of school Christer Windeløv-Lidzélius, is that they learn to see themselves as chaos pilots: "We believe everyone has unlimited potential, but tapping into that unlimited potential begins with your perspective." Graduates have gone on to create Tibet's first football team, live video-casting platform Bambuser, and a global coding program for refugees.

The foundational arm of the first-aid cross for uncertainty is Reframe, because our ability to navigate it well turns on a fundamental shift: "uncertainty is inherently bad" (evolution response) becomes "possibility always brings uncertainty" (transilience response). When we focus on the possibility from the outset, calmly recognizing that uncertainty will attend every possibility, we team up with the upside of uncertainty. That doesn't mean we champion every risk or uncertainty as worthwhile. Bad things happen to good people, and good people do bad things. This book is less about those things and more about tools for facing uncertainty well—the ones worth facing *and* the ones that we wouldn't have chosen to face but that happen to us anyway.

To start reframing uncertainty (including your situation and your current preparation or lack thereof) as the shadow of possibility, we encourage you to use the tools briefly summarized in the table below. Short chapters with exercises for reflecting on and practicing each tool follow.

The Reframe tools are largely cognitive in nature, meaning they are about how you make sense of the world. They have a good deal of overlap with Sustain, the other tool kit on the north-south "thinking" axis of the first-aid cross. The main difference is that the Reframe tools are more proactive, long-term strategies to help you step into uncertainty, whereas the Sustain tools are more short-term, reactive tools to deal

Tool	Description
Framing	When you frame uncertainty as possibility, your ability to navigate it increases because your experience shifts from the fear of loss to the anticipation of gain.
Reverse Insurance	An instinctual fear of uncertainty sometimes leads us to forget that we also *need* uncertainty. Humans need surprise, spontaneity, and change—and those things are inherently uncertain.
Frontiers	Frontiers can feel daunting, but they are where we do our best work. There are myriad accessible frontiers awaiting us that could transform our daily lives.
Adjacent Possible	Adjacent possibles are the infinite ways in which the future can be reinvented, hovering at the edge of our awareness, waiting to be discovered.
Infinite Game	Infinite players learn to question the boundaries, the rules, and the game itself, reinventing both the games they are playing and themselves.
Stories	We live by stories, but you need to think about what kind of story you are writing each day and what you would like to be able to pull off the shelf at the end of this year—or at the end of your life.
Regret Minimization	How do you make decisions when you don't know the outcome? Simple frameworks used by innovators help you to make wise choices.
Aplomb (Doubting Self-Doubt)	Self-doubt accompanies the unknown. What we don't realize is how many people, including our heroes and geniuses, share it. There is a better way.
Uncertainty Manifesto	A personal uncertainty manifesto or aspirational beliefs in the face of uncertainty can provide resilience when the going gets rough.

with setbacks, disappointments, failures, and misfortunes. For this reason, we use the emblem of the compass to illustrate how Reframe tools consistently remind you of the upside of uncertainty. But the beauty of both of the "thinking" tool kits—Reframe and Sustain—is twofold. They have the power to change our perspective immediately, like a light switch being turned on in a dark room, but they also develop like muscles—so as we practice reframing and sustaining, we strengthen our uncertainty ability over time.

Chapter 1

Framing

For better or for worse, human beings are wired to fear uncertainty. Psychologists argue that fear of the unknown may be the fundamental fear underpinning all other anxieties, and neuroscientists have demonstrated that we have multiple neural alarm systems that fire in the event of uncertainty.[1] This presents a challenge for us because, despite being wired to fear the unknown, the only way we get to new possibilities is by first facing uncertainty. The good news is that if we can learn to frame uncertainty as the doorway to possibility, we can actually use the same wiring in our brain that warns us against the unknown to help us get excited about, and even embrace, uncertainty. In fact, some people have become so skilled at this that they have learned to see uncertainty as a good thing, even choosing to create more of it on purpose because they realize it helps them access new possibilities.[2]

The mechanisms behind this are what behavioral researchers call the *framing effect*, which affects whether we perceive something as a loss or a gain. Daniel Kahneman and Amos Tversky won a Nobel Prize for their work demonstrating that people make different choices based on how something is "framed" or described.[3] When presented with a choice—such as a medical treatment with a 5 percent chance of failure or a different treatment with a 95 percent chance of success—people are consistently gain-seeking and loss-averse. We strongly prefer the treatment presented as a gain (the 95 percent chance of success) even though the one framed as a loss (the 5 percent chance of failure) probabilistically has the exact same success rate.

Loss, especially the kind of loss that arises from uncertainty, sparks deep and powerful reactions. Empirical research suggests we are motivated by the fear of loss more than by the potential for gain (at least twice as much).[4] And fMRI imaging studies that peek into our brain's reactions reveal that it takes vastly more mental energy for our brains to make sense of a loss than a gain, even if it is a certain loss that is objectively easy to understand. If we are facing time pressure, our difficulty dealing with potential losses gets even more extreme.[5] Our desire to avoid losses is so great that we will even violate our own ethics and be dishonest if it helps us keep what we have.[6] In other words, there is a great deal of empirical work supporting a core human tendency: we gravitate toward gains, particularly when they feel certain, and struggle to make sense of loss, risk, and uncertainty.

The good news is that we can use this same framing effect to reframe uncertainty as a potential gain, rather than a loss, thereby changing how we respond to it. Begin by framing yourself as someone who has enough courage to stand at the edge of opportunity. This definitely can sound easier than it is, except the mindset shift does have a light-switch quality to it, as illustrated by the example of our expat friends during the Covid-19 summer of 2020. It was a tense time for most families, even those who had a place to live and stable jobs, but for Amy and Michael—who didn't know what was next—that summer was brutal. Earlier his company had let them know they were cutting his position, but just as he seemed to be locking in on several tantalizing job offers, the pandemic erupted, and one by one, every single offer was rescinded. They had no jobs, nowhere to live, and no idea where to go next except that they had flights to leave, the final concession from his old company for his expat service. For weeks their home life was a high-tension zone, with everyone walking on eggshells. Their teenagers harangued them, "You are the worst parents ever! How can you have no clue where we are going next?" Well-meaning friends and parents texted anxious questions like, "Do you guys have any plans yet?" The only bright spot was a mixed blessing: a job had opened up but in a place and a role neither of them wanted.

It was on a drizzly July 1 that Susannah met Amy for lunch. Amy confided that their family had tickets to leave the country in two days and a hotel reservation back home for a couple nights, but they still had no jobs and nowhere to live. At that very moment Michael was interviewing with a French company, raising the question of whether they would get on the flight if he got an offer quickly enough. They were exhausted by the stress and worry of how to move forward.

After listing the grim facts, Amy asked Susannah, "Are we terrible parents? Should we just take the bird in the hand? I feel like we are such losers!" Susannah, fresh from researching and writing about framing effects, was thrilled to be the bearer of good news. She responded, "Not at all! You guys aren't losers—you have the courage to explore the possibilities, to wait for the things you really want. You are heroes standing on the edge of possibility. You guys are doing a master's degree in uncertainty!" Amy conceded a smile, then took out a pen and started jotting down notes on her napkin as Susannah explained that uncertainty has upsides but that we can't achieve anything new without also facing the unknown that comes with it. Then she tried to help Amy reframe her abilities and be bolder about looking for frontiers and adjacent possibles (concepts we'll discuss in chapters 3 and 4). At the end of the lunch, she encouraged Amy, "This is graduate-level uncertainty, so go tell your kids how lucky they are to have such cool parents, who are bold enough to believe in, and wait for, what they really want." It was a victorious moment for Amy, who felt rejuvenated, but also for Susannah, who witnessed framing work in an instant.

A few months later, Susannah received an interesting text from Amy: "Good morning! Things have slowly worked themselves out here. I'm working for a neighbor's mortgage company. Michael took a great job in Boston but can work remote for now, so we'll evaluate moving in spring. We bought a fixer-upper in a fun neighborhood full of kids so they can skateboard, bike, jump in the river, swim at the pool, etc. Christina leaves for New York next week to spend the year nannying!" Framing their ongoing uncertainty as the normal, foggy by-product of the pandemic, and not as an indicator of personal weakness, enabled them to wait out the discomfort that felt like it would never end. Ultimately, they found a situation that resonated for everyone.

Reflection and Practice

Reframing uncertainty as the arena for possibility can be practiced.

1. Do a brief review of some of your finest achievements, most important experiences, and most meaningful relationships. You most likely experienced uncertainty on the way there. Try to

remember what it felt like. Were you nervous, scared, unsure, or tempted to give up? It's highly unlikely that you were certain you would achieve these wonderful outcomes you now might be taking for granted. When we remind ourselves of how facing the daunting waves of prior uncertainty brought us achievement and happiness, we strengthen our upside of uncertainty frame.

2. Next, focus on a current uncertainty you face and consider how you are framing it. Is it a threatening one filled with supposed loss (failure, deadends, ruin) or a more optimistic one in which you focus on what could be gained rather than what might be lost? Jot down both the worries you have and the possibilities that could be awaiting you on the other side of the uncertainty. If you are struggling to see any benefits that may be attached to the current uncertainty, remember that at the very least, struggle is the gateway to growth and change. Even if the only upside is that you navigated the uncertainty with more ease than the last time, your muscles for uncertainty ability are getting stronger!

3. When you find yourself stuck in a negative loop about uncertainty, try an exercise developed by author and speaker Byron Katie.[7] Katie uses a simple interrogation process to reveal the deeper complexity inherent in any limiting belief by asking four questions: (1) Is your negative belief true? Can you absolutely know that it's true? (2) How do you react—what happens—when you believe that thought? (3) Who would you be without that thought? (4) Could the opposite of your original thought be as true as, or even truer than, the original thought? You can apply these questions in any situation that feels like failure (joblessness, rupture of a relationship, diagnosis of illness, and so forth).

    In the example above, when Amy feels like a "loser," she could start by asking, "Is it really true that we are terrible parents? That we are losers?" The answer would be simple enough—of course not. Next, Amy might evaluate how she feels when she sees the world this way—that is, terrible. Then she could ask herself, "What if the opposite were true? What if we are displaying immense courage in the face of the unknown?" That reality would feel awesome and bring more energy for the hard work of navigating the current uncertainty.

4. What if the current uncertainty you face, even the unwelcome kind, might have a silver lining? Consider the loss and uncertainty Charles Dickens faced when his father was thrown into debtors' prison, forcing him to drop out of the school he loved and work in a miserable factory to make shoe polish.[8] Through years of toil, Dickens faced profound uncertainty about whether he would ever escape a life of poverty and return to school. When he did, the experiences from those years became the raw material for *David Copperfield*, one of the greatest English novels.

Chapter 2

Reverse Insurance

Many of us feel anxiety in the face of uncertainty and so we try to avoid it. But a world with too much certainty becomes a boring, repetitive cycle from which we long to escape. We forget that we actually need uncertainty, and if we don't have enough of it, we will even pay to introduce more into our lives. As the leader of a major gambling organization explained it to us, "We sell reverse insurance. . . . Our ideal target customer is the forty-five-year-old person who wakes up in a job they hate, a relationship they hate, and realizes their life is always going to be the same."[1] They gamble to give themselves the chance that something new could happen.

Although most of us spend an immense amount of energy trying to make our lives more certain, in the process we forget how much we also crave uncertainty. In a recent survey of sixteen thousand people changing fields in mid-career, most didn't give up their hard-won success because they wanted to make more money or they had a bad boss—they changed because they were bored![2] The boredom predicament invades our personal lives, too—as relationship counselor Esther Perel has found, the major challenge for maintaining relationships is reintroducing the uncertainty that keeps the spark alive.[3]

Clearly, too much uncertainty is overwhelming, but often in our quest to avoid uncertainty we forget that we need it to feel alive, happy, and challenged. Most of us are taught to create a predictable, stable life plan, forgetting that with every certainty we nail down, we eliminate other possibilities and add certainties that will be frustrating. For example, although we may aspire to buy a house, we forget that buying the house reduces the possibilities of living in other cities, discovering new areas, or making new friends while adding the headache of repairs, yard care, and taxes.

We aren't claiming that the increased responsibility isn't worth the benefits of owning your place but consider how doggedly pursuing certainty everywhere leaves no room for the invigorating "reverse insurance" sort of uncertainty that comes from not having every hatch battened down. Cautious and predictable choices often feel safer or morally right but when stacked up *ad nauseum*, they can leave you unfulfilled.

The same is true for organizations—they need uncertainty as well. In a recent study, Harvard professors found that when companies instituted quality-control systems like ISO 9000 to increase certainty in their production processes, they also eliminated the innovation that arose from mistakes, changes, and uncertainty.[4] Tim Little, the entrepreneur who reinvigorated legacy shoe company Grenson, explained that reinventing the brand was only possible if he could, "take risks. If I hadn't . . . it would have been a long, slow road to mediocrity."[5]

Uncertainty is an essential ingredient for new things to happen. The innovation teams at some of the world's top restaurants actually encourage uncertainty, injecting it into their processes by forcing themselves to use unknown ingredients, try new cooking techniques, reinstalling new kitchens, or adopting undefined roles for chefs.[6] Likewise, Hamilton Mann, the head of transformation at Thales, which builds high-performance systems for space stations and electrical systems for megafactories told us, "To innovate, we have to seek risk, we have to seek uncertainty. If we try to avoid it like in other parts of the business, we won't innovate."[7]

When we start reframing uncertainty as a necessary reverse insurance against a boring checklist life, we will take bigger risks, tapping into *uncertainty possibilities*, which are the most interesting, valuable, and instructive possibilities. Jamie Rosen is an entrepreneur whose unusual journey taught him how important uncertainty really is to a fulfilling life. After finishing an undergraduate degree at Harvard, he had the sense that he wanted to do something different from the familiar career tracks in medicine or business. But he didn't know what that something different was, let alone what to call it. As a student he had written travel guides for the Let's Go series, and when a coworker suggested creating one for East Asia, they decided to write about Mongolia. Sadly the project fell through just before launch, so Rosen fished around for "that something" he felt was missing and came across a new program on invention and creativity that was sponsored by Jerry Lemelson—the late inventor who held 606 patents.

Rosen joined the innovation program and later worked with Lemelson, inventing creative toys like giant foam Lego bricks that could be used to build castles or ships. After his experiences with inventing, Rosen went on to found several entrepreneurial ventures, including WayBetter, which leverages behavioral science to encourage people to pursue healthier lifestyles. When we caught up at a small café, Rosen observed, "I used to see life as trying to get straight to my objective. And the periphery—those were the uncertainties, those were the distractions."[8] Then he hesitated, coffee cup in hand. "But, you know, the most wonderful and important things in my life have always come from the side, from the periphery. Every good and great thing that has happened to me—meeting my wife, meeting Lemelson, starting my businesses—it all came from the periphery." Nodding to himself, Rosen concluded, "I still go toward an objective, but now I'm looking for the periphery, I'm looking for those surprises. That's the good stuff. It all comes from the uncertainty. That's the point of the journey."

Not only do we need uncertainty, to introduce surprise, change, and enthusiasm into our lives, but uncertainty may be the only pathway to the possibilities many of us dream about. Uncertainty possibilities are easily forgone since they entail even *more* uncertainty and *more* of the unknown, but they are more satisfying and potentially life changing. They tend to come only after you face the unknown and, instead of backing down, live it into possibility.

Reflection and Practice

Reverse insurance reminds us that we can't thrive without uncertainty. When thinking about our individual capability, or uncertainty ability, when facing uncertainty, it can be helpful to imagine a thermometer that registers the current temperature of uncertainty you are living with. To take the temperature of your uncertainty, consider both the planned and the unplanned uncertainties you are experiencing in five areas: relationships, career, health, personal growth, and time/money resources. Planned uncertainties could include starting a new venture, making a career change, moving to a new location, getting married, or undergoing some other exciting but potentially stressful change in your life. Unplanned uncertainties are any unexpected threat or disabling circumstances, such as a job loss, relationship breakdown, serious illness, natural disaster, depression, or other shock.

Taking your uncertainty temperature is subjective and requires some imagination and intuition—it will not be an exact measurement. Now consider that the heat of the uncertainty you are facing likely puts you into one of three development zones described by Tom Senninger (based on psychologist Lev Vygotsky's original model): panic, learning, or comfort.[9] If the heat of uncertainty is too high, then you are likely in the panic zone, in which case, your intention should focus on bringing the temperature down, as you would with a dangerously high fever. Simply reframing the unknowns you are facing—by finding ways to move them into the realm of possibility—often lowers your temperature a bit, bringing you down to the learning zone, where growth begins. If, on the other hand, the heat of uncertainty is too low, then you are probably squarely in your comfort zone and thus not really learning, growing, or developing. Obviously, the ideal is to introduce some novelty and uncertainty so you can reach the learning zone, where you grow and develop. We will discuss how to do that effectively in the discussion on frontiers in chapter 3. However, for most of us, the real problem is that we are so used to being in the comfort zone that just a little uncertainty ruffles our feathers. We then react by trying to escape from it in order to get back to our comfort zone rather than seeing how the uncertainty might be leading us to the learning zone. As you look at the uncertainties you face, is it really true that you are in the panic zone? Or is it possible that you are just feeling the normal discomfort of the learning zone? Ask yourself, What could I be learning from this? How is this making me more resilient, capable, and wise? Perhaps you will realize that you are actually in the learning zone, building your uncertainty ability and developing important lessons for the future.

1. We coined the phrase *possibility quotient* to describe one's likelihood of enabling positive change and transformation. Like all Reframe tools, reverse insurance increases your possibility quotient in the way it defangs the downsides of uncertainty and reveals the human need for uncertainty. Imagine our surprise when we googled "possibility quotient" and found Harvard assistant professor

Srini Pillay using the idea in a slightly different way, one that is as informative as a temperature-taking exercise. He created the following checklist to measure factors that "could be masquerading as impossibility" and depleting one's possibility quotient.[10]

- How burned out are you?

- How lost do you feel?

- How much have you given up on your dreams?

- How hard is it for you to change?

- How depressed or anxious are you?

- How much of a pessimist are you?

- How difficult is it for you to clearly imagine what you want?

If you have been avoiding risk and uncertainty at all costs, your possibility quotient will be low. If you are burned out, depressed, and have given up on your dreams, it may be that you aren't allowing enough uncertainty into your life, which is the only way to imagine and live new ways of being into reality. We try to control situations to feel safe, but this chapter's tool is a reminder that certainty in everything is overrated, making life dull and depressing. If we live all areas of life in the comfort zone, our uncertainty temperature will be low and our uncertainty temperature upper limit will remain equally low, since we aren't taking steps to become comfortable at higher temperatures.

2. Often innovators and others adept at navigating uncertainty get tired of high possibility quotients and "retire," opting for calmer days within the comfort and learning zones. Taking breaks from introducing uncertainty can be a great idea, but reverse insurance is there to remind us not to stay there long. The most fascinating and inspiring individuals continue to learn and grow right up to the end of their lives, preferring learning zones over unfulfilling existences.

Chapter 3

Frontiers

"Anyone can achieve their fullest potential[;] who we are might be predetermined, but the path we follow is always of our own choosing. We should never allow our fears or the expectations of others to set the frontiers of our destiny."

—Martin Heidegger

We often think of frontiers as wild places at the edge of the known world, full of risk and danger, and so while they might make a great movie setting, we tend to avoid frontiers in our own lives. We forget that they are also the places where we learn, discover, and grow—and we find them everywhere, not just in faraway lands. A frontier is really any boundary between where we feel comfortable and where we don't. And there are an infinite number of frontiers available to each of us, because every aspect of our lives includes a comfort zone that we have taken as a given and that constricts the possibilities available to us.

Born into humble origins, Denis O'Brien had already achieved a great deal by his family's standards when he was hired by the local bank after attending university. Always restless, however, O'Brien cold-called Tony Ryan, founder of Guinness Peat Aviation and Ryanair, landing a job as his personal assistant. Later, as mobile phones started to mature, he left Ryan to create his own mobile company, ESat Telecom, which he later sold to British Telecom. Still looking for the next frontier, O'Brien founded Digicel to lead the development of mobile networks in over thirty Caribbean and Pacific islands.

When we asked O'Brien about navigating the uncertainty of so many frontiers, he answered by recounting his experience creating a mobile network in Haiti, one of the poorest nations in the world, crippled by underinvestment and corruption. "No one wanted to invest, absolutely nobody," O'Brien told us. But he flew to Haiti anyway. "It took me two hours driving around Port-au-Prince to see that we could do it. Everywhere, people were transacting—selling food, car parts, and other stuff. I could see people had a few dollars to invest in something that could transform their lives."[1]

Despite his optimism, O'Brien could only convince one other investor, who in the end dropped out, leaving Digicel to fund the full $160 million up-front costs to establish the network. Digicel Haiti has since weathered earthquakes, fuel riots, hyperinflation, and other uncertainties to become the first mobile operator in a place where everyone thought it was impossible. "So in answer to your question," O'Brien told us, leaning in close with a smile and a wink, "all anyone could see were the risks, but I saw possibility." Pushing into the frontier has made O'Brien one of the wealthiest entrepreneurs in the world, allowing him to build over two hundred schools in Haiti and to rebuild its famous Iron Market after it was flattened by the 2010 earthquake.

However, for most of us the frontier will be found not in other countries but much closer to home. Clare and David Hieatt are a creative couple who cofounded the clothing brand Howies while working jobs at advertising agencies. But when Howies started to take off, they left their high-paying jobs in London to focus full-time on their eco brand, ultimately selling to Timberland in the hope that they would have greater impact with more support. Imagine their devastation when Timberland chose to go a different direction, moving the company to the United States. The Hieatts left the company, and while the financial exit made them comfortable, they missed the entrepreneurial frontier.

One weekend, hanging out with friends, they wondered aloud, "How can we keep learning, like we did when we had Howies?" Remembering that one of the hardest things about being an entrepreneur is feeling alone, they started to think about developing an "encouragement network" to help others trying to do new things. In some ways, it didn't make sense for the Hieatts to lead an encouragement network. They had moved to Cardigan, Wales, a tiny town of four thousand people on the remote western edge of the UK. What could they do from such a small place? But they had bought a farm, with old chicken sheds and large fields. What if they could attract top-notch speakers, provide great coffee, let attendees camp in the fields, and broadcast the resulting encouragement to the world?

The idea grew to become the Do Lectures, the SXSW of the continental innovation world. Featuring lectures from people like Sir Tim Berners-Lee, Marion Deuchars, Tim Ferriss, and Maggie Doyne, it created a global impact—there are now Do Lectures in the United States, Australia, and Costa Rica. The experience not only expanded their frontier as a couple but led to the creation of a new business, Hiut Denim. Looking back on the journey, David Hieatt now champions frontiers: Although they can be scary or intimidating, "you can only do your best work when you are at the frontier," he argues. "You have to be at the frontier if you want to do something new."

Frontiers can also be personal internal boundaries with equally transformative rewards. Benjamin Gilmour is an author, filmmaker, and paramedic who has worked, written, and filmed all over the world. His film *Jirga* is about an Australian soldier fighting the Taliban who, during a village raid, kills the innocent father of a family of three. Racked by guilt, he returns to the village three years later to make amends and is put on trial by the village elders. The film's climax is as touching as it is surprising: the oldest son holds a knife to the throat of his father's murderer and forgives rather than seeks revenge. The village elders, Afghani tribespeople who many Westerners have been taught to fear, then express the film's valuable lesson: "forgiveness is mightier and more honourable than taking revenge."

When we asked Gilmour why he wanted to flip the script on so many of our Western stereotypes, he said, "I wanted to push the boundaries of empathy, of what people can feel for someone who is so different from them, even someone they have stereotyped as bad."[2]

Not all frontiers have to be emotionally charged, entrepreneurial, or daringly adventurous. Signing up for a new workout session, trying a new haircut, and even going to a restaurant that you assumed you wouldn't like are all frontier-expanding pursuits. When we spent time with author Brad Modlin during his visit to Paris, we had a hard time meeting up with him on several occasions. What we didn't know is that this nationally recognized author and poet was either lost or just running a couple minutes late. Why? He didn't have a map . . . because he doesn't carry a smartphone . . . on purpose. He welcomes getting lost because he knows it means he will discover new places and see new things. It's something he learned walking the Camino de Santiago, the ancient pilgrim trail that cuts through the heart of France and Spain. Amid the sudden rainstorms, blisters, and faulty gear, he found his most interesting experiences happened when he got lost or had setbacks. "I learned to love it," Modlin told us, "and now I let myself get lost just to see what I find. It's so fascinating!"[3]

Reflection and Practice

There are frontiers all around us, in both the small things that can be tweaked (morning rituals, exercises, work practices) and the bigger, long-anticipated events (going to college, first real job, marriage, childbirth, retirement). A frontier is simply the boundary between the known and the unknown. None of us can explore all the frontiers but waking up to their existence can be a powerful tool for transformation, and the most important ones are those that hold the most possibility for your personal growth or satisfaction. If frontiers in your life are ignored or even underexplored, the chances of capturing a new opportunity in that aspect of your life are low.

1. Start by listing the frontiers in your life. Some of the most obvious are areas like career and relationship. If you think there is no longer a frontier there, take a second look: Empty nesters go back to medical school. A grandma we know is still doing the splits at age ninety in a yearly dance production. Those of us who doggedly seek the "what" of our career, like being CEO or the boss, may be seeing the frontier too narrowly. Social, emotional, skill, activity, and geographic frontiers are also tethered to our career frontier and impact our quality of life.

2. When asking "How can I expand the frontier in my career?" consider the options broadly: Could you work with new people? Would you like to do this same job but in a different company, or with this company but in a different location? Would you enjoy creating your own project or company? Can you start a side project in your free time? How can you expand the frontiers of your responsibilities at work?

3. Beyond career, consider physical, intellectual, emotional, social, spiritual, and other frontiers, which often overlap and inform each other. Whichever neglected frontier you approach agitates others into momentum. For example, when you start to expand the frontier of learning a new skill, you will undoubtedly discover a new world of people and resources that love and live for that skill you are just discovering.

4. Go deeper with your questions. Choose one or two frontiers that are most motivating to you, and start imagining options: How could you take the first step? Would it start in conversation with a leader or mentor? Do you need to research more about how to begin? Which practices can you start now, and which will take more preparation? From the list of action items that you start now, choose one and make a commitment to yourself to begin today (e.g., send the email, buy the book, sign up for the class). Often, just taking ten minutes to sniff around the edges of a frontier can reveal the path beyond your comfort zone.

5. If you are feeling uninspired about which frontier might hold the most meaningful change for you, consider starting with the emotional frontier. Who among us would not enjoy the improved relationship that would come from better understanding a partner, child, or friend? Or even closer to home, what if you embarked on a journey of deeper self-knowledge? Any self-reflective inner work (meditation, journaling, therapy) will reveal clues to what might be holding you back from all other frontiers.

Chapter 4

Adjacent Possible

While frontiers are about expanding the current boundaries of your life, the *adjacent possible* is about the untapped opportunities nearby, ready to be discovered. Author Steven Johnson calls it "a kind of shadow future, hovering on the edges of the present state of things, a map of all the ways in which the present can reinvent itself."[1] Biologist Stuart Kauffman introduced the term to describe how evolutionary adaptations often find surprising new uses, such as how feathers, evolved for warmth, turned out to be useful for flying or how the complex jawbones of fish, no longer useful on land, proved useful for hearing. But Kauffman has since applied the term to underscore that although we may perceive a finite world, there are actually infinite possibilities hidden in the world around us. His favorite example is the screwdriver. Most of us see a single use, but in fact there are infinite ways it can be used! It can turn screws, wedge a door, be used in sculpture, be rented for spearfishing in exchange for 5 percent of the profits, and on and on.[2]

How do we tap into this expansive field of opportunity hovering just out of sight? First, we start by *paying greater attention.* In the nineteenth century, surgeon Joseph Lister noted something curious: carbolic acid that was used to treat the sewage spread on fields reduced the number of parasites in the cattle grazing there. He wondered if carbolic acid could also decrease the amount of bacteria in wounds after surgery. He experimented and discovered that using antiseptics reduced mortality rates after major operations from 40 percent to less than 3 percent by 1910, saving as many lives as were lost in all the wars of the nineteenth century.[3]

Adjacent possibles also reveal themselves when we *look thoughtfully at problems* we face. When Barbara Alink and her aging mother passed a group of elderly people sitting in wheelchairs, Alink's mother announced, "Over my dead body will I ever use one of those." Baffled by her mother's statement, Alink realized, as she put it, "we live in a society that has caused a divide between people with and without disabilities. . . . Mobility devices emphasize the disability."[4] Alink is quick to clarify that wheelchairs are "amazing" for people who need them, but 60 percent of wheelchair users still have some use of their legs, and she wanted to make a device that gave greater freedom for that 60 percent.

Alink set about designing a device "so cool that it overcomes the discomfort other people have with the disability."[5] Using available bicycle parts, she designed the Alinker, which has a tricycle-like frame that allows users to remain at eye level, get around using their feet, and keep their hands free. The device required years of prototyping and she funded multiple iterations on personal credit cards, but in the end, she succeeded in creating a device that allows users to engage with others at face level while also giving them greater mobility. Alinker users can't express enough gratitude. For ten-year-old Luca, who required 24/7 care and was always lying on his side, the Alinker has given him his childhood back: snacking from the countertop, being excited about school, engaging with friends, and even learning to swing a cricket bat.

Adjacent possibles also reveal themselves when we *question assumptions*. Vicki Saunders, a successful executive, recalls discovering this as a young woman living in Europe when the Berlin Wall came down. She jumped on a train to Prague, where "every sentence was, 'Now that I'm free, I'm going to do this. Now that I'm free, I'm going to do that.' Every person was dreaming . . . it was absolutely intoxicating." Amid the elation, Saunders suddenly thought, *Oh my god! I'm free too! What am I going to do?* When she reframed her own situation, it allowed her to "recreate myself," helping her see new and bolder options. "I ended up staying for four years, and it completely changed my life," she concludes.[6]

After a career in Silicon Valley, including taking a company public, Saunders started to question assumptions again. She began to wonder why for her it "felt like a burden to be a woman in business. It felt like a burden to be a woman in society." One day she realized, "I'm not surprised it is hard . . . because nothing was designed by [women]. . . . We were not at the table to design this world." Only 4 percent of venture capital money goes to women founders, and five men hold as much wealth as 3.5 billion people. "How do you solve this?" Saunders asked. "Where are the acupuncture points in the system where you could create disruption so you could open up everything? For me, it was three: finance, education, and media. We need to fund women's ideas."[7]

Inspired by the Native peoples of the United States and Canada, whose wealth was demonstrated by how much they gave away, Saunders began to experiment with "radical generosity." She founded SheEO, a perpetual investment fund where women give $1,100 to become "activators," loaning to female entrepreneurs at a 0 percent interest rate. This fund is built on "the sanity of women looking at something, saying, 'That makes sense to me. It is doing good in the world. I'd like to support it,'" Saunders explains. "Fifty percent of the population have had innovations sitting on the sidelines for generations. We have ideas on how to change things, and we haven't been able to get funded." Curious about the kinds of projects SheEO funds? It funded the Alinker!

Adjacent possibles reveal themselves, too, when we *purposefully recombine* things. Van Phillips enrolled in medical school because he was curious about creating a better prosthetic after losing a leg in a boating accident. His professors discouraged him, claiming all the prosthetic advancements had already been made. But Phillips argued that while existing prosthetics looked like a leg, they didn't function like one. More interested in function than form, he borrowed principles from diving boards, pole vaults, and cheetahs to create the Flex-Foot, a carbon fiber prosthetic that works like a leg. It works like a spring to help wearers move in ways—including running and jumping—that other prostheses don't. It has even been used in professional athletic competitions.

Adjacent possibles can also reveal themselves when we *ask what's missing*. Designer Adrien Gardère is famous for the Melampo Lamp, for which he borrowed the folding mechanism of an Opinel knife to create two positions—straight down for diffuse indirect light or inclined for direct light. Today he designs spaces like the Louvre-Lens museum in France and the Egyptian Museum in Cairo. Recently he was asked to reimagine Chinese-French artist Huang Yong Ping's installation in Paris's Grand Palais, which featured a dragon's silver skeleton wrapping around shipping containers. The exhibit, a commentary on China and global commerce, was well received, and the group supporting the exhibit made five to-scale models to recoup some of the exhibit's cost. When none sold, they asked Gardère to explore why. He observed the model and noticed something critical was missing: the model did not capture the play of light and shadow through the glass ceiling of the Grand Palais. Gardère set about designing a projector system that recreated the light of the Parisian sun as it passed over the windows of the historic building. The results were stunning, and the five models quickly sold.[8]

Sometimes adjacent possibles reveal themselves if we're facing a tempting but risky choice, when we *ask what the worst-case scenario is*. Steve Blank, the serial entrepreneur and father of the Lean Startup movement, started his career as an engineer. He recounts visiting Silicon Valley for a work assignment and being shocked upon opening the *Mercury News* to find page upon page of job listings. Blank decided right then to quit his job and stay. His colleague thought he was insane—back home, positions were scarce. But Blank asked himself, "What's the worst that could happen? I knew that in this country I wouldn't starve, so why not try?"[9] Reframing the choice this way, Blank saw a viable adjacent possible, which gave him the courage to face one of life's scariest uncertainties— joblessness—and ultimately enabled a much more dynamic career than if he had stayed with what was comfortable and certain.

Finally, adjacent possibles reveal themselves by *questioning the status quo*, like where we can live, how much we need to earn, or our definition of a good life. Lynne Curran, a tapestry artist featured in the Uffizi Gallery in Florence, Italy, and David Swift, an artist and educator who has worked with refugees and people with mental illnesses, are a creative couple who challenge norms. Rich in life but poor in resources, they bought an old house in Edinburgh, Scotland, so decrepit that the assessor suggested they demolish it. Instead, they transformed it into a gem regularly featured in design magazines with a gorgeous garden. But when a correctional facility opened next door, young men out on "good behavior" started breaking in, lighting cars on fire, and throwing stones through the windows.

The anxiety interrupting their work demanded a change. Unable to afford anything with any potential remotely close to Edinburgh, they at first searched the suburbs, but then asked: Why stay here? They considered Japan but settled on Tuscany, a place they had visited before and loved, and where they found an ancient farmhouse in Chiusi della Verna, the mystical mountainside of Michelangelo's youth, just down the hill from where Saint Francis of Assisi experienced his stigmata. They moved in, again after significant renovations, and now can wake in the morning to see the mist clinging to the hills, walk past the rock Michelangelo painted into *The Creation of Adam* in the Sistine Chapel's ceiling, and take fresh water from the springs that cover the mountainside.

Like frontiers, adjacent possibles require a willingness to look for them and the courage to pursue them. Moreover, they build on each other, in that each step you take into the unknown reveals yet more adjacent possibles in the future. Using the metaphor of a house, you can't walk straight from the entrance to the tenth room. Rather, you reach new rooms by walking through each room successively, with each new room revealing new doors or new possibilities. Thus, while possibilities are infinite, we have to move forward to reveal the full range available to us. As Steven Johnson describes it, adjacent possibles are "intelligently curtailed at every step by the limitations of the present."[10]

This may be no better illustrated than by the life of Buckminster Fuller, who suffered a series of defeats that left him contemplating taking his own life. After getting kicked out of Harvard twice, he married and then cofounded a company, only to be pushed out of that same company a few years later after losing his three-year-old daughter to spinal meningitis. With no job prospects and a second baby on the way, he wandered the streets of Chicago, thinking of drowning himself so his family could at least collect the life insurance payments. Then, in an inspirational flash, he considered a shadowy "what if"—an adjacent possible he described in almost religious terms. Rather than giving in to despair and despite his powerless position, what if he tried his best to simply change the world for the better. From that starting conviction, Fuller went on to write more than thirty books, register more than two dozen patents, invent the geodesic dome, and influence tens of thousands as a thought leader for reinventing the future.

The year he died, Fuller continued to describe himself in the humblest of terms as "guinea pig B," summarizing his life by saying,

> I am now close to eighty-eight, and I am confident that the only thing important about me is that I am an average healthy human. I am also a living case history of a thoroughly documented, half-century, search-and-research project designed to discover what, if anything, an unknown, moneyless individual, with a dependent wife and newborn child, might be able to do effectively on behalf of all humanity that could not be accomplished by great nations, great religions, or private enterprise, no matter how rich or powerfully armed.[11]

As you consider the potential of adjacent possibles in your own life, recall Fuller's injunction, "We are called to be architects of the future, not its victims."[12]

Reflection and Practice

Unlike frontiers that are personal and knowable, adjacent possibles are not obvious, even when hiding in plain sight. They require a creative sideways glance that often starts with a hunch that something might be there. One thing we have noticed about adjacent possibles is they are usually discovered by individuals who have a deep interest or need. These people tend to be curious, puzzling about the possibility for reasons other than fame or reward. Lynne Curran and David Swift were more likely to see the Tuscany option because they had spent time there before. Van Phillips was more likely to see the possibility of Flex-Foot because he wore prosthetics and wanted a leg that performed, not one that looked like a leg. Vicki Saunders walked through the "rooms" of her career in male-dominated industries for decades before she could recombine the elements that led her to create SheEO.

Of course, adjacent possibles are open to all, but we are more likely to find them when we are motivated to really pay attention. Below are some questions to help you explore the adjacent possibles hovering at the edges of your life. These questions can easily be adapted to an organization setting too.

1. What am I curious about? How can I delve deeper into that curiosity?

2. What do I long to do? If I rank-ordered the list, which would be persistent and recurring?

3. What do I care about? What am I already involved with that begs for more of my attention for greater change?

4. What interactions or processes that I am a part of feel inherently broken? Which might be open to change that I could effect?

Once you have alighted on the adjacent possible you want to explore, the following questions will inspire you to be more creative about the resources you may or may not have, as well as about the roles others play in either helping or hindering your discovery and rollout of adjacent possibles.

5. What are the skills and talents I have? Could I use them in new ways?

6. What kinds of people interest me or leave me feeling uninspired? What qualities or activities do I admire or dislike them for? Do I share some of those positive or negative traits, and could I start to nurture or diminish them?

7. What could I stop doing to free up time and energy to explore an adjacent possible? What would be the path to stopping it? Do I have obligations, relationships, or tasks that could be put off, finished, or delegated to free up energy?

Sometimes the most interesting adjacent possibles reveal themselves when we challenge our most quotidian assumptions. These could be simple assumptions, like how things are supposed to work. Once, Nathan and his roommate realized they rarely received guests, so they moved their beds from the cramped bedroom to the spacious living room, where they awoke to the rising sun. But there are even bigger assumptions we live by. What if we could unframe our lives to see them in new ways? Here are a few questions to help:

8. What beliefs (family, cultural, religious, and so forth) have I inherited that might be limiting my ability to find the adjacent possible? If you were born into a family of creatives, innovators, or risk takers, experiments might feel natural to you. If not, you might assume that the life you are living is the only one available. Take courage from Fuller's guinea pig B moment, when from a sense of total unworthiness, he intuited that money, fame, and power weren't required to change the world.

9. Go spend some time around people who have lived across cultures, and ask them: How has their sense of what's possible changed as a result? One of the greatest perks of being an expat is the way it reveals the made-up quality of much of what we do and how we do it. Take the idea of vacation. In France, schoolchildren have two weeks off every six weeks (with affordable childcare options available to parents who work), and everyone gets at least two weeks off in August (and most take the whole month). Another Reframe activity: Ask contrarians, who don't believe in any system, what they think about the adjacent possible. They might say it's their middle name.

Chapter 5

Infinite Game

In his quirky philosophical treatise, *Finite and Infinite Games: A Vision of Life as Play and Possibility,* New York University professor James Carse describes life as a game with two types of people: finite and infinite players. Finite players accept the roles life gives them (e.g., college student, manager, lawyer, parent, spouse) and play by the received rules in an effort to win. Infinite players play *with* the roles and bend the rules, not to win the game but for the joy of playing.

For example, rather than buy art for a collection, New York City–based art collective MSCHF purchased Damien Hirst's painting *L-Isoleucine T-Butyl Ester* for $30,485, cut out its eighty-eight colored dots "so everyone can have a spot" (priced at $480 each), and then auctioned the "spotless painting with 88 holes in it" for over $250,000. This stunt is just one of many MSCHF has pulled off that break rules and challenge the game.

For finite players, uncertainty is the enemy because it creates unknowns about the ability to win. For infinite players, uncertainty is the realm of opportunity, and they play with the "expectation of being surprised!"[1] As Carse argues, "To be prepared against surprise is to be trained. To be prepared for surprise is to be educated." There are many ways to live as an infinite player.

Infinite players *challenge their roles.* Carse writes that we tend to identify ourselves by the roles we play in life, such as our job, relationships, or status (student, consultant, parent, etc.). But when we identify with a role, we are less likely to experiment with it because failure to "do it right" implies failure as a person. By contrast, if we view roles as temporary, changing, and separate from who we really are, then we are more free to experiment, reinvent, and transform them. For example, when a finite player loses their job or gets divorced, it crushes their identity, whereas an infinite player, after taking time to absorb the loss, views it as an invitation to reinvent their role.

Eleanor Roosevelt illustrates the reinvention of roles in the face of difficult challenges. Raised by an alcoholic father who died by suicide, then a stern grandmother who suddenly passed away from diphtheria, Eleanor recalls feeling like a displaced ugly duckling that didn't belong. Imagine her elation when she married the jovial, charismatic star of the Harvard social scene, Franklin D. Roosevelt, and settled into her new family as wife and mother. It was only after bearing six children and while unpacking Franklin's suitcase from his trip to Europe, she discovered love letters between him and her secretary, Lucy Mercer. Eleanor offered Franklin a divorce, but his controlling mother, whose house adjoined theirs via sliding doors, threatened to cut Franklin off from the family fortune if he did.

After a period of deep grief in which Eleanor "faced myself, my surroundings, my world, honestly for the first time," she decided to reinvent her role.[2] She started business school, learned to drive, and took cooking lessons. She fired the servants, or "spies," hired by her mother-in-law and surrounded herself with friends, including African Americans and others deemed inappropriate in her social circle. She started working for the League of Women Voters to fight for unemployment insurance, the abolition of child labor, and wages-and-hours legislation.

Eleanor's own political career was just taking off when Franklin came down with polio, and she put everything on hold to massage his legs, roll him in bed, and administer catheters and enemas. Despite her mother-in-law's demand that Franklin retire from political life, Eleanor insisted he continue and traveled the country speaking on his behalf, writing a nationally syndicated newspaper column, and hosting a weekly radio show. After Franklin's death, she both advocated for the United Nations and became America's first delegate, helping to frame the Universal Declaration of Human Rights. When she died, the *New York Times* noted she was "the object of almost universal respect."[3] She could have stuck to the roles of obedient wife, rejected lover, submissive daughter-in-law, but she did not. If she had, Eleanor knew she would have become "a completely colorless echo of my husband and mother-in-law, and torn between them, I might have stayed a weak character forever."[4]

Infinite players *challenge the rules*. Too many of us take the rules for granted without realizing they are made up. As filmmaker David Lynch describes it, "We think we understand the rules when we become adults, but what we really experience is a narrowing of the imagination."

The most distinctive characteristic of Tesla CEO Elon Musk is his willingness to challenge the rules. "The one thing you can never do is tell Elon, 'That's the way things are done,'" said Sterling Anderson, former head of the Model X.[5] Musk's approach is to "boil things down to the most fundamental truths in a particular area, the things you're really sure of are base truths, or highly sure of, and then you reason up from there."[6] For example, batteries have long been a bottleneck to affordable electric vehicles. Musk challenged the industry standard of $600 per kilowatt hour by breaking batteries down into raw components and demonstrating that the materials could be purchased on the London Metal Exchange for $80 per kilowatt hour. "Clearly, you just need to think of clever ways to take those materials and combine them into the shape of a battery cell, and you can have batteries that are much cheaper than anyone realizes."[7]

Likewise, George Yancopoulos and Len Schleifer, founders of Regeneron Pharmaceuticals, observed that one reason for the exorbitant cost of developing new treatments is that so many therapies fail in the transition from animal to human testing. They challenged this bottleneck by splicing the human genome to develop a mouse that bridged the animal-human divide. This new mouse allowed them to radically improve their testing accuracy, lowering development costs by 80 percent, as compared with competitors.[8] Reflecting on the origin of their remarkable breakthrough, Yancopoulos told us, "We challenge everything. Every concept. Every scientific principle. Nothing is unchallengeable and you don't take anything for granted. Most of what we believe are facts are not."[9]

Another way to challenge the rules is to *rethink the way you interact with other players*, even the competition. While at Cisco, Kate O'Keeffe observed that some of the most interesting and valuable opportunities happen at the boundaries between industries. She created the Cisco Hyperinnovation Living Lab, an outside-the-box forum to bring together uncommon partners like Visa, Nike, Costco, and Lowe's to find opportunities at their intersections, including reimagining retail and supply chain.[10] O'Keeffe reenvisioned the boundaries of the game, intuiting that competitors could work together to create new opportunities beyond the grasp of any individual company: "We are all each other's customers and face common problems, so why not work together to create something more?"[11]

Infinite players also *challenge the game itself.* Zach Klein, cofounder of Vimeo, recalls learning this lesson the hard way. "In the current cult of startup, it is a perfectly reasonable idea of success to start a company just to sell it very soon after for gobs of money."[12] After Vimeo took off, Klein and his cofounders did exactly that, making a fortune. But today Klein laments, "As soon as I sold my company and I was standing safely on the ground, I wanted nothing more than to have those wings again. I just wanted to keep flying."

Klein set out to look for others playing the game differently and came across Yvon Chouinard, founder of billion-dollar retail brand Patagonia. Chouinard, a self-described "dirtbag" climber who got his start selling rock-climbing equipment out of the back of his car, challenged the rules of business by treating his employees well, telling customers to repair their products rather than buy more, and donating 10 percent of profits or 1 percent of sales, whichever is greater, to grassroots change and sustainability efforts. As Chouinard summarized his approach in his inspiring manifesto, *Let My People Go Surfing*, "I learned at a young age that it's better to invent your own game, then you can always be the winner."[13]

All of us, due to living within a cultural setting, are handed a set of metrics by which we are told we should live—a game and a set of rules. One of the things that expats often come to realize when living between two cultures is that these rules are largely made up. Recognizing that you can choose the rules you live by can be incredibly liberating. As legendary innovator Steve Jobs famously said, "Everything around you that you call life was made up by people that were no smarter than you, and you can change it, you can influence it. . . . Once you learn that, you'll never be the same again."[14]

What makes a startup disruptive is its willingness to challenge the rules. Airbnb challenged the idea that people would only rent rooms from a hotel, Wise (formerly TransferWise) challenged the assumption that currency could only be exchanged by big banks, and Uber challenged the idea that only taxi drivers can give rides. Imagine for a moment how amazing it would be if companies, more generally, could be even more inventive in challenging the game, and thereby create better outcomes regarding sustainability, employee well-being, and humanity as a whole.

Infinite players *play for the sake of continuing the game* and for discovering new surprises. One of the things that characterizes a Kaospilot student is their more holistic view of the game. "None of them would work eighty hours a week and do what they are told to earn $5 million a year. . . . They look for something different," says head of school Christer Windeløv-Lidzélius. "They believe they can create something better than that. It's OK to have more than one goal, more than one dimension of success. Our students learn to work with moving objectives and multiple objectives, and they are rarely happy if they achieve just one!"[15]

Most importantly, *infinite players are ready for uncertainty.* David Hornik, a leading Silicon Valley venture capitalist who ranks on the Midas List of the world's top investors, struggles with dyslexia. "Because I'm dyslexic, I always have uncertainty," he says. "The world doesn't make sense the way it does for everyone else."[16] Hornik learned to play the game differently while attending Harvard Law School. "Going to law school as a dyslexic was a dramatically stupid thing to do," he told us, laughing. "If I had to read everything, I was dead."

Instead, he says, "my goal in year one was to understand the game so I could play it my own way." For example, rather than cram for an exam by forcing himself to read, he prewrote an essay based on the professor's interest in philosopher John Rawls. His roommate chided him, "You are insane. You have just wasted so much time. You should be studying and instead you've written a useless essay." But when the professor handed out the exam—a paper on Rawls—Hornik simply handed in his prewritten essay. "I have to understand the system, because if I have to play by your rules I lose, but if I can play by my rules, I can do anything." Hornik went on to earn high marks and become editor of the *Harvard Law Review.*

Infinite games might seem risky or counterintuitive to many, but Karen Arnold's fourteen-year study of valedictorians reminds us that "college grades aren't any more predictive of subsequent life success than rolling dice." Why? "School has very clear rules . . . but life doesn't. Life is messy."[17] So challenge your roles, the rules, even the games you are playing, and create a life of continued play and new possibilities.

Reflection and Practice

To start applying the infinite player reframe, pick one professional or personal "game" you currently are playing and ask yourself:

1. *What have I assumed is essential about this role that is actually made up or nonessential?* When CEO adviser Saj-nicole Joni helps top leaders develop breakthrough thinking, she starts by asking

them questions about why they see the world the way they do.
But she also encourages freewriting to reframe what things could
look like. To help Nathan imagine what he really wanted from
his career that balances academic and practitioner research, Joni
advised him to be playful in his freewrites: "What if you made
this easier and more fun? What if you broke all the 'rules'—[be]
concise, precise, [use] vision, [be] forward-thinking, [focus on]
challenges, etc.—and made it fun for yourself, like jamming, then
stepped back and asked if there were critical things you left out—
noticing, not judging?"[18] The nature of finding a more infinite
way to play requires a playful stance—a not-taking-yourself-too-
seriously lens—which can be hard but increases with practice.

2. *How can I play with the game?* Infinite players play for love of
   the game, more than for external rewards or outcomes. Donald
   Winnicott, one of the most influential psychologists of this century, talked about play being essential to healthy development
   and creative living. He argued that play should be something
   that continues into adult life, and as an old man he used to ride
   his bicycle to work downhill with both hands *and* feet on the
   handlebars.

   Winnicott also spoke about "transitional objects," such as a
   beloved teddy bear, that help kids make the shift from earlier
   to later phases of childhood. Upon learning of Winnicott's fun-
   loving nature, Nathan wondered if we could find a "reverse"
   transitional object to introduce more fun and creativity back
   into our overserious lives. He bought a whimsical bicycle with
   old-school handlebars and pedals that brake when you push
   backward, like the bikes he learned to ride on; now Nathan can't
   help smiling every time he walks toward his bike. We also bought
   matching wool jackets to sew old national park patches and other
   cool felt patches onto, both to bring out a playful element in
   our relationship and to add to our curious collection of matching clothing items for when we want to go "twin," the word we
   give to wearing the matching pajamas, shoes, shirts—and now
   coats—we own.

3. *What are the rules for this game? What ways could I challenge
   them?* Tim Ferriss is a controversial figure because he challenges
   rules and boundaries. Sometimes what he does is contentious,

like how he won the national kickboxing title by leveraging a rule that disqualifies participants who step outside the ring, but sometimes he identifies rules worth breaking. For example, he challenges the idea that everyone must work eight hours per day to be effective. He also asks if there are ways you could compress your work, or work in different ways or locations, to allow yourself to develop other things you want to pursue. You can ask similar questions in your life.

4. *What are the boundaries of the games I am playing?* Like Kate O'Keeffe challenging the idea that big corporations can't work together, can you challenge limiting beliefs in how or with whom you play? For example, can you find ways to make your work pay twice? Consider that SXSW, the world-famous creativity festival, emerged from an effort by musicians and creatives in Austin, Texas, to get global exposure for their work, which turned into a craft-supporting source of income.

5. *What is the purpose of the game I am playing?* If you interrogate the things you believe about your life, could you come up with a more infinite game view? What would it look like to play instead of work? What would it look like to play the game just to play, versus trying foremost to win? What would it look like to see work as a chance to help others? What would it look like to add a new game? After Zach Klein sold Vimeo, he and friends went and built wood cabins, just because they wanted to. Their first cabins were poorly made, but they got better, and their efforts led to the "cabin porn" movement. That led to another effort, DIY.org, where people can upload videos to teach and share their projects, like building a tree house.

6. *How can I find and play an infinite role in difficult games?* There is no doubt that life forces us into games that take us by surprise or that we wouldn't choose to play. We aren't trying to discount how hard these things are, but it is helpful if you can envision the infinite path. When our oldest child came out as transgender, we had a hard time navigating our complex emotions, all the conflicting advice, and our own conservative upbringing. When we asked, "What is the infinite game role for parents?" we immediately knew that "unconditional love" was the guiding star to base

our decisions on. This more infinite role created immediate calm and new possibilities for healing and trust.

7. *How much effort will be required to challenge the game?* In one of the most influential models of change, sociologist Kurt Lewin describes the process in terms of unfreezing, making the change, and then refreezing. Unfreezing takes immense effort because you have to convince yourself it needs to change and then get others on board before you can even start the often uncomfortable and time-consuming unfreezing phase. The change phase can feel awkward until it becomes more familiar. And finally, freezing the new changes takes time. Challenging any finite role, rule, or game is hard and requires sustaining yourself while you wait for the change to refreeze.

8. *How do I tap into the joy of playing even when I don't win?* Watch Gabe Polsky's documentary *In Search of Greatness* for a motivational tour de force in the arena of athletic genius. While celebrating sports legends, the film continually reminds us that the beauty and entertainment of sport is so much more enduring than who won. "If the outcome is always to be number 1 no matter the sacrifice . . . what's the point? We aren't robots. We are people driven by feelings and inspiration and a sense of possibility. Creativity is the essence, not an inconsequential aspect of humanity."[19]

Chapter 6

Stories

Stories awaken possibility because they inspire curiosity and help us imagine what might be possible. Ursula K. Le Guin, one of the great science fiction writers, wrote stories to "dislodge my mind, and so the reader's mind, from the lazy, timorous habit of thinking that the way we live now is the only way people can live."[1] Stories also motivate us to take action, even in the face of uncertainty. Indra Nooyi, the CEO who led Pepsi through a massive health and sustainability transformation, told us in a 2018 interview that stories were her primary tool for change: "I could fall back on a lot of personal stories, you know, talk about my own experiences growing up with water shortages and electricity shortages . . . examples of issues related to health and wellness that were very personal and stark."

When facing uncertainty, the most useful stories encourage imagination, hope, curiosity, and purpose. If we can imagine a narrative about our personal uncertainty with characters, conflict, and resolution, we are on our way to a powerful reframing of the possibility at hand. When Clare and David Hieatt moved back to the tiny town of Cardigan, Wales, they could feel the negative effects caused by the collapse of the jeans industry when jobs had gone overseas twenty years earlier. For David, this kind of loss felt personal because a similar closure happened when he was a boy. He recalls riding the school bus and seeing the dirty faces of the miners returning from work, until one day, when the mine closed, "they were gone. Just like that, they vanished."[2]

The Hieatts were determined to do something to change their town for the better. When David tells the story, he starts with his beliefs: "I've always loved business, but . . . I've always thought a business could be a tool for some kind of change you believed in."[3] Upon discovering that

Cardigan had been the headquarters of jeans manufacturing in the UK, leaving hundreds of skilled makers behind, he knew what they were going to do: instead of making low-cost jeans, they would make a great pair of jeans, sustainably, get people their jobs back, and show that "you can make in Britain and you can do it really, really well."[4]

But how do you get people to believe in something that already failed? Again, use your story. When it's told truthfully, with heart and purpose, customers rally with your brand and respond. The Hieatts' "getting people their jobs back" story is powerful because of the authenticity of its characters, conflict, purpose, and optimism. But it also sells their jeans. Every year they are able to hire back more of the "grand masters," and customers have responded. Even Meghan Markle, the Duchess of Sussex, wore a pair, promoting their cause. Today the Hieatts operate from the same factory that shut down two decades ago, and from that remote place at the edge of the sea they inspire a network of influence and change.

According to neuroscience studies, stories have a remarkable ability to change our thinking, for example by demonstrating how our minds literally sync with each other as we hear a story.[5] But decades before neuroscience proved it, philosopher Søren Kierkegaard wrote about the importance of imagining what we can do as the first step in eventually taking action. Kierkegaard believed deeply in our potential, if we could just imagine it, writing that "there is nothing with which every [person] is so afraid as getting to know how enormously much he/she is capable of doing and becoming."[6] It is an inspiring thought and worth reflecting on, given Kierkegaard's conclusion after a lifetime of reflection on human possibility: "If I were to wish for anything, I should not wish for wealth and power, but for the passionate sense of the potential, for the eye which, ever young and ardent, sees the possible."[7]

How can you get started on creating your own story to guide you through uncertainty? Begin by paying attention to what social entrepreneur Mike Smith calls "the tiny whisper that tells us we can do something incredible." Looking around his isolated, rural town of two thousand people with a poverty rate above 40 percent, Smith heard that whisper. His idea was to create an indoor skatepark that could serve as a resource for kids like the one he had been: creative, a bit rebellious, on the fringes but needing community. He didn't even have a checkbook, but he assembled a group of advisers and started fundraising to support the park. Today, that skatepark has welcomed over 10,000 skaters, served over 250,000 meals, and helped over 1,000 youth with its services. Smith's many humanitarian projects are sponsored by major brands like Vans, Jostens, and Red Bull.

Reflecting on finding his story, Smith argues it's not about traditional success metrics but finding what you are good at.

> Look, I'm a white guy from Nebraska who graduated with a 2.4 GPA, an 18 on my ACT test, and was accepted to one small college to play sports because my grades were bad. I'm the most average human being. If I can make stuff happen, so can others. But we have to ask what's driving us. It cannot be money. . . . People always say do what you're passionate about, [but] you should do what you're good at, what you have a good skill set for. For me, it was gathering a community around an issue, networking, and speaking.[8]

Melinda Thomas, cofounder of multiple companies including Octave Bioscience, CardioDx, and ParAllele, and New York City's first entrepreneur in residence, takes this advice a step further, arguing that you should systematically explore your strengths. Part of what helped her through the uncertainty of multiple startups—the "foggy whiteout conditions without a road map . . . [where] you don't quite know what to do or how to move forward"—was having a sense of her skill set.[9] "Pay attention and be introspective," she advises. "Take every test you can take. Myers-Briggs. Superpower. StrengthsFinder." Pay attention to what resonates and then "pilot the hypotheses" in low-risk situations to build your confidence around what you like and are good at. It is on the back of these "certainties" that you have the strength to step into the unknown.

If you are struggling to find a story, trust curiosity. Journalist and author Elizabeth Gilbert recounts how after her fourth book, *Eat Pray Love*, sold twelve million copies, she set to work on another memoir. But when she finished, she concluded, "Truly, the book was crap. Worse, I couldn't figure out why it was crap. Moreover, it was due at the publisher [and] I had absolutely no passion for writing. I was charred and dry. This was terrifyingly disorienting."[10] A friend advised, "Take a break! Don't worry about following your passion for a while. Just follow your curiosity instead." Gilbert admits she was curious about gardening—not passionate, just curious—and so she spent the next six months planting vegetables. "I was pulling up the spent tomato vines when—quite suddenly, out of nowhere—I realized exactly how to fix my book. I washed my hands, returned to my desk, and within three months I'd completed the final version of *Committed*—a book that I now love."[11]

Curiosity is indeed a tiny whisper that we hear when we pay attention and that grows stronger when we follow it. Paul Smith grew up dreaming about and preparing to become a professional cyclist. But when a biking accident put him in the hospital for six months, he had to change course. He began to get curious about clothing design, and when out of the hospital, he took a class on tailoring clothes. That led to a job on Savile Row and then to opening his own small store, a mere thirty square feet. Today he is an internationally recognized designer with stores all over the world.[12]

It can be empowering to remember that whatever happens to us, our life is the story we tell from it. When we asked Benjamin Gilmour what led him to ride a motorcycle through Pakistan, save lives in an ambulance in Mexico City, and make films featured at Cannes and the Oscars, he simply said, "I grew up getting read to every night. . . . I love the stories where the protagonist makes remarkable choices, not the safe choice. . . . I wanted my life to be a remarkable story."[13]

Reflection and Practice

Like all Reframe tools, the power of stories lies in finding and harnessing new possibilities. A powerful story will encourage curiosity, help you imagine what's possible, and create the desire to get you moving forward. Imagine your life as a shelf holding several books full of potential stories, and ask, "What story do I want to pull down off the shelf and read? What do I wish the main character of my story would do?" It's your turn to create a story to guide you through uncertainty. Here are some ways to start:

1. *Imagine speculative personal fictions.* Alone or with the help of friends, develop a handful of short paragraphs about what your life could look like in five years. Alternatively, at the beginning of the year, write the holiday card that you would love to be able

to send at the end of year. What would it look like to live an intentional year you felt inspired by? Use these to start breaking boundaries about what the future could be. If you find yourself getting stuck, try the inverse and write a story about what you don't want. Remember that great ideas may start as tiny whispers.

2. *Focus on values, questions, and problems to be solved rather than specific outcomes.* Most of us think of stories in terms of outcomes (e.g., I want to be a CEO, I want to be married and have two kids by age 38). Try to focus instead on the values and passions that are important to you (healthy relationship, meaningful work) or the problems you could solve that would be most interesting to you. For example, why do you want to be the CEO? Do you have a different vision for how the company should be run or how it should treat its people? Infuse your story with verbs like *help*, *inspire*, *shape*, and *change*, rather than lists of achievements.

3. *Develop a narrative, not a vague mission statement.* We are motivated by narratives—with characters, conflict, and resolution—more than by mission statements. Stories about who we are and the future we are trying to create will be more powerful than any vague "strategy."

4. *Take time for introspection to uncover the tiny whisper.* Ask yourself, "Under what circumstances do I do my best work?" Also, ask friends, colleagues, parents, and partners what they see as your strengths and capabilities.

5. *Use your strengths in new ways.* As you think about strengths, you may want to play with the level of abstraction. For example, perhaps you like working in teams, but the bigger-picture thing you enjoy is helping people.

This book is the product of applying this tool. We met early in life, fell in love, and had four children quickly. Sometimes we only had a hundred dollars at the end of the month, and so to survive we specialized, Nathan in his career and Susannah in the family. But we shared an intellectual curiosity from the very beginning, taking courses together at university (Susannah always scored higher). And even though she completed graduate school just after our third child was born, Susannah decided to start her own clothing line instead of pursuing a PhD like Nathan. As our kids grew and Nathan's tenure-track positions required more focus, we specialized further, culminating in an almost *Leave It to Beaver* division of tasks by the time we moved to France.

While Nathan continued investigating how innovators navigate the uncertainty that comes with doing new things, we shared many passionate discussions on uncertainty over dinners and long walks because we were living it: leaving our faith tradition, moving to France, navigating parenting challenges. For example, our children's schools in Fontainebleau turned into daily torture, and in the space of two weeks we relocated to Paris, increasing the uncertainty (and maladaptive specialization). Now Nathan needed to make more money to pay for school tuition. Scarcity meant Nathan said yes to every opportunity for extra income, and he began traveling nonstop. It was taking a toll on us and our friendship, but we didn't know how or what else we could do.

We started to work on our fading friendship and the imbalance of our pursuits but we were both overworked, Susannah in particular, with boring, thankless tasks. Both of us felt underappreciated. We worked with life coaches and a marriage therapist, but we still didn't know how to put down the story we were living and go back to the one we dreamed of when we met. When Covid-19 erased Nathan's entire calendar overnight, his distress hit the roof. He intuited it was the right time to sit down and write the uncertainty book but was frantic to use his grounded time well. *What would this book be about? What was the angle?*

Susannah had ideas and started imagining this book—the one we ultimately wrote—explaining that he should write it for everyone, not just for managers, because uncertainty is a human condition. Uncertainty could be navigated, not just "managed," she argued. Even though it became obvious how much Susannah was contributing intellectually, Nathan (he is embarrassed to admit) still hesitated. He had just been granted tenure at a top school and had a streak of three bestselling books published by Harvard Business Review Press. What would it mean to publish with his spouse? Would people take it seriously? Meanwhile, Susannah wasn't sure she could stomach his dismissive, "I can do it myself" antics. She knew she had great ideas and would steer the book in a more authentic, helpful direction . . . if he was lucky enough to have her join.

In some ways, the story upon which we originally formed our relationship had grown dusty on the shelf, pushed way back, forgotten. When we both listened for the tiny whisper, we knew working alongside each other as researchers and writers was a shared dream, and we decided to try. It was like the early days of university, and we naturally found an exhilarating rhythm that felt right. Be forewarned: We still fell into old stories and suffered through lots of rounds of frustration and feeble threats about leaving the project. If Susannah was going to be a coauthor, it meant Nathan needed to pitch in more with household tasks and time-consuming French bureaucracy. Nathan recalls imagining the books on the shelf of his life. When he considered pulling down a book coauthored by Susannah, its story buzzed with curiosity and possibility.

Chapter 7

Regret Minimization

Recently one of Nathan's former students lamented, "I spent all summer coming up with business ideas, but in the end, I couldn't make the decision to go for it." This indecision highlights a predicament we all face: How do you make the decision to do something uncertain? How do you know whether an opportunity is real or imagined, and if it is real, whether it's worth the risk? The truth is, you can't know in advance of trying. That's part of the uncertainty. But you can figure out if you should try.

When Jeff Bezos came up with his idea to sell books online, it wasn't obvious that it would work. The year was 1994, long before the dot-com boom of 1999, and most people didn't even know about the internet—there were only two thousand websites in the world (compared with almost two billion today). Hotmail, the home of most people's first email address, wouldn't be founded until two years later. Bezos had a high-paying job at one of the most prestigious Wall Street investment firms, and when he pitched the idea to his boss, investment legend David Shaw, Shaw agreed about its merits but advised "it would be a better idea for someone who didn't already have a good job!"[1] He encouraged Bezos to reflect for a while before making the leap.

Bezos admits he struggled with the decision until he found what he called a *regret minimization* framework that made his decision "incredibly easy." Bezos clarifies, "I knew that when I was age eighty, I was not going to regret having tried . . . to participate in this thing called the internet, which I thought was going to be a big deal. I knew that if I failed, I wouldn't regret that." Then with emphasis in his voice, he continued, "But I knew the one thing I might regret was never having tried. I knew that would haunt me every day."[2]

Bezos wasn't the first to come up with such a framework. Years earlier, researchers Amos Tversky and Daniel Kahneman argued that the one remedy to the biases introduced by maladaptive framing (i.e., framing that leads you to interpret an event in a negative way) is to ask "How will I feel in the future?" rather than "What do I want right now?"[3] But there are some nuances to applying the regret minimization framework. After graduating from Stanford, Nathan had a comfortable job at a US university, close to grandparents and cousins and with great public schools, when he received his dream job offer from INSEAD in France. Accepting would mean a lower salary in a more expensive location, a higher tenure bar at a more demanding school, a disruption to the children's schooling, and the challenges of living in a foreign country. He wondered, "Is it wrong to put our family through the stress of dramatic change just for this supposed dream? Will we regret pulling our kids out of their schools?" We didn't know if he would be able to get tenure or if we were up to the loneliness of expat life far from our networks. The complexity of the uncertainties had us spinning in circles. Here is a list of clarifying frameworks—some we have used and others we wish we had used—to make sense of uncertainty you are facing.

> *Risk versus regret minimization.* Most of us are taught to minimize risks, but that's different from minimizing regrets. Minimizing risks reduces negative surprises, but it also reduces the chances of new things happening. Regret minimization, on the other hand, is about identifying the right risks to take, the ones that define who you are now or who you want to become. When we were deciding whether we should risk disrupting our children's lives to move to France, clarity arrived when Nathan's grandmother said, "Parents teach their children to live their dreams by living their own dreams." Staying put might reduce our risks, but it would greatly increase our regrets.

> *One-way versus two-way doors.* Bezos talks about decisions in terms of one-way doors (irreversible) and two-way doors (reversible). Innovators try to turn "one-way door" decisions into "two-way door" experiments, usually by breaking a big decision into smaller decisions, taking short-term options on a longer decision, or creating backup plans. When we framed moving to France as a permanent change, it was terrifying. But when we reframed it as a three-year experiment after which we could always move back

and pick up where we left off, it became much easier to make the decision.

Independent versus interdependent decisions. Some decisions affect us alone and some affect others. We should be thoughtful about the harm we may cause to others through our decisions, but also honest about it. Moving to France meant pulling our oldest out of high school. Would it disrupt his education? We concluded that it probably would, and hesitated. But then we found a compromise we felt good about: for our children, perhaps the greater education would be in facing and overcoming hard things. That has proved true, perhaps too true, as our children have become so bold and independent that we sometimes bemoan their daring.

Apples versus apples. Lastly, one of the biggest mistakes people make is comparing the certain benefits of their current situation with the uncertain risks of the unknown. For example, in deciding to move, we compared our known comforts (e.g., salary, current schools, family) with the uncertain risks (e.g., culture, new schools, workload). This is an unfair comparison—one that's particularly hard for our brains—because it compares known gains with risky losses. As Tversky and Kahneman's research revealed, we tend to overestimate the benefits of preserving the status quo.[4]

For us, making the decision to join INSEAD proved difficult when we compared certainties with uncertainties. The known benefits of our comfortable position, good schools, beautiful home, and family proximity were powerful weights when compared with the big risks of lower pay, a higher performance bar, an unknown education system, and a small row house. But that unfair comparison didn't take into account the possible upsides. Being at a top-tier school could actually offer new income opportunities, and tenure at such a school could open other intellectual frontiers. The European lifestyle would teach us new things about ourselves, and the international experience could increase our resilience. When we reframed the unknown as a source of possible gains, we could see why the innovators we studied love the unknown: because they see it as full of opportunity.

What happened? We moved—and at first, we did make less money, the children were bullied mercilessly by peers and even teachers, and we struggled with homesickness and the frustrations of being foreigners. But we learned so much! Nathan got tenure, published two more books with Harvard Business Review Press, and his speaking career took off. The children adapted, learned a new language, and we found a better school. Susannah took intensive French lessons, learned embroidery and jewelry making from expert craftspeople, and felt liberated by the anonymity of living in a big city. In the end, we wrote a book together. Our move to France, and then to Paris, brought new opportunities we never could have discovered from the old status quo. We are so happy we took those risks and are even more daring now about making decisions we will not regret when we are age eighty!

Reflection and Practice

Ultimately, making remarkable and satisfying choices for ourselves and those who depend on us involves asking a pair of questions: (1) Will I regret trying and failing? and (2) Will I regret never having tried? Usually the answers to these go hand in hand: It can be an incredibly valuable lesson to try something and discover you don't want it. So if you wouldn't regret trying and failing, then that is a good sign you should try. If you would regret never having tried, that is another indicator that you should take action. Bezos's experience does not mean that the answer is always to try: sometimes we ask the question and realize that we would regret either what we might lose or what it would mean for others impacted by the risk. In that case, regret minimization would mean not taking the risk. But recall that one of the top five regrets people express at the end of life is not having taken more risks.

Here are a few more tactics that might help you reach a good decision:

1. *Write yourself a letter from your imagined eighty-year-old self.*
   What advice would you give from that perspective? When Susannah did this exercise, she instantly channeled a more compassionate, wisdom-filled older self that reminded her of the current things she was taking for granted (mobility, health, youth). She was also surprised at how feisty her eighty-year-old voice

was—encouraging her to be bolder, have more fun, and be more contrarian.

2. *Advise the main character.* If your life were a novel, what choice would you want the main character to make? What advice would you give him/her?

3. *Compare apples with apples.* Imagine what could go right on both trajectories—deciding to move forward or not—and compare those, as well as what could go wrong on both trajectories.

4. *Consider multiple dimensions of performance.* It is easy to get stuck on one dimension, such as money. But remember that Kaospilots see multiple dimensions of the value of a decision. Moreover, consider performance dimensions thoughtfully. Although our children's performance in math was temporarily disrupted by moving to France, they learned something more important: grit and independence.

5. *Be careful about extraneous elements.* When Bezos quit Wall Street in the middle of the year, he left his bonus on the table. For Bezos, who had already made plenty of money, hanging around for a bonus ran the risk of creating regrets. For others, that money might be what allows you to actually try something new. How do you tell the difference? What really is essential to helping you move forward in the uncertainty? What is your soul whispering for you to do?

6. *The right choice isn't always to go for it.* There are many things we have turned down and are happy that we did. Many advisers on decision making, for example, talk about opportunity costs, or the cost of the opportunity you give up. Before you make a final decision, you may want to review the next section of the book to help you make informed choices about where you excel in uncertainty and where you struggle.

7. *Adopt a decision framework.* If you are still struggling, perhaps dig a little deeper by using well-thought-out decision frameworks. For example, a year before the offer to join INSEAD arrived, Nathan received a tempting offer from another, nearby university. He used the "Making Smart Choices" framework to think through the decision. The framework consists of eight elements:[5]

(1) Frame the problem accurately, acknowledging complexity, assumptions, and option-limiting prejudices. (2) Specify your objectives and how they help you get to your goal. (3) Create imaginative alternatives so you have the full choice set. (4) Understand the consequences and how a particular choice impacts all your objectives. (5) Recognize and accept trade-offs. (6) Clarify the uncertainty of a particular future happening. (7) Consider your risk tolerance. And (8) think about how decisions link together. Applying this framework, it became clear that in this case we should stay put and wait. And we are so glad we did because the offer to join INSEAD came just a short time later.

Chapter 8

Aplomb (Doubting Self-Doubt)

When facing uncertainty, self-doubt almost always shows up. Even innovators, entrepreneurs, and pathbreakers doubt themselves, and not just once but over and over. At the core of this recurring fear is the nagging worry that you may not be smart (or clever, or daring) enough, your ideas may not be good enough, and that trying anyway might reveal this fact for all to see. If you buy into that fear, it is almost certain that you won't try anything uncertain. Because self-doubt is such a natural part of facing uncertainty, feeling it is a sign not that you should stop, but rather that you're in territory requiring triage—digging deeper to that place inside yourself that believes your offering is worthwhile. We named this chapter and tool "aplomb" because it's such a great word, coming from the French for a plumb line, denoting steadiness, confidence, poise. When something is done with aplomb there is self-assurance, even nonchalance.

Consider the experience of two Nobel Prize laureates, one a pioneer of quantum physics and the other of literature. When Richard Feynman arrived at Cornell University for his new job as a physics professor, he didn't realize how burned out he was due to his work in the race to beat Nazi Germany to build an atomic bomb and the loss of his wife to tuberculosis. As the months passed, Feynman found himself suffering from a crippling self-doubt. "When it came time to do some research, I couldn't get to work," Feynman recalled. "I simply couldn't get started on any problem. . . . Here I was, burned out, reading the *Arabian Nights* and feeling depressed about myself."[1]

Despite his struggle to produce, Feynman started receiving job offers from other universities and companies. "Each time I got something like that, I would get a little more depressed. . . . They expect me to accomplish something, and I can't accomplish anything! I have no ideas." When Feynman got an offer from Princeton's Institute for Advanced Study, led by Albert Einstein himself, he balked: "The other offers had made me feel worse, up to a point. They were expecting me to accomplish something. But this offer was so ridiculous, so impossible for me ever to live up to, so ridiculously out of proportion."

The prestigious offer felt so absurd that Feynman took a new, almost roguish angle on his self-doubt: he moved to aplomb. "I thought to myself, 'You know, what they think of you is so fantastic, it's impossible to live up to it. You have no responsibility to live up to it!' It was a brilliant idea: You have no responsibility to live up to what other people think you ought to accomplish. I have no responsibility to be like they expect me to be." He decided to quit trying to do "important" research and just spend time having fun with physics, which is what originally attracted him to the field.

A few days later in the dining hall at Cornell, someone tossed a plate in the air. Feynman noticed that the Cornell medallion on the plate went around faster than the plate wobbled. He developed a series of equations to calculate the ratio of the spins. When he showed them to his department chair, Hans Bethe, another Nobel laureate, Bethe admitted it was interesting but asked, "What's the importance of it? Why are you doing it?"

Feynman laughed and replied, "There's no importance whatsoever. I'm just doing it for the fun of it." Because he had reframed his work based on his curiosity, he was able to be calm and collected in the face of the skepticism and dismissal.

As Feynman kept working, driven by curiosity and setting aside the notion of importance, the simple work started to transform. "Before I knew it (it was a very short time), I was 'playing'—working, really, with the same old problem that I loved so much, that I had stopped working on when I went to Los Alamos: my thesis-type problems, all those old-fashioned wonderful things. It was effortless. . . . There was no importance to what I was doing, but ultimately there was. The diagrams and the whole business that I got the Nobel Prize for came from that piddling around with the wobbling plate."

Feynman's vulnerable account is rare for its transparency, but it's a type of experience shared by many creatives and innovators tackling the unknown. Nobel Prize winner John Steinbeck won a Pulitzer Prize for his novel *The Grapes of Wrath*, but while writing it he experienced overwhelming self-doubt on a daily basis. He documented his experience in a journal that he requested be kept private during his lifetime and be given to his two sons, so they might "look behind the myth and hearsay and flattery and slander a disappeared man becomes, and to know to some extent what manner of man their father was."[2]

His journal reveals shocking levels of self-doubt, frustration, and fear while writing what many people consider the greatest American novel. At every stage he doubted himself, worrying, "If only I could do this book properly, it would be one of the really fine books and a truly American book. But I am assailed with my own ignorance and inability." At one point he decides, "I'm not a writer. I've been fooling myself and other people. I wish I were." Even when he manages to encourage himself to keep going, his journal documents a continual struggle to maintain hope that it would be good: "Sometimes, I seem to do a good little piece of work, but when it is done it slides into mediocrity." His doubt did not abate even as he neared the end. He concluded: "This book has become a misery to me because of my inadequacy."[3]

These firsthand accounts of self-doubt by two Nobel Prize winners illustrate the intensity and regularity with which people who had great ideas and produced important work still doubted themselves. Indeed, when we step into the unknown, self-doubt may be the first instinct we have: what if we aren't right, what if others think we are foolish, what if things don't work out? There are many, many faces of self-doubt. We may tell ourselves that we don't have the time, we don't have the money, we are too old, others have had the idea before, someone else could do it better, and on and on until we convince ourselves not to try. But aplomb is moving forward anyway, knowing others have felt what we feel. And when paired with the concept of prioritizing values over goals, which we discuss in chapter 19, aplomb becomes truly powerful.

Reflection and Practice

Few, if any, people have all the capabilities they need when they start something bold, new, or uncertain. Instead, they get what they need by starting. When self-doubt arises, welcome it, separate it from yourself, focus on what makes you curious or inspired, and get back to work.

There are a number of tactics to increase self-confidence in order to bypass the self-doubt that arises with uncertainty. Acting with aplomb takes nerve, nonchalance, collectedness, and self-assurance.

- *Call it what it is.* When you are experiencing self-doubt, recognize it quickly and externalize it—it's a natural human response to the unknown, not a measure of your ability or the idea's merit.

- *Work regularly and frequently.* Both Feynman and Steinbeck simply got to work (or "play" in Feynman's case). Steinbeck committed to a daily routine: "There is no possibility, in me at least, of saying, 'I'll do it if I feel like it.' One never feels like awaking day after day. In fact, given the smallest excuse, one will not work at all." Steinbeck advised himself, "Just set one day's work in front of the last day's work. That's the way it comes out. And that's the only way it does."[4]

- *Separate the self-doubt from idea doubt.* In his book *Originals*, Adam Grant argues that innovators are able to separate the value of their idea from their value as people, making them more curious and more robust against self-doubt. "The difference between high-output geniuses and the rest of us is the attitude they take when something flops. . . . When many of us would internalize that realization and think, 'I'm crap,' they think something like this: 'The first few drafts are always crap, and I'm just not there yet.'"[5]

- *Go rogue on the doubt.* The beauty of Feynman's example is that he flips the self-doubt on its head and lets it liberate him. Part of what creates self-doubt is the question of whether our idea is worthwhile and our attempt is any good. Not caring so much about either liberates us to do our best work.

- *Revisit your story.* When self-doubt comes up, go back to your story: Why are you doing this? Recalling your reasons for doing it in the first place will bring aplomb to your work.

- *Argue both sides.* Rather than letting self-doubt cripple you, argue your case like a defense attorney would. Remind yourself why what you are doing has merit. Explain why you should take action now versus later. Sometimes you need to put the thing you were working on in the drawer for a while, but if you can convince yourself that now is the time, don't let the doubting of your own capabilities drive the decision.

- *Stop letting self-doubt rob you.* It may help to remember what self-doubt has stolen from you and will steal from you if you listen to it. Yes, doing new projects is uncertain, but the one certain thing is that if you never try, you will never achieve anything. Self-doubt, if you reframe it, is robbing you in broad daylight of the things you want most: conversations, experiences, projects, curiosities—all of it!

Chapter 9

Uncertainty Manifesto

"The world is more magical, less predictable, more autonomous, less controllable, more varied, less simple, more infinite, less knowable, more wonderfully troubling than we could have imagined being able to tolerate when we were young."

—James Hollis

Reframing how you feel about uncertainty includes becoming aware of your foundational beliefs about your work and your purpose. Though guiding motivations are and should be personal, we have noticed some remarkable similarities among individuals adept at facing uncertainty. They call it by different names (e.g., stoicism, mindfulness, faith), attribute it to different forces (e.g., God, the universe, luck, timing), and it manifests in different ways, but it often comes down to a similar philosophy. Quite simply, the ability to calmly face uncertainty seems to be related to whether you view your goals as *internal* (i.e., doing your best, being your best, learning) rather than *external* (i.e., being the best, being the most famous) and whether you view outcomes as partly *outside your control* versus completely *inside your control*.

John Winsor, the founder of multiple companies and a fellow at Harvard Business School's innovation lab, describes developing this perspective after being caught in an avalanche. Before the climb, Winsor and his fellow climbers had trained extensively and checked the weather. But despite their best preparations, as they traversed a glacier, a crack appeared on the hillside above them and the snow started to slide under their feet. Winsor stayed calm, grabbing the climber next to him as they had been trained to and shouting, "Let's ride this out! It's not going to be any big deal."[1]

What they couldn't see was that the fracture line above them was nine feet deep and a thousand feet across. Suddenly the whole of the mountainside came rushing down like a gargantuan tidal wave, filling the valley with a deafening roar. The snow hit the team from behind, tumbling them head over heels in a blind white flurry until suddenly it stopped, hard as cement. Everyone had been buried, the fortunate ones partway. Thanks to their training, and some luck, the entire team was rescued, but that sort of close call, Winsor reflects, "shakes everyone up so much [that] there are these long lingering effects in . . . the psyche of each individual person, in what they are willing to experience, in the confidence to go out there and do it again, and in how they are willing to accept risk."[2]

As he looks back on his career, Winsor compares his experience as an entrepreneur, and disruptor, to that avalanche. You go into this terrain and there is opportunity there," he says, but even if you do "all the analytics to approach it safely . . . everything can be going along and a massive disruption happens."

The unexpected, or fear of the expected, can dent your willingness to try, depending on how you look at uncertainty.

> We have this perception in business: we think we control the world. I think what is probably more correct is it's more about timing . . . and interpreting the world instead of trying to say we control it. . . . It would be much healthier to think about it in the context . . . of trying to be in the right place at the right time and to create something. . . . A really good surfer finds themselves at the right place at the right time to take off on a wave, but then always flows and does maneuvers to stay where the most powerful part of the energy of the wave is.[3]

Winsor's example illustrates the importance of finding and holding on to a foundational belief about uncertainty and your relationship to it. We suggest creating an *uncertainty manifesto*, a motto or intention that can carry you through any uncertainty you face. Derived from the Latin for *easily recognizable or obvious*, a manifesto is a statement, often shared publicly, that makes clear your intentions or position about something. When Winsor talks about the people and organizations that can face uncertainty, he talks about doing one's best and leaving the rest up to timing. Straightforward. Likewise, when Jeff Bezos talks about leaving a great job to start Amazon, he describes a focus on living a life he wouldn't regret, regardless of whether his startup succeeded or not. Simple. How helpful would it be to have a straightforward and simple uncertainty manifesto to cut through the confusion and noise the unknown usually brings?

Harnessing a guiding belief system can be empowering. David Heinemeier Hansson, the serial entrepreneur behind Ruby on Rails and Basecamp, acknowledges that while he understood these principles intuitively, developing an explicit view—in his case by borrowing from stoicism—has helped him immensely:

> Having some external philosophy of life has helped. Because prior to me discovering stoicism, [my company] didn't really have a great vocabulary to talk about this. We were sort of on the same page, but there were still certain times when things happen, like "What if a competitor does something?" but this is one of those things you almost get liberated from when you realize, "Worry about the things you can control." Right, so what if a competitor comes out with a competing product? That is what competitors do, and they do their thing, and we will do our thing: put out a great product, treat our people well, and deal ethically with the market. Doing that releases you from the stress, from the ends having to justify the means, and the outcome becomes of third or fourth importance. It releases you from all that stress of failure.[4]

The idea that outcomes are partially outside your control can be hard to swallow, but the truth is that in an uncertain world, a lot of things are outside your control. The founders of YouTube weren't brilliant visionaries who saw something no one else saw. There were video-sharing startups founded by smart, dedicated founders before and after them. The YouTube founders initially wanted to create a dating site, but found that people were only uploading videos. They got lucky to be in the right place at the right time when falling storage costs and rising consumer adoption of online video created a perfect storm for their success.

If we adopt a perspective that the goal of life is external—such as money, position, and power—and that the outcome of our efforts is within our control, we can get trapped in an unsatisfiable, *Machiavellian obsession* with being the best. We'll measure ourselves against a constantly moving target because there will always be a dimension on which someone else outstrips us. And if we believe that the goal of life is external but the outcomes are partly outside our control, we tend to get stuck in *mercurial fatalism*, where we believe the world is unfair and we just didn't get the breaks we deserve. By contrast, if we can adopt the view that the goal is internal—our own learning and progress—we will already be better off, even if we still think the outcome is completely within our control. Why? Because the internal goal will be more sustaining even if we make *ruminating progress*, obsessing about everything that goes wrong and mistakenly thinking that it was all up to us.

The most resilient people in the face of uncertainty—the ones who feel the least anxiety, the ones who are more likely to take the most worthwhile risks, the ones who get back on the horse when they get knocked off—adopt the perspective that the goal of life is internal and that the results are partly outside their control. These are the *enlightened pathbreakers*. As Heinemeier Hansson describes, they can let go of the worry that if they don't do things perfectly they might fail, and instead focus on doing their best work.

Certainly, many people have succeeded via Machiavellian obsession or mercurial fatalism, and we all fall into those traps from time to time. Moreover, no innovator we studied had unmitigated success—all of them failed in some respect or did something they regretted. But the most powerful and liberating view you can adopt for your own uncertainty manifesto may simply be to do your best and let the chips fall where they may.

Reflection and Practice

To clarify the different approaches to uncertainty we observed, we use the 2x2 matrix shown in figure 9-1. While it is impossible to maintain a perfect perspective all the time, remembering this framework is helpful for proceeding calmly and hopefully in any situation.

As it turns out, this 2x2 has some deep foundations. The ancient Greek Stoics argued that because many things are outside our control, if we can move beyond obsessing about why things happen and focus in-

FIGURE 9-1

Goal versus control orientation

		Control orientation	
		Inside Events are entirely within my control and outcomes are entirely up to me (success, prestige, recognition)	**Outside** Events are partially outside my control and outcomes are not entirely up to me (success, prestige, recognition)
Goal orientation	**Internal** My goals are internal outcomes (learning, best work, contribution)	**Ruminating progress** My goal is to be my best, but when things work out, I immediately move to the next goal. When things do not, I obsess about what I did wrong.	**Enlightened pathbreakers** My goal is to be my best and do my best work in a way that contributes to the world. What happens as a result is a bonus (when good) or just luck (when bad).
	External My goals are external outcomes (money, position, and so forth)	**Machiavellian obsession** My goal is to be *the* best. I'm constantly plotting how to win, and if I don't win, I am the only one to blame. I will never be satisfied.	**Mercurial fatalism** My goal is to be the best, but circumstances keep getting in my way. A lot of the time, others get the breaks I deserve.

stead on our response, we will be much happier. Likewise, perspectives from mindfulness and Zen Buddhism suggest focusing on being present to what is happening and choosing our best response; trying to control the situation leads to suffering.

But this framework also has roots in psychology, particularly the views espoused by Alfred Adler, a contemporary of Sigmund Freud. Adler rejected much of his colleague's view that what happens to us in the past determines our present (e.g., that an abusive relationship dooms you to a life of abusive relationships). While Adlerian psychology empathetically acknowledges the pain caused by past events, it argues that our response to these things determines our future. If life deals us a hand of cards, instead of blaming our actions on what cards we got, we can instead ask, "What hand can I play now?" Whatever the past or the future holds, it is our response that holds power.

Likewise, Nassim Taleb, a former investor who writes about risk, volatility, and uncertainty, argues that attempts to control uncertainty are doomed to fail. But modern psychology underscores that they can also be dangerously counterproductive. Stanford psychiatrist Irvin Yalom observed that "feeling helpless and confused in the face of random, un-patterned events, we seek to order them and, in so doing, gain a sense of control over them."[5] But instead of gaining control, Yalom says, we end up creating patterns that are incorrect and serve us poorly, creating an "illusion of control" that we repeat to our own detriment. Below are some different approaches for developing your uncertainty manifesto. Focus on those that resonate for you.

1. Read thoughtful reflections to develop your uncertainty mani-festo. A few of our favorites include:

    - *The Manual: A Philosopher's Guide to Life*, by Epictetus

    - *The Three Marriages*, by David Whyte

    - *A Guide to the Good Life*, by William B. Irvine

    - *Finding Meaning in the Second Half of Life*, by James Hollis

    - *The Marginalian*, a blog formerly known as *Brain Pickings*, authored by Maria Popova (who originally called our atten-tion to Irvin Yalom)

2. Interrogate your beliefs to discover your knee-jerk reaction or philosophy—though it may be subconscious—about uncertainty.

    - When you started reading this book, what were your beliefs about uncertainty? When something bad happens, how do you respond (e.g., blame yourself, blame circumstance, re-frame what happened, get curious)?

    - How might your relationship with uncertainty be changing? For example, could you adopt statements like "I am curious about the possibility waiting for me beyond the uncertainty I currently face," "Uncertainty attends every possibility," and "I trust I can find possibility in adjacent possibles, in-finite games, and my personal frontiers."

    - Writing out an uncertainty manifesto will help ground you when facing the unknown. Your manifesto should be written on a human scale: It isn't the stuff of superheroes or pompous arrogance. It can and should acknowledge the emotions it is triggering for you but should reframe uncer-tainty in terms of possibility. A powerful uncertainty manifesto can offer an infusion of energy and courage. If you can't think of one, try this one: "Uncertainty brings both chaos *and* possibility, but I am a chaos pilot! I will find the possibility."

3. Acknowledge paradox: Everything we've talked about in this chapter involves a dose of paradox, a quantum physics idea that two things can be true at once and that there are irresolvable tensions we have to accommodate. On the one hand, things are partially outside your control, but on the other hand, you aren't helpless—you should try to be your best and hope to affect the outside world. This is a paradox. There is a small but growing literature that acknowledges paradoxes. For example, if top leaders want their companies to innovate but also survive, they have to accommodate the competing demands for running an efficient business with the differing demands to innovate. Likewise, entrepreneurs need to build coalitions with a shared identity to create new industries while also carving out a distinct identity within those coalitions. In chaos theory, this idea is known as the *edge of chaos*, a paradoxical zone in a state of disequilibrium where change happens. If you find such ideas helpful, read deeper into chaos and complexity theory. But for many of us it is probably most helpful to acknowledge that uncertainty is not easily tied up with a bow, but involves trade-offs, competing objectives, and paradoxes.

Section Two

Prime

P riming is about getting ready for what's next. You prime a water pump so it provides a steady flow of water, an engine so it can run, and the walls of a room so that the paint adheres. Psychology research has even demonstrated that we can be primed using tools such as power poses, breathing exercises, imagining an ideal performance, or repeating positive phrases to prepare ourselves for challenging situations, like a negotiation or a presentation.

In this section we describe tools that help you prepare for uncertainty. Whereas the Reframe tools lie along the "thinking," or cognitive, axis of the first-aid cross for uncertainty, the Prime tools are situated on the "doing" axis, inviting you to start taking steps toward any uncertainties you face. These include both the uncertainties you choose, such as starting a new project or venture, and those you don't, such as an unexpected loss or downturn. As we explained before, there is always some overlap in the tools—they feed into and inform each other. Thus you may find that as you start taking action, the way you think about uncertainty may change, enriching your ability to reframe and sustain what is happening to you as you face uncertainty.

The table provides a brief summary of the Prime tools, followed by short chapters with exercises for each.

Tool	Description
Know Your Risks	Most people are attracted to some types of risks and are averse to others. Knowing your risk profile helps you fortify where you feel weak and make the most of your affinities.
Personal Real Options	Research on hybrid entrepreneurs reveals that risking it all is often counterproductive. Having a portfolio of both certain and uncertain projects helps reduce anxiety while increasing your chances of success.
Uncertainty Balancers	Even innovators who claim to love risk balance the uncertainty they face by incorporating more-certain things into their lives.
Dumbo Feathers	People, places, and things can be your biggest helps or greatest hindrances. How do you find the "Dumbo feathers" that will help you fly to your dreams and avoid the quest destroyers that will pull you down?
Runways and Landing Strips	Runways and landing strips are the money and time to get your ideas off the ground and the networks that give you new opportunities.
Reimagining Resources	Too often we let constraints limit our imagination, but there are ways to reimagine resources to transform overlooked abundance and use constraints as fuel for creativity.
Fait Sur Mesure	Sometimes we fall into the trap of following someone else's plan for our life. We forget that we can, at any time, customize our lives in bright and beautiful ways. Your life should be, as the French say, *fait sur mesure*—made to your measure.
Don't Force Machinery	The anxiety created by uncertainty can trap us into prematurely settling for suboptimal certainty. Sometimes the best preparation is to be patient. We must learn to entertain the unknown long enough to let a better future emerge.

Chapter 10

Know Your Risks

Have you ever felt that maybe you just aren't a risk-taker, or that you would rather avoid uncertainty altogether? Before you categorically dismiss yourself as incapable of taking risks, it can be helpful to see that there are actually different types of risks. Understanding your natural aversions to some types, and your affinities for others, helps you be more effective at facing uncertainty.

Nathan learned the importance of understanding his personal risk profile when he was a student at Stanford, where the heroes of Silicon Valley are the entrepreneurs, not the academics. Nearing the end of his PhD, with a mountain of student loans and four kids in tow, Nathan had a bit of an identity crisis: maybe he should quit and join a startup? He began to beat himself up for his lack of courage until a fortuitous lunch at the faculty club with one of his mentors, Tina Seelig.

"Let's face it, Tina, if I really had any courage I would become an entrepreneur, but I'm just not a risk-taker," Nathan confessed.

Tina looked up from her salad. "I don't agree at all. I think you are a risk-taker," she said.

"What do you mean?" Nathan asked.

"Do you really think there is only *one* kind of risk?" she pressed.

"I don't know, risk is risk, right?"

"No," she said. "There are different kinds of risks. There's financial risk. There's intellectual risk. There's social, emotional, and many others." Tina paused. "In my view, you aren't comfortable with financial risk—and I'm glad. As a single-income earner with four children, I don't want you to take financial risks, for their sake! But I see you as someone very willing to take an intellectual risk or a social risk."[1]

Midbite, Nathan's perspective changed. He could see how if he quit the academic track to become an entrepreneur, his best intentions might become distorted by an obsession to assuage his financial anxiety, rather than following the desire to create the meaning and impact that characterize the most durable ventures. Moreover, the academic path now seemed like a wise choice because it gave him opportunities to take the intellectual and social risks that energized him.

When we know our natural risk aversions and affinities, we can preemptively prepare for the risks outside our comfort zone so we can handle them more easily. To become familiar with their risk profiles, Seelig encourages her students to create a "risk-o-meter" that assesses their comfort with the major types of risk: financial, emotional, social, physical, intellectual, and political. As an example, see Seelig's own risk-o-meter in figure 10-1.

When thinking about your own risk aversions and affinities, it can make sense to choose strategies that help you fortify in areas where

FIGURE 10-1

Tina Seelig's risk-o-meter

Seelig encourages her students to create a "risk-o-meter," a tool she developed in partnership with her colleagues at Stanford's d.school, which assesses their comfort with the major types of risk: financial, emotional, social, physical, intellectual, and political.

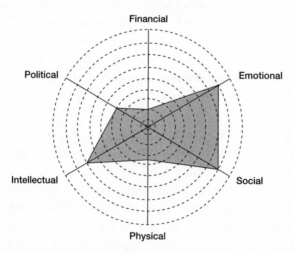

Source: Tina Seelig, *What I Wish I Knew When I Was 20: A Crash Course in Making Your Place in the World, Tenth Anniversary, Expanded Edition* (New York: HarperOne, 2019).

you have a *risk aversion*, rather than tackling risk head-on. This could include setting up a protective mechanism (e.g., savings, a backup plan, life coach sessions, or additional training) or partnering with someone more comfortable with that risk. Serial entrepreneur David Heinemeier Hansson admits he hates financial risk, so to facilitate being an entrepreneur he always has a consulting gig or other income stream that pays the bills while he works on his startups on the side. Notably, one of his side projects, Basecamp, has become one of the most popular team collaboration tools and now pays the bills for other ventures.

At the same time, you also want to proactively embrace areas of *risk affinity*, which are those areas of natural strength where you can push the boundaries more easily. Recognizing your risk affinities can help you make wise career choices, as well as see where you may not be playing to your full capacity. For example, Nathan often holds on to new ideas for too long before sharing them. Recognizing his affinity for intellectual risk has helped him be more proactive in sharing ideas openly and advancing new projects. By more proactively taking such risks, Nathan has discovered new collaborations, publications, and teaching opportunities.

What Do You Care about Most?

Simply because you feel risk averse in a domain doesn't mean you shouldn't ever take such risks. Sometimes we may actually be missing out on the things we care most about because we are letting a risk aversion hold us back. Nathan learned this lesson at Stanford, too, from another mentor, Bob Sutton. The goal of most PhD students is to do great research, land a university position, and earn tenure—the job for life that gives you the freedom to ask even bigger, riskier questions. But being a PhD student is hard, financially and intellectually. You have very little money and a lot of uncertainty about your research ideas. Imagine the surprise when Bob announced in class, "Well, when I was a PhD student like you, I took out a loan to hire people to help me finish my dissertation."[2]

The students all looked at Bob agog. They were packing homemade sandwiches to save a few dollars.

"You took out a loan?" Nathan asked skeptically.

Bob cracked one of his jovial smiles. "When I looked around me at who got great jobs and tenure, the common factor was the quality and speed with which they published their dissertation. I thought to myself, 'If that's the bottleneck, then why not spend some money on it?' So I took out a $10,000 loan and hired assistants to help me gather my data so I could get a head start on publishing."

Bob had seen the real risk—a slow start on the most important ingredient in winning a great job—that Nathan, in his financial risk aversion, had failed to see. Still curious, he asked Bob why he had seen what these Stanford PhD students had all missed. Bob replied matter-of-factly, "I came from a family of entrepreneurs. Taking risks was part of how they created their lives. To me it was obvious—you have to take the risk to create the life you want." While Nathan loves this story for the way it revealed how financial risk aversion might be holding him back, Susannah loves Sutton's ability as a student to take on the role of an academic and expert by hiring assistants *before* he was officially in that role. He was acting *as if* he was already a bona fide researcher and lived it into reality. (For more on this idea, see chapter 28.)

If the PhD student experience seems too abstract, consider a much more common predicament: staying in a job you don't like. Serial entrepreneur Melinda Thomas says this is the most common risk she comes across: "[People] tell me, 'I can't afford to leave my job.'" But Thomas argues that the risk of staying in a job you dislike has a dangerous hidden cost. Doing unfulfilling work can lead to lower performance, which leads to lower raises and bonuses. Moreover, any resulting negative feedback can dent your confidence, putting you in danger of taking any other job that comes along, even one far below your skills, just to get out of that situation.

Thomas quantifies this negative downward spiral with what she calls "grumpy math." She proposes that it would be better to quit, borrow $50,000 to live on, and give yourself a year to find a better job than to stay put and let the negative spiral ensue. She calculates that the better job, with a 10 percent pay increase, would enable you to pay back the loan in just a few years. "Not only have you paid [the loan] off, but you have probably enjoyed those . . . years, and you are on a better trajectory. So get out before you get cranky. That's how you preserve your confidence."[3] We suggest an alternative approach in chapter 11, but you get the point.

Expand Your Risk Tolerance

The good news is that you can also increase your tolerance for risks. Seelig advises taking small risks to build your confidence. A big risk can be overwhelming, creating disabling fear. By contrast, we can usually tolerate a small risk, and when that risk pays off, our confidence in taking on risk increases. For example, Seelig normally likes to keep to herself on a flight, but once, wanting to build her social risk tolerance, she decided to speak to the gentleman next to her. He turned out to be a publisher, and when she mentioned her book proposal, he gave her valuable feedback (though he declined to publish it). However, he did agree to visit her class, and on a later visit, one of the other executives who came to campus with him saw great promise in Seelig's book and ultimately did agree to publish it.[4]

As Piet Coelewij, former senior executive at Amazon and Philips Electronics, explains it this way, "Over the course of my career, as I moved from entry-level positions into leadership, I had to shift from avoiding risks to taking them. It requires courage to do that. Courage is the ability to confront your fear." Coelewij believes that courage can be trained like a muscle and that once you build it up in one area of your life, it can actually help you in another. When he took on a new role as a managing director at Sonos, he decided to take up kickboxing to build his courage. "I am naturally fearful for physical confrontation, so it was very logical to start training for one of the most brutal forms of martial arts, kickboxing," he says with an ironic laugh. But confronting that fear in a controlled setting, "made me more comfortable with higher risk decisions in other settings with less complete information. Once you are in a cycle of lowering fear and developing courage, you create a virtuous circle that allows you to continuously improve. For me, confronting this very specific quality has been transformative. And fun."[5]

Reflection and Practice

1. *Create a risk-o-meter.* Score yourself from 1 to 10 in terms of your risk affinities (1 = very high aversion and 10 = very high affinity) and fill in your scores in the figure. To explain briefly,

social risks involve your public and community relationships; emotional risks involve your intimate, personal relationships; political risks describe your advocacy efforts; physical risks describe your willingness to put life and limb in peril in activities; financial risks are about money; and intellectual risks include your comfort with seeking further learning, different perspectives, or new ideas. If a category doesn't make sense to you, replace it with one that does.

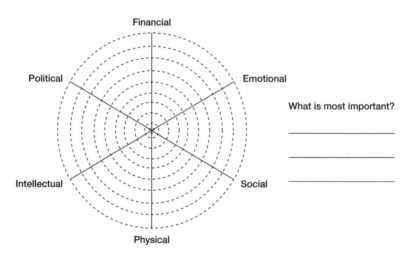

What is most important?

_____

_____

_____

Source: Tina Seelig, *What I Wish I Knew When I Was 20: A Crash Course in Making Your Place in the World, Tenth Anniversary, Expanded Edition* (New York: HarperOne, 2019).

2. *Consider the things that are most important to you.* Ask yourself, How is an affinity or aversion holding you back from them (like in the Bob Sutton example)? Write these things down under "What is most important?" For example, you may long for a relationship but are too scared to take emotional risks.

3. *Think about ways to increase your risk tolerance.* How can you fortify a risk aversion so you could feel more comfortable stepping into the unknown? How could you take small risks to build up your tolerance in an area of risk aversion? For a risk affinity, are you really playing to the full extent of your strengths?

4. ***Explore life goals through the lens of risk.*** Make a list of your current top three priorities (e.g., projects, life stages) and pass them through the lens of your risk zones. Imagine how you might pursue a priority differently if your aversion zones were expanded. And in zones where you feel comfortable, consider how you might be willing to introduce more risk to create more possibility for that priority (e.g., health/robustness of business ideas, parenting methods, empty nest, retirement).

   For example, as a couple we charted one of the shared priorities we hold most dear, the parenting of our four children into adulthood, and discovered some valuable insights about how enlarging our emotional and financial risk would promote growth and closeness with our kids. We also charted our readiness for our coming empty nest phase and recognized there was a lot more we could be doing to prepare for the complex emotions (and newfound freedom) it will bring. For example, we are both curious about hiking Mont Blanc but need to start building our comfort with physical risks first.

5. ***Apply it to your story.*** Thinking back to the Stories tool in chapter 6, pick one of the versions of your future life that you would like to pull off the shelf someday and take it for a spin around the risk-o-meter to see which risk zones might be obstacles to its fruition. Where do you need to prepare for or develop your risk tolerances if you want to achieve that?

6. ***Apply it to the group.*** You can apply this tool for a group or organization, although the risk zones on the outside of your circle may change. In an organizational context, you may use labels like intellectual, social, psychological, financial, political, operational, innovation, and so forth. In that setting, intellectual risk might mean the ability to be intellectually honest. Psychological risk could mean the psychological safety of the organization.

   Choosing the labels could be a group activity. Then after having group members fill out a profile, hold a discussion about organizationwide strengths and weaknesses. You might also ask a focal group (e.g., legal or finance) to fill out a profile for their own group and then have other groups fill it out to give them feedback on how they are perceived.

Some risks may have mixed blessings. For example, a high operational risk tolerance could facilitate innovation but could also expose you to mistakes. Recognizing the collective risk profile could help you have richer conversations about how to address what may be holding an organization back or helping that organization. For example, due to their financial risk aversion, a major manufacturer recently needed to expand production on their corporate campus but had delayed calling back the space they had subleased to other companies for so long that they had workers hired but with nowhere to work. They ultimately delivered the products late, much to their clients' frustration. Having a conversation about their risk aversions helped them realize that their financial risk aversion was holding them back from their ultimate goal.

You can even apply the chart to your family. Our youngest is the least afraid to engage in transactions, even awkward ones, with strangers . . . in French to boot! Seeing this makes us all want to be a bit braver about approaching a stranger, even in a foreign language.

When we take time to share risk affinities as partners, with our families, or as teams and colleagues, we can celebrate the ways our collaboration works well. It can be a powerful moment to recognize personality strengths we have been taking for granted.

Chapter 11

Personal Real Options

Many of us think we need to go all in to succeed. But research suggests that putting all your eggs in one basket may actually decrease your chances of success while also multiplying the accompanying anxiety. Pursuing a portfolio of interests, rather than going all in on one thing, can be a much more effective strategy. Whether you have two or more career interests, projects, or hobbies, adopting a *personal real options* approach will decrease your anxiety in the event that something doesn't work out. It also decreases the potential regret of missing out on meaningful aspects of your personality or skill set.

While adjacent possibilities are the hovering opportunities that await discovery, a personal real options perspective helps you prioritize and move forward on your interests, hunches, hobbies, projects, and ultimately, bring adjacent possibilities to life. The term *personal real options* emerged during an interview with Nobel Prize–winner Ben Feringa. Back in 1999, Feringa made a profound scientific breakthrough when he discovered how to create molecular machines ten thousand times smaller than a human hair. This foundational technology could one day be used to create tiny machines that roam the body's bloodstream to eliminate threats, repair the pipes inside a house from the inside, or increase the capacity of your phone battery so that one charge lasts for weeks.

When we asked Feringa if he encountered uncertainty during the journey to a Nobel Prize–winning breakthrough, his eyes lit up as he responded, "You can't discover anything new if you don't step into uncertainty. Science is full of uncertainty!"[1]

"How do you help your students deal with it?" Nathan asked.

"Striving for certainty will lead you down false paths or lead you to commit too long to projects that won't work, or to uninteresting projects that will work," he explained. That's why he coaches his students to have multiple projects at once.

> If you have only one foot to stand on, you will ride it all the way to the bitter end because you don't want to fail, even if it means you will ultimately fail. Instead, you want to have multiple pathways, multiple projects, and in a way get some certainty out of the portfolio of uncertainties. I usually advise my students to have at least one risky project and one less risky project so you have the confidence that at least something will work out."

Intuitively, Feringa tapped into wisdom that goes back at least as far as the ancient Greeks, when philosopher Thales of Miletus purchased an option on the region's olive presses. By paying a small amount of money in the spring, when his calculations predicted a large harvest, he had the right, but not the obligation, to use the presses that fall. When a massive olive crop matured, he made a fortune with his monopoly on olive presses.[2] Options are common in finance and can be an important tool for taking risks. When Michael Burry, the investor featured in the film *The Big Short*, purchased an option on mortgage defaults (the right to be paid back if mortgage-backed securities defaulted), he earned $700 million in the Great Recession of 2008.

The options approach helps lessen the risks of either going all in and losing everything or missing out entirely by not daring at all. Ricardo dos Santos, former head of the disruptive innovation at Qualcomm (one of the world's largest semiconductor firms), illustrated this logic well when he reflected on his experience: "If I could teach people just one thing, it would be the word *maybe*. . . . I have watched executives do a big analysis about the opportunity in something like server chips, put 100 engineers on the project, get spooked, pull 100 engineers off the project, wait for years until a competitor was doing it, and then go from zero to 100 engineers all over again." Dos Santos says it would be better to adopt a "maybe" approach, going partway in with a few engineers and treating the project like an experiment to see where it could go.[3] He has applied this wisdom in his role as head of ResMed's innovation incubator, where he recruits intrapreneurs "according to the stage of their idea. First as part-timers when the idea needs some initial exploration, then offering a sabbatical—a one-year break from their job—if the idea is looking promising, then offering them a full-time job once the major risks and upside are identified."[4]

Empirical studies support the wisdom of personal real options, demonstrating that at least half of new startups are created by hybrid entrepreneurs who keep their day jobs while starting something on the side—and that those who first start as a hybrid entrepreneur before jumping into a full-time new venture are 33 percent less likely to fail.[5] One of the major reasons they are more successful is that they have more time to discover what works with less stress due to uncertainty. When Felicia Joy quit her job to start a seminar business with a partner, she ran out of money in six months and had to find a new job to pay the bills. Failing "shook me to my core," Joy admits, "but it also gave me strength. It was not that I could not pursue it, but I needed to be smart about it."[6] Later, she founded Ms. CEO Media, a venture providing support for female entrepreneurs, but this time she kept her job until the company could stand on its own, giving it the time it needed to succeed. The hybrid approach can help you take a small step into the unknown to learn about it, helping you be more successful in the future. Nathan's research about companies responding to disruptive technologies has shown that the hybrid approach proved effective in helping them build a bridge to the future.[7] The same is true for individuals.

The personal real options approach also helps avoid many of the dysfunctional behaviors that all-in risks can create. A large body of research—which has uncovered biases like sunk costs bias, confirmation bias, and escalation of commitment—highlights the dangers of going all in. In a famous experiment, MBA students were asked to invest in one of two business units. When it was revealed the business unit in which they had invested had lost money, they counterintuitively invested even more money in the failing business than a successful one in the next round. Moreover, if they felt personally responsible for the consequences, they invested even more money than before, in hopes of recouping the underperforming investment.[8] This effect, known as escalation of commitment, affects many real-world settings, including the National Basketball Association, where higher-paid draft picks are given more playing time even if they underperform, and in the Vietnam War, when as Under Secretary of State George Ball predicted, "Once we suffer large casualties, we will have started a well-nigh irreversible process. Our involvement will be so great that we cannot, without national humiliation, stop short of achieving our complete objectives."[9]

The personal real options approach, then, is simple: as Feringa advised, don't put all your eggs in one basket. The value of this approach applies to all kinds of projects, not just science or business. Author Roald Dahl wrote an essay called *Lucky Break* in which he observes that most authors have a day job to pay the bills. Dahl worked for Shell Oil and in a number of other positions until his writing career took off. Similarly, the extremely prolific Victorian author Anthony Trollope held a job with the postal service for decades, writing every morning from 5:30 to 8:30 before work, a routine that produced forty-nine novels in thirty-five years! He argued that creative work should be as "common work to the common laborer. No gigantic efforts will then be necessary. [An author] need tie no wet towels round his brow, nor sit for thirty hours at his desk without moving."[10]

Personal Real Options on Dreams

While we have focused on the pitfalls of going all in on an uncertain project, the truth is that most of us have the opposite problem: we are all in on a safe path. We tell ourselves that when we have everything nailed down, then we will try the thing we feel calling us. This deferred life plan violates the principle of personal real options just as much as going all in on the uncertain option. There are times in life where we need to wait to act on possibilities, such as while in school or at the start of a career. But even then we can be tiptoeing toward possibility. Although we had few resources while Nathan earned his PhD, Susannah started her clothing line anyway. She recalls looking in the mirror and asking, "Should I wait?" After all, we were living on student loans with four children in eight hundred square feet of on-campus housing. But the resounding answer was, "No, start now." She is so glad she did! Not only did she benefit from the startup vibe of Silicon Valley, but she learned about designing and manufacturing, joined an incredible network of women entrepreneurs, and found a creative, rewarding pursuit during those years of raising four tiny kids.

We observed the dangers of waiting in a case study of two professors in the same English department. They both dreamed of living in Europe during the summers, writing in cafés, and then returning to their Midwest university to teach in the fall. One of the professors, our friend Eric Freeze, started on the dream early, first by taking on the unglamorous role of directing summer programs for high school language students, then years later by scraping together the down payment for a rathole of an apartment in the city of Nice, which he and his wife slowly renovated and rented out the rest of the year. Eric juggled credit card offers to earn points for free flights and learned to spearfish to cut down on grocery bills. Today he and his wife, Rixa, who is a global expert in breech birth, live with their four children part-time in Nice and part-time in the Midwest, which he recounts in his enjoyable memoir, *French Dive*.

One of the most challenging parts has been managing the jealousy of the other professor, who, by waiting for everything to line up perfectly, is still dreaming about living in Europe. While Freeze slowly cobbled together a personal real option, the other professor trusted that it would come together after he got tenure, saved up some spare funds, and hopefully landed a glamorous chaired position that might give him more flexibility. By keeping the France idea on a low burner from its inception, Freeze has benefited from the European real option all along. Although it has required many sacrifices, including at times accepting half-time salary, the dream has gained momentum over years, and now it is a permanent option. Indeed, they recently purchased the apartment below theirs and have started renovations to rent it out as an extra source of income.

One of the best ways to develop personal real options is to start them as side projects, a name used in the excellent how-to guidebook from the Do Lectures, *The Side Project Report*. This report recounts the story of Rhys Newman, cofounder of the Omata, a quirky analog speedometer for cyclists who appreciate the charm of old technology. Newman worked for years as a designer in Europe and Silicon Valley, eventually becoming head of advanced design for Nokia. While working full-time, he made sure to keep drawings of his "mechanical machine" posted around his desk, working on it bit by bit. One November evening at a party in Big Sur, entrepreneurs and wealthy friends encouraged him to quit and start working on it full-time, but the pressures of supporting three children made it too scary for Newman and his wife, Naomi. Two weeks later, Nokia canceled his project and made him redundant. The severance gave Newman the runway, and the nudge, to make Omata his primary project.

Newman offers helpful advice about starting side projects: (1) Give your project a space that doesn't have to be cleared away at dinnertime. (2) Create visual reminders for yourself. (3) Open your eyes to how the other things you are working on could contribute to your side project. And (4) don't be afraid to talk about it, since the advice and help you get along the way vastly outweigh the near impossibility that someone will steal your idea.[11]

Sometimes a side project creates a conflict between your main focus, whether paid or unpaid, and what you are feeling called to do (e.g., go back to school). But even in this challenging scenario, explore whether there are creative ways to develop a personal real option. You might take a sabbatical from your job, work part-time, or take classes in the evening. Of course, none of these are easy, and the answer isn't always so simple, but giving ourselves permission to pursue personal real options is liberating.

Reflection and Practice

Juggling personal real options requires keeping an eye on each project, or option, even though each option won't necessarily get equal attention. But if it adds value to your sense of self, it deserves space and time. Here are some ways to strike that balance between your options:

1. *Take stock.* The creator of *The Side Project Report*, David Hieatt, recommends pausing every few months and asking yourself: "Is the project still providing enough value for the effort I'm putting in? Am I still excited about this project, or has it become a chore? Am I still learning enough to make it worth it? If no one else found out about it, would I still do it?"[12]

2. *Set up a sanctuary.* Remember, your project will never exist if you don't do anything with it, so dignify the option by letting it take up space in your world. This could be a drawer, shelf, or folder where you collect inspiration, ideas, to-do lists, and research pertaining to that project. Keeping it well organized and handy is a way of honoring its place in your life as well as enabling a quick start whenever the moment allows.

3. *Schedule check-ins.* Plan a meeting with your project and use that time to research, think, doodle, or discuss it with someone else.

Set deadlines and hold yourself to them. Sometimes you can find a bridge between your current paid work and your side project so that working benefits both options. If you can find a friend who wants accountability for their personal real option, you can encourage each other to push forward concrete action items.

4. *Avoid doing nothing.* Options can start small and still be legitimate. Among urban adults who missed out on the tranquility of growing up in nature, there is a growing trend of seeking out time outdoors. Few will muster an off-the-grid life in a van or tent. But it is possible to plan a summer camping trip, to take half-day hikes that don't require extensive supplies, or to rent a cabin without Wi-Fi for a weekend. The coffee-table book *The Outsiders: New Outdoor Creativity* hilariously assures its readers that a connection with nature can even start as small as "capturing the retro chic of Edmund Hillary through the gear you wear. . . . There is no set of rules other than to respect and enjoy the outdoors."[13]

5. *Create a personal skunk works.* Some of you might be ready for something more radical to jump-start your effort. Could you take cues from the Skunk Works, the secret division at Lockheed Martin where employees worked at a radical pace to deliver on critical tasks without respect for the rules? They created the U2 spy plane in 143 days, as well as the SR-71 Blackbird, which is still the fastest, highest-flying manned aircraft. In a similar manner, could you take a couple months away from your job or set up a space to work at a furious pace to test one of your personal real options?

6. *Respect the timing.* Timing is real, and some options do need to wait. Nathan had to wait to pursue some projects until later in his career. As Håkan Nordkvist, head of sustainability innovation at IKEA, said, "Sometimes you have to put it into a drawer and come back to it if it is the right thing. We do live in an external environment independent of your idea. If it doesn't happen today, it could always happen tomorrow."[14] Often the retired option we worked on still turns out to be valuable.

Chapter 12

Uncertainty Balancers

We've observed a surprising contrast between what innovators say about their relationship to uncertainty and what they actually do behind the scenes. When we asked for their feelings about uncertainty, we heard responses such as "I love uncertainty" or "I live for uncertainty," sentiments that can be intimidating and hard to relate to. But when we dug a bit deeper, many of those who claimed to love uncertainty had also gone to surprising lengths to create a great deal of certainty in other parts of their lives. These *uncertainty balancers*, in the form of habits, routines, rituals, objects, humor, and relationships, served to counteract, or balance, the unknowns they faced.

Sam Yagan has been one of *Time*'s one hundred most influential people, is the founder or cofounder of four companies (including Spark-Notes and OkCupid), and was CEO of Match.com when it disrupted its own business with Tinder. When we asked Yagan about uncertainty, he said boldly, "I love uncertainty. It's fuel for me."[1] But when we asked about other parts of his life, Yagan revealed a concerted effort to minimize uncertainty elsewhere. "I'm drawn to low-drama relationships, stability, etc. My best friends are from junior high and high school. I married my high school sweetheart. . . . I already have a natural comfort with ambiguity, but I do think that given how much ambiguity I traffic in at work, I do look for less in other areas of my life."[2]

It is a well-established fact that having something familiar helps people to accept the unfamiliar. Technologists have exploited this tendency for centuries in the form of skeuomorphs—familiar elements from older technology that help people accept newer technology. For example, e-commerce sites use shopping carts like physical retail, digital cameras make an audible click like the shutter in analog cameras, email is represented by a paper envelope icon, and early digital notepads looked like real paper (the original iPhone Notes resembled a yellow legal pad). None of these elements serve any functional purpose except to make us more comfortable with the unknown by linking it to something familiar. In fact, when Thomas Edison introduced his electric lighting system, he intentionally dimmed the light bulb to match the brightness of a gas light so it would be easier for people to accept.[3]

Similarly, we can use uncertainty balancers to help us face the unknown in our lives. Uncertainty balancers take many forms, including habits and routines. For example, when we interviewed Lindsay Tauber, former head of Novartis's Digital Acceleration Labs, which is responsible for creating new internal startups, she announced, "I eat uncertainty for breakfast!" But when we inquired more deeply, she revealed some unusually routine habits. When she travels, she always chooses the same seat on the plane, stays in the same hotel, and carries the same granola for breakfast.[4] Likewise, fashion designer Paul Smith, known for his risky, bold color combinations, stays in the same hotel, and even in the same room, whenever he travels.[5] Artist Georgia O'Keeffe would arise at the same hour and eat the same breakfast, and Apple cofounder Steve Jobs had a closet full of enough black turtlenecks to last him a lifetime. Even objects can act as uncertainty balancers. Architect Tadao Ando said "we need unbreakable passion to survive the unknown," but then went on to describe his "unbreakable" passions: the fountain pens he loves, his typewriter, cherry blossoms in spring, and the Hotel d'Angleterre in Paris, where he loves to stay.[6]

Still others adopt rituals. In 1914 anthropologist Bronisław Malinowski observed that the inhabitants of the Trobriand Islands of New Guinea attributed their fishing success to skill in familiar waters and performed rituals when fishing in unfamiliar waters to give them confidence.[7] Although you may be tempted to discount ritual, know that recent studies show up to 70 percent of college students perform small rituals before a big exam, as do a similar percentage of athletes before a big competition.[8] What these and related experiments reveal is that such rituals aren't useless mumbo-jumbo but actually serve the real purpose of helping us deal with the anxiety of uncertain situations.[9]

Research also suggests that humor can be useful for dealing with uncertainty.[10] "Gallows humor," a term that can be traced back to the 1848 revolutions in Germany, is a technique for dealing with stressful, uncertain situations.[11] Paramedic Benjamin Gilmour recalls the frequent use of gallows humor to deal with stress and uncertainty in his work. He remembers one emergency visit where his team found a man, unconscious and in cardiac arrest, lying in front of the TV. As they frantically tried to revive him, his wife said through tears, "Well, I knew you didn't like that show, but I didn't know you disliked it that much."[12] Although morbid on the surface, the ability to use gallows humor, according to sociologist Antonin Obrdlik, "is an index of strength or morale."[13] Author Catherine Ingram recalls how the singer Leonard Cohen was a master of gallows humor, explaining that its power comes from allowing "a sideways glance at the gathering clouds while one is still sipping tea in the garden. . . . In sharing gallows humor, it is also comforting to know that your friend sees the tragicomedy as well. There is an amortizing of the burden when we share a heavy load."[14]

Of all the uncertainty balancers, relationships may be the most powerful. Mike Rhodin, who led IBM's artificial intelligence project Watson from its early days as little more than a computer science experiment, said, "I love uncertainty. I was a competitive athlete in the past, so I love the thrill." But when we asked about how he managed the inevitable anxiety that attends uncertainty, he was very open. "I have a stable core—I've been married for thirty years, and my wife chose to stay home with the kids. That stability really helps me do all the other crazy stuff."[15] Likewise, Morten Karlsen Sørby, a senior executive who has acted in CEO and leadership roles at some of the world's largest telecom operations, reflected that "you think that when you become a leader, your life will become more certain, but actually it becomes more uncertain."[16] When explaining how he deals with uncertainty, he too pointed to his family.

Friends and communities can play a similar role in more long-term relationships for balancing uncertainty. Dallas Roberts, an actor who has been in TV shows such as *Law & Order* and *The Walking Dead*, told us about the importance of the community he met at the Juilliard School for enduring the uncertainty of his job: "I have a community of friends who are also actors, and we all email each other and talk to each other. That community is immensely helpful in dealing with the uncertainty of not knowing if you will get the next role."[17]

In sum, navigating uncertainty well isn't about living in chaos all the time. A better strategy is to find uncertainty balancers to lower the anxiety of facing the unknown. Former UK Prime Minister Winston Churchill provides an inspiring example of using such balancers to endure a decade of uncertainty when it appeared his "destiny envisioned but not yet attained" would never materialize.[18] Churchill had already faced a great deal of uncertainty in his life: His teachers described him as a "lazy little wretch." He failed his military school entrance exams twice and just barely managed to get into the cavalry, which his father dismissed as second-rate, concluding that his son was "a social wastrel . . . one of the hundreds of the public school failures."[19] Even after Churchill established a promising political career, his oversight of the disastrous World War I attack at Gallipoli, which had half a million casualties, appeared to be the definitive end of his ambitions.

Dismissed from the cabinet and the war room, Churchill retreated to his estate, Chartwell, where to deal with the disappointment and uncertainty he began "laying bricks, digging ponds, sculpting terraces, planting gardens, and painting in oils."[20] He adopted a rigid, if eccentric, schedule and spent a great deal of time writing, all while waiting out the grueling period until, with the advent of World War II, he was called back into the political arena and ultimately became one of the great leaders of freedom in the Western world.

Reflection and Practice

Recall the thermometer metaphor we used to chart our uncertainty ability and possibility quotient in chapter 2. There is an optimal area (the learning zone, between the comfort and panic zones) for most of us, below which we stagnate and above which we malfunction. One way to prepare for, or deal with, uncertainty is to use uncertainty balancers to bring us back into this optimal area.

Two important categories of uncertainty balancers to explore include (1) small traditions and routines that bring comfort and (2) predefined choices that create efficiency (e.g., breakfast, wardrobe, schedule, exercise routine). This is not about creating rigid systems, so build in flexibility. If your balancers stop working, adjust or drop them. To find the gaps where uncertainty balancers will be most meaningful, do an audit of the existing routines you live by.

1. ***Examine your routine.*** Jot down your daily or weekly schedule, paying special attention to time slots that introduce decision breakdowns or stress.

   - Do you feel like you suffer more from a lack of renewal (e.g., traditions, things you look forward to) or a lack of efficiency (e.g., menu and chore planning, repetitive tasks)?

   - Are there repetitive tasks you can automate, delegate, or stop worrying about?

   - Are you spending too much energy making decisions? Consider psychologist Barry Schwartz's research on the paradox of choice, which reveals that too much choice decreases happiness and satisfaction and can even lead to paralysis.[21]

   - Are you spending swaths of time on entertainment (e.g., binging on shows, games, or social media) to avoid dealing with uncertainty? What could you do instead to help you rejuvenate rather than just check out?

   - Are there spots where you get stuck? If you are dreading getting out of bed every morning, could you create a morning routine that feels kinder to yourself—time for eating a more nourishing breakfast, reading something inspiring, or choosing an outfit that helps you look your best?

2. ***Adopt new rituals.*** Even the simplest traditions bring comfort and meaning to our lives. Don't underestimate the power of setting aside time—with friends, family, a club, or by yourself—to do something you enjoy. Some of our favorites over the years: pancakes for lunch on Sundays, watching the *Avatar: The Last Airbender* TV series from beginning to end during the winter, bridge walks that crisscross the Seine to mark important milestones, biweekly morning soccer, "family church" where we aim to promote vulnerable and spiritual conversations at home with our kids. If you have a hefty list of rituals, keep going with them—they are providing much-needed certainty to your life! If you feel like you are missing out, add new traditions or elevate the ones that are on life support.

3. *Adjust for your context.* Consider your need for uncertainty balancers in relation to the heat of the uncertainty you face currently. If you are living in an uncertainty panic zone, you might need to implement more extreme measures to rebalance yourself, such as taking a mental health day or finishing your work early enough to do something you love. Removing optional tasks from your plate if they're proving to be toxic—even if you originally said yes to them—can balance the uncertainty you are living with.

Chapter 13

Dumbo Feathers

When preparing to face uncertainty, it's important to surround ourselves with helpful people who believe we are up to the task. The premise of the entire field of social psychology is that outcomes are affected as much by our surroundings as by our free will. When we have encouragement from our friends and family, our confidence grows. Thus, who and what we spend time with become either Dumbo feathers—recall the cartoon elephant Dumbo, who gained the confidence to fly by holding on to a "magic feather" (really just an ordinary feather)—or quest destroyers that hold us back from achieving our dreams.

Like many of us, Kate Bezar wondered if she was on the right career track. After working in management consulting for years, she took a two-year sabbatical, taking classes and trying new things, only to discover that she didn't want to do any of the things she explored. Having "burned through [her] savings like nothing else," she approached a newsstand one night wanting to "read about people who were doing great stuff, who had found their passion in life, who were living their fullest potential."[1] All she found were "pretty pictures of dresses, and clothes, and houses and cars." That night she had an epiphany. Her journal entry captures her euphoria: "I know what I'm going to do. I'm going to make a magazine with soul and passion and heart, and it's going to be about living a rich life and not about material possessions but about experience and fulfilment and all of those magic things." She named the magazine *Dumbo Feather*, a nod to "magic" things that can inspire us to believe we are capable of greatness.

There are many kinds of Dumbo feathers that you can rely on to give you confidence to do new things. In fact, the definition of "noun" comes to mind: people, places, and things all have the power to inspire us to reach our highest potential. People encourage, believe in, and support you like no other Dumbo feather can; places can be powerful instigators and reminders of change and authenticity; cherished objects can give you a boost, helping you feel grounded, prepared, and loved. Our job is to find and hold on to Dumbo feathers, letting them work their magic in our lives, because their opposite, quest destroyers, are an unfortunate reality we must guard against.

We were reminded of this reality in the Chyulu Hills of Kenya, where we spent time with the Maasai guide Kuroyi, who gave our family a pep talk about achieving dreams. Using the analogy of becoming a pilot, he advised, "If you want to be a pilot, you need to dress like a pilot, act like a pilot, and spend time around pilots."[2] Then he added with emphasis, "You have to convince *yourself* most of all!" As we walked behind him, deliberating whether wearing the pilot outfit could really make a difference, he said, "Don't spend time with people who don't believe in you." Standing tall in his bright-red tunic under the setting December sun, he pantomimed what happens if you do. With two hands raised as if holding imaginary reins, he moved his wrists in three distinct stepping-down movements in sync with his warning. "Otherwise, they will bring you down, bring you down, bring you down." By the end his hands were at an unnaturally low position, below his knees. We stood there transfixed. We knew it was true. Let Kuroyi's hand gestures become a reminder that people, places, and things can raise you up or bring you down.

Identifying quest destroyers is sometimes easy, but sometimes they might be hiding behind a guise of trying to help. How can you know if someone is genuinely trying to help or is acting as a quest destroyer?

Sarah Mouchot and Nico Alary are the cofounders of two well-loved restaurants in Paris. On weekends you can expect to wait up to two hours to taste their delicious food. But to get to that point, they had to learn the difference between Dumbo feathers and quest destroyers.

Mouchot and Alary spent several years outside their native France, working in restaurants and cafés around the world, but in Melbourne they fell in love with the spirit of delicious, unpretentious food served in a friendly atmosphere. On their days off, they took long walks on the beach, dreaming of starting such a restaurant together in Paris. But when they returned home to France, they met stiff resistance. Banks wouldn't lend them money because they didn't have collateral or formal credentials from a cooking school. Family members questioned them, filling their minds with all the things that could go wrong. Mouchot remembers, "Everyone attacked it. The menu was too small. We didn't go to school to be chefs. We had stars in our eyes."[3] Alary synthesized the dilemma: "We love and respect our parents, but should we listen to them?" And what about the banks? What about the people who said they needed expensive training at cooking schools like Le Cordon Bleu or Ferrandi?

The banks, they realized, were risk-averse institutions with a narrow set of criteria that made them myopic to this kind of possibility, and so the rejection did not reflect on the quality of their idea. Many of the acquaintances who questioned their formal credentials were reflecting their own fears about doing new things, as well as the larger French cultural focus on credentials. Even the advice of their parents needed to be taken in context. "Our parents were just trying to protect us because they love us," Mouchot reflected. "They were coming from the perspective of people who had worked as employees, not entrepreneurs." There is compassion and wisdom in their observations—they had to sift through the motives of the people giving advice so that they could defend themselves against the quest destroyers, even if those people were well intentioned.

Though discouraged by the naysayers, Mouchot and Alary were willing to take the risk. "We knew it was possible. We wrote our idea down, and whenever we felt discouraged, we went back to that," Alary remembers. Their manifesto wasn't poetic or lengthy, just three sentences about what they believed Holybelly (the name of their two restaurants) could be. When negativity was fierce, they went back to that statement, relying on their friendship and belief in each other as the Dumbo feathers to keep them going.

Dumbo feathers don't eliminate the risk or the hard work. Opening the restaurants required their entire savings and workdays that started at 6 a.m. and ended around 11 p.m. Alary laughs remembering how "we would come home from a workday so exhausted that we would just eat a handful of peanuts and go to bed." But Dumbo feathers help you believe in yourself. Today, Mouchot and Alary are successful entrepreneurs, but they still hold on to a Dumbo feather, a motto printed on all their menus, mugs, and T-shirts: "It's good because we care." That simple idea has guided them through tough times, including endless citywide strikes and three Covid-19 closings. Everything they do has a touch of magic about it because of this one guiding principle.

When the French government closed all restaurants in the first Covid-19 confinement, the Holybelly restaurants had two days to deal with two weeks of food that would spoil. They gave away twenty thousand euros' worth of prepped food to neighbors and customers. The generosity, the goodwill, and the feeling of warmth they created in that gesture is indescribable. But their generosity didn't stop there—after an exhausting day of handing out this food, they went home and created Instagram stories with detailed instructions explaining how to cook each item, including techniques, temperatures, and cooking times. When they were finally allowed to reopen for takeout, their fans in Paris quickly overwhelmed them with orders and their admirers from abroad cheered them on.[4]

Ideas, memories, and stories may be some of the most powerful Dumbo feathers we have. As we recounted in the discussion about regret minimization in chapter 7, when we had the chance to leave a steady and comfortable life in the United States for a job in France, we took courage in the feather Nathan's grandmother offered him when she advised, "Parents teach their children to live their dreams by living their own dreams." We held on to that through the fears of moving and the challenges of settling in. Whether your feathers are people, places, or things, don't forget the ultimate truth: you already have the ability to fly, you just need a little encouragement.

Reflection and Practice

There are many people, places, and things in your life that could become Dumbo feathers. Here's how to think through what they could be.

1. Dumbo feathers can be people you have never met, even those who have passed away, such as authors, poets, artists, mentors, and ancestors. What matters is that they inspire you.

2. In a similar way, identity-forming memories and insights from your youth that were revelatory in some meaningful way can serve as Dumbo feathers if you remember and revere them.

3. Imagining yourself in a more fulfilled future state could also be a Dumbo feather that helps you make good choices today. In his

poem about an ancient saint in Ireland, poet David Whyte encourages us to think and act based on the future we want to create: "Live in this place as you were meant to and then, surprised by your abilities, become the ancestor of it all, the quiet, robust, and blessed Saint that your future happiness will always remember."[5] In other words, it could be a Dumbo feather to imagine your future happiness and then make the noble or good choice today (make the call, quit the job, apply for the position, and so forth) that lays the foundation for that future happiness.

4. Create a list or canon (defined as a collection of rules or texts that can be considered authoritative) of the defining people, places, and things (memories, objects) that inspire you to live courageously. Remember, a Dumbo feather is personal; you can't use someone else's unless it resonated powerfully when it was shared. And sometimes you may acquire Dumbo feathers from an experience that others didn't have. Not to worry. They are valid and should be cherished if they keep you soaring.

5. Make a collage of your Dumbo feathers—a visual reminder of these wonderfully inspiring people, places, and things can give an instant dose of staying power and motivation for facing uncertainty.

The opposite of Dumbo feathers, quest destroyers, can knock the wind out of you and your dreams. They exist as part of the human experience, but the degree to which they get us down or destroy us can be mitigated.

6. Consider someone who is a current quest destroyer and take into account their background, experience, and motivation. Do they have a background in what you are trying to do, and how does it inform their comments? What is their own experience? Is the person giving you advice as a tired veteran resigned to riding it out, a staunch defender of the conservative approach, or a generous, open-minded innovator? Are they trying to protect you, empower you, or discourage you? These questions will help you separate quest destroyers from a potentially helpful voice.

   If you can avoid the truly harmful quest destroyers, then do so. If you cannot control their participation in activities of mutual interest, prepare and fortify yourself beforehand for their negativity.

Stop asking their advice and stop listening if they demand to share it—and if they do share it, notice how the questions above can reveal the foundation of their naysaying.

7. Quest destroyers can also be things or addictions (substances, video games) that steal from our health, clarity, time, money, or relationships. Whatever the source, we need to clean up the toxic energy spills to protect our quests. (For more, see the Reflection and Practice tools in chapter 8 and chapter 26.)

8. The most challenging quest destroyer most of us will face is the critical inner voice that continually badgers and shames us for mistakes we make and opportunities we miss. We replay moments of weakness or failure over and over, and far from being inspiring or motivating, these bad memories and negative self-talk are abusive and carry devastating results.

9. For quest destroyers that are part of the physical and emotional experience of being human (fear, stress, aging, fatigue), consider setting firm boundaries. Author Elizabeth Gilbert does this for her relationship with fear. Admitting that fear seems to be the "conjoined twin" to creativity—showing up alongside all of her best and most interesting ideas—she wrote a sort of speech to her fear, granting it the right to come along on the "road trip" of her life and to have a voice but to never "have a vote and to never drive." Giving yourself these kinds of guidelines about to what extent you are going to let things get you down is critical.[6] For example, if you hold negative beliefs about aging and what you are going to be able or unable to do at certain ages, you limit what's possible.

10. Last but not least, are you a Dumbo feather or a quest destroyer for others? Or both? Add more Dumbo feather energy to your relationships! Pay attention to how your positive and generous treatment of others can energize you as well.

Chapter 14

Runways and Landing Strips

Sitting in the Silicon Valley office of famous venture capital firm Draper Fisher Jurvetson (DFJ)—renowned for investments in companies like Tesla, Skype, and Baidu—the cofounder of Livescribe pitched for funding. The entrepreneur described how the company's digital stylus captured pen strokes and audio, allowing users to replay the recorded audio simply by touching the pen to the notes. Warren Packard, managing director of DFJ, listened closely and then posed one of the most familiar questions in the entrepreneurial world: "What's your burn rate?"[1] The entrepreneur tossed out a number, and Packard's eyes wandered to the ceiling as he divided the startup's remaining cash by the burn rate. "So you have sixteen months of runway left?" he asked.

For those unfamiliar with this world, it's worth explaining. In a startup, your "burn rate" is how much you are spending a month (in excess of any income) and your "runway" is your remaining cash divided by your burn rate. Runway refers to how long your startup has to take off, like an airplane, before it runs out of cash. One of the most important startup survival tactics is to lengthen your runway, either by reducing your burn rate or by bringing in money, giving you more time to figure things out and ultimately to succeed.

Thoughtfully adopting tactics to lengthen your runway is helpful when priming for uncertainty. Thomas Ramsøy was working as a professor at a leading business school when he began to see how his specialty in applied neuroscience could have useful applications in the real world. He started dreaming about starting his own company but had to weigh the massive uncertainty of becoming an entrepreneur against the comfort of a predictable academic salary. When Nathan asked him how he got the confidence to leave a coveted position and step into the unknown, he said, "Frankly, the key was reducing my personal burn rate."[2] Doing so helped give him the courage to launch his company, Neurons, and the time to make a few mistakes without the anxiety that his home and family were in peril. It turned out to be critical to his success: after a slow start, the business took off, growing over 10x a year eventually winning contracts from Google, Lego, and IKEA.

Decreasing your burn rate might feel grim unless you see it through the lens of possibility. When Sarah Mouchot and Nico Alary moved from Melbourne to Paris to start their first Holybelly restaurant, they wanted to do everything they could to give themselves more time to succeed. "We tried to find the cheapest apartment possible," Alary said. "I remember we found this horrible place for a couple hundred euros." Mouchot winced. "I mean, it was really terrible."[3]

"I was like, 'no way,'" Mouchot chimed in. "It was the kind of place that our friends would just shake their heads in disbelief at."

Alary interjected, his voice going into a higher register, "Yeah, but I told Sarah, 'What's our goal, though? This will help us get the best chance of getting started.'"

"It was true that we weren't going to spend much time there, and the dream of starting the restaurant was more important," Mouchot admitted.

There are often creative ways to lengthen your runway (or to get started with what's available—see chapter 23 for more). One entrepreneur we know had the idea to sell Rice Krispies treats. He wasn't sure if the idea would work, since it was before the era of packaged treats, so to keep his burn rate low, instead of building or leasing a kitchen space he contacted the owner of a local Marie Callender's restaurant to see if he could use the kitchen during their off-hours. He delayed leasing his own kitchen until the demand was so high that there was no choice. In the end he sold the business to Kellogg's, the company that makes Rice Krispies, all of it based on the recipe on the back of its own box.[4]

It may be easier to cut your burn rate if you can flip the lens from focusing on what you are going without to focusing on how much you already have. Cristina Mittermeier, founder of the International League of Conservation Photographers, recounts her fascination when a young man who grew up in a shack in Hawaii, surfing with friends and surrounded by family, told her, "I never knew I was poor until somebody from the mainland told me. I always thought I had enough."[5] Mittermeier reports that after traveling to almost one hundred countries, she concluded that only about 10 percent of happiness comes from material goods. "Where does the other 90 percent that makes us feel good come from?" Mittermeier asks. "Contentment is something that is long-lasting, it comes from inside, and it is basically the satisfaction of knowing our place in the universe. So if I had to define enoughness, I would say it is an internal yardstick and it is something only we can develop."

Empirical studies confirm Mittermeier's hypothesis that although we believe a little more money, time, or success would make us happy, as soon as we achieve a new level, we want more. Research shows that lottery winners are no happier than anyone else after they adjust to their new level of wealth.[6] Anecdotally, a tax lawyer working with high-net-worth individuals told us that although his clients differ in many ways, there is one way in which they are all the same: people with $10 million in wealth think they would be happier if only they had $50 million, and those with $50 million think they would be happier if only they had $100 million.[7]

This tendency is what psychologists label the "hedonic treadmill," or the tendency to adjust to a new positive event, absorb it as the new normal, and then want more. One way out of the hedonic treadmill is to start challenging yourself to see that you already have enough. You don't need to have more to be happy. There is even an "enoughness" movement underfoot, first described by Marcus Barber when, in a major consumer study, he observed that "enoughness is an emerging attitude that sees people choose NOT to buy into the 'buying' paradigm. In particular, it overturns the 'upgrade' and 'replacement' model of consumer behaviour."[8] By seeing you already have enough, you may find it easier to lengthen your runway to do the things you most care about.

Landing Strips

Sometimes what holds us back from stepping into new possibilities is our fear of losing what we already have—our current job, position, prestige, or the trajectory we have planned. This is particularly prevalent in corporate jobs, where it often feels like doing anything out of the ordinary could threaten your path up the ladder. One of the most surprising things that we observed in our interviews was that the people pursuing the most interesting possibilities weren't afraid of losing their jobs! How were they able to be so bold? Rather than letting the fear of losing their current jobs hold them back, they saw how taking a risk could open up other jobs and possibilities—more landing strips where they could touch down than just their current employment.

For example, when Nathan's coauthor Kyle Nel was working as a junior manager at Lowe's, most people were afraid to participate in innovation projects because they worried that failure would derail their corporate career. But Nel adopted a different view of taking risks: "I knew I could take what I'm learning and get another job, maybe even a better job."[9] This view helped Nel have the courage to speak up, suggest, and then try something that seemed crazy to his peers: Why not use science fiction writers to create some "speculative organizational fiction" about what the future could look like for their company in five years? To his surprise, they returned with a fairly consistent vision of how customers could use augmented and virtual reality tools to plan and communicate a remodel. Although these tools are common today, at the time they were a very new idea. Nel synthesized the stories into a strategic narrative—a story of customers using the tools to remodel a beloved home—and then hired graphic artists to create a comic book telling the story. Although senior leaders thought it was a joke at first, the story had real power, and Nel won the support to build augmented reality remodeling tools, in-store robots for taking inventory, and exosuits to protect workers, and eventually founding the Lowe's innovation lab.[10] Ultimately, although these ventures won awards and made money, Nel found a new landing strip—cofounding his own consulting firm to help other companies use speculative fiction, a firm that was later acquired by Singularity University.

Taking risks may lead to you losing your current job, but it could open up better opportunities somewhere else. But taking risks might also be the key to getting a better job in your current company. A recent analysis of over sixteen thousand people found that innovators were promoted faster and paid more money than the noninnovators in the same company![11] At the core, seeing your landing strips isn't only about taking risks; it's really about broadening your view beyond your current situation to realize that you may have many more possibilities.

Finally, consider how seeking multiple landing strips enriches your portfolio of personal real options. When you are too laser-focused on keeping your current job, you may be blind to the other interesting landing strips available to you. Let's be honest, even failure can lead to a new landing strip. Can you think of a time you failed, but it led to new possibilities? Nathan has had several "failures," like the time he got rejected from all the graduate programs to which he had applied. It led to a reevaluation of his career and to new and fascinating landing strips, including working in strategy consulting, a PhD at Stanford, and a life in Europe!

Reflection and Practice

To lengthen your runways, there are a few things you can do:

1. *Reduce your burn rate.* Financial gurus and the FIRE movement (financial independence, retire early) provide many creative ideas, from the basics like eliminating costly debt or expensive consumables, to more creative tactics such as enjoying staycations instead of vacations, biking instead of driving, and gardening instead of shopping.

2. *Increase your enoughness.* Mittermeier outlines the key factors that build enoughness: responsibility, humor, a sense of connection, being in the present moment, and pursuing meaning. She admits that living in the first world, with all the stress of social comparison and peer pressure, makes enoughness far harder to attain. Still, she urges us to ask ourselves daily "How much is enough?" and to let it guide our consumer choices, knowing that we can be happier with less if we adjust our perspective. Our runways might stretch so far into the future that we never have to worry about money again! We will be grateful for what we have, and we will be living more sustainably.

3. *See the greater possibilities.* Like Mouchot and Alary, defining the possibility we want to create can make it easier to let go of the things standing in our way. Mouchot and Alary wrote down their manifesto and returned to it at night, reminding themselves

of their goals when they came home to their crummy apartment to literally eat peanuts for dinner.

To envision more landing strips, take a few steps:

4. *Look for them.* Go out and see what kinds of roles are available, or what you might qualify for if you take on a new task. Grab coffee with friends in related roles at other companies or people in areas you might be interested in exploring. Just getting a sense of what is available can be helpful.

5. *Join or form an uncommon partnership.* Nel is a master of seeking out connections to other people and organizations, including "uncommon partners," the kinds of people you might not normally get to know in the narrow scope of your activities. Working to build connections, including uncommon partners, multiplied Nel's ability to see landing strips and increased his confidence that even if he took a risk, he would always have somewhere to land. Uncommon partners enable a view into another world. For example, you might try volunteering to mentor at a local startup accelerator, joining up with a group pursuing new things that interest you, or inviting someone from a different company for coffee.

6. *Revisit your portfolio of personal real options.* Could any of your personal real options offer viable landing strips? Does looking at your portfolio through the lens of landing strips encourage you to spend more time on certain options? Maybe you would like a different landing strip better than the one you currently assume you will touch down on.

Chapter 15

Reimagining Resources

Many of us believe we can't take action because we don't have the resources (e.g., time, money, education) to pursue a new project or idea. However, there may be overlooked abundance—something we have so much of that we take it for granted—waiting to be put to use in valuable ways. Likewise, sometimes the constraints we curse can actually fuel creativity and possibility. We take inspiration from the recent discovery that all the known matter in the universe actually represents only about 5 percent of the actual matter that exists. The other 95 percent is dark energy and dark matter, which we can't directly see.[1] If we become curious about the resources we think we have or think we need and the constraints we see as problematic, we prime ourselves for finding possibility, which may be hiding in plain sight.

When Rob Adams landed a job as head of city planning in Melbourne after graduating from Oxford with a degree in urban design, he was given a seemingly impossible task: reverse decades of urban decline, and do it without a budget. The city had been laid out during the gold rush of the 1850s in large rectangular blocks connected by broad roads. Over the decades, speculators subdivided these blocks into smaller parcels, adding narrow service lanes like wormholes in each block. Over time these grimy, poorly lit laneways multiplied, serving as parking by day and harbors for trouble at night. As crime increased, people working downtown fled to the safer suburbs, the wide boulevards becoming little more than clogged arteries out of the city's emptying heart.

Adams began searching for resources that might have been overlooked because they were so abundant. What about the proliferation of laneways? As an experiment, Adams blocked one laneway with a pylon and turned the street over to the nearby cafés in exchange for their cleaning up and maintaining the space. For the restaurants, it meant a doubling of their square footage, and soon tables appeared, illuminated by hanging bulbs. As people lingered, the streets began to feel safer. Adams started blocking more laneways, encouraging street art in some, restaurants in others. Slowly the city's laneways began to transform, today becoming hangout spaces, tourist attractions, and part of Melbourne's unique heritage.

And when a recession pushed down the already depressed property values, counterintuitively, Adams celebrated because he saw the unwanted space as an opportunity. At that time, most people believed Australians didn't want to live in the city. But Adams had seen the popularity of mixed-use buildings in Europe (commercial on bottom, apartments on top). So he approached the owner of an empty old Victorian building and made a proposal: Adams would renovate the building to create mixed-use space, keep the rent until it paid off the renovation costs, then give the building back to the owner—improvements and tenants included. With no other alternative, the owner accepted. Shockingly, people flocked to the now-restored grand old building, and it proved so popular that Adams paid back the loan in half the time, allowing him to repeat the process, one building at a time, until the central business district had become a vibrant residential zone as well. By the 2020s, Adams's team had helped increase the number of occupied apartments downtown from 650 when they started to over 45,000.

We'll mention one final example. Adams argues that "if you design a good street, you design a good city."[2] Few people would have seen Melbourne's wide boulevards, clogged by traffic, as a hidden resource. But he slowly started converting the boulevards, a lane here and a lane there, into pedestrian space. Adams built small kiosks and attractive cafés, renting them out at cost to coffee shops, florists, and other vendors as long as they kept an eye on the street. Then he planted trees and installed durable outdoor furniture so people could sit down and enjoy their coffee. Today there are more than six hundred coffee shops (there were but a handful when he started) and over seventy thousand trees. You can even download an app—Urban Forest Melbourne—to find out about any given tree or report a problem. What Adams didn't imagine was that the app would go viral, and that the trees would receive love notes via email. One representative email read, "As I was leaving St. Mary's College today, I was struck, not by a branch, but by your radiant beauty. You must get these messages all the time. You are such an attractive tree."[3] Melbourne has been voted the most livable city in the world seven years in a row, a transformation Adams helped achieve by seeing the value of overlooked abundance.[4]

Many times, recognizing this abundance requires challenging an assumption, such as how Adams didn't believe Australians didn't want to be downtown. Sometimes discovering the value of abundance requires moving an abundant resource to another location. For example, in the 1800s, Boston's "Ice King" created a global empire by connecting New England's winter ice, leftover sawdust from the many lumber mills, and ships returning empty to the West Indies—things no one saw any value in because of their abundance—to provide ice in the hot climates of the tropics.[5] Other times, we can trade our abundance with partners to get access to what we need. For example, when Kyle Nel led Lowe's foray into augmented reality, he realized the company had an abundance of stores that could be great testing environments, trading access with partners like Google in return for their technical capabilities.[6]

Although there may be abundance we have overlooked, there are still often very real constraints. Few of us have all the resources we would like. But sometimes constraints can push us to do things in different ways, which ends up being a good thing. When Marissa Mayer was a vice president at Google, she purposely imposed constraints on the teams—for example, introducing limits to the size, speed, or richness of a product—because it increased their creativity.[7] "Creativity loves constraints, but they must be balanced with a healthy disregard for the impossible," she explained.[8]

Likewise, David Heinemeier Hansson says that "constraints are your friends . . . constraints force you to do way less and different than your competition. . . . The fact is, when you restrict yourself, when you put up constraints for yourself, when you say . . . as I had to do when we were building Basecamp, 'I'm going to work ten hours a week,' you have no choice but to underdo your competition. You are not going to out-effort Microsoft or Google."[9] What Hansson discovered was that his constraint turned out to be an asset. "The number one feedback we have . . . is that 'We love how simple your product is. We love how easy it is to get started.' . . . We love all the things that come from doing less."

Consider an even more extreme scenario of constraint: prison. Beverly Parenti, cofounder of Last Mile, an organization dedicated to teaching coding skills to inmates, believes that "constraints equal fuel." Parenti faced innumerable constraints in creating Last Mile, from lack of internet access in prisons to some inmates' limited education. But she believes that constraint

> causes one to think deeply about the problem, to be open to ideas that you may never have thought of when you had such an abundance of resources. It makes you try harder and harder. . . .
> For me personally I found that learning how to work within the constraints and learning how to navigate in a very controlled environment made me a better leader, a better listener, and made me really step back from the way I looked at situations and challenges in my own organization.[10]

A constraint can force you to think deeper about what you are doing, to discover your commitment to it, and to deliver it with greater inspiration. Despite being so poor that he couldn't afford canvases, part of what helped artist Jean-Michel Basquiat make his mark was his willingness to use whatever was at hand: postcards, discarded doors, windows, and even scraps of foam rubber. Ultimately, these constraints informed the subjects that brought attention to his work: the dichotomies of race, class, society, and wealth.

The unexpected benefits of overlooked abundance and constraints don't always negate the need for tried-and-true methods or requirements. Sometimes we have to pay our dues, such as by taking the time to pursue a certification or degree to establish credibility for certain careers. But even then, we should probably challenge the idea that there is only one safe route. Look hard at the resources you have, and when a lack of resources is your reality, don't forget—the constraint may be the door into possibility.

Reflection and Practice

Reimagining resources has some overlap with chapter 4, about adjacent possibles, since it is about seeing the overlooked possibilities. In this case, though, we focus more narrowly on seeing the unrecognized opportunities hidden by abundance. But "resources" can mean many things, including tasks, skills, locations, people, and so on. The table below asks specific questions to help you explore those resources and gives some examples.

Revealing questions	Examples
Can you repurpose a task to do two things at once or to pay yourself twice?	Employees at Trader Joe's are allowed to listen to podcasts, learning while they work. On a more personal level, maybe walking the dog or doing the dishes is a time to connect with your child or listen to an audiobook.
What are your inherent capabilities (even if they may not be certified or trained)?	At the start of our careers, we didn't have much money, but we had moxie. We bought a tiny, oddly shaped, broken-down apartment outside Boston. Then, leveraging Susannah's design skills, low-cost items from IKEA, and a lot of do-it-yourself energy, we renovated the apartment—selling it two years later for a profit.
Do you have access to a place, knowledge, or resource that people desire?	When David Whyte left his job as a marine biologist to become a writer, he could no longer afford to visit family in his native England. He came up with an idea to lead walking tours in the country's Lake District. For thirty years, his tours have paid for his travels, encouraged other creatives, and built a rich community of readers.
Do you know people who are undervalued but eager to engage in meaningful work?	Bunker Roy founded Barefoot College in 1986 on the principle that the poor in India had time, capability, and desire that was underutilized. Today, Barefoot College has taught predominantly illiterate women how to assemble solar electricity systems, construct houses, and perform dentistry—and to pass their skills on to other women.
Can you repurpose a space to serve a new need?	One of our favorite restaurants is a sort of pop-up shop that uses the kitchen of a café that closes after lunch. The low rent and his commitment allow the chef to prepare amazing meals in an environment that he describes as "inviting friends over for dinner."
Can you flip a constraint into an asset?	Often the most fashionable people are the ones who don't have the money for designer brands. They are able to creatively mix and match what they can afford, and the look is ultimately much more interesting and vibrant.

Chapter 16

Fait Sur Mesure

Learning a foreign language can be exhilarating but also comes with frustration, confusion, and exhaustion. Having lived in France for six years, and despite studying French in high school and college, we often bemoan the fact that we aren't more fluent and still find it difficult to follow the subtle subplots in movies. ("I know the guy is starting an affair, but is it with the editor or the best friend or both?") But one benefit of this translation soup is the discovery of a French word that illuminates an idea, enriching our understanding in a way English cannot. One example is the French way of saying "custom" when referring to anything made to your specifications. *Fait sur mesure* (literally *made to measure*) is the three-word phrase for anything North American speakers of English would call custom, whether it's referring to a tailor-made dress or kitchen cabinets. Somehow the English word misses the real power of the idea, but the French words highlight the special quality of getting to choose and the joy of having something made to *your* exact needs.

Likewise, in life, many of us forget that we really do get to choose for ourselves, that we can make a life fait sur mesure. Rather than following the program, we can decide what, when, why, where, and how we do things. Designer Stefan Sagmeister, whose memorable ads include typography carved into his own skin and inflatable graphics, is a great example. On one occasion, he created a wall of bananas that spelled out "Self-confidence produces fine results." As the bananas aged, the message disappeared for a time, only to be revealed again as the bananas ripened in different stages. Khoi Vinh, former design director of the *New York Times*, marvels at "how he gets away with it." In a blog post titled "The Sagmeister Phenomenon," Vinh writes that "you rarely get the idea that he's weary of his assignments, or that he's doing anything less than having the time of his life."[1]

It is clear to all that Sagmeister is living fait sur mesure. But how does he do it? The way he pursues his career, with deliberate choices about what life can look like, provides important clues. Sagmeister had a hunch that waiting until retirement to explore his interests, as society implies, was a limiting idea. He decided instead to work five years more before retiring but to add five one-year sabbaticals in the middle of his career.[2] He has since taken three one-year sabbaticals, putting himself in places he is curious about, doing things he is drawn to, and collaborating with people he meets along the way. This hasn't been without challenges. During one sabbatical in Bali, feral dogs attacked him almost daily—inspiring a series of T-shirts depicting the wild dogs with the line "So Many Dogs, So Little Recipes" as a gallows-humor way to counteract the frustration.

Although Sagmeister provides an inspiring example, living fait sur mesure can feel out of reach for the rest of us. But a trip we took in 2020, during the brief interlude after the first wave of the Covid-19 pandemic in Europe, opened our eyes to new possibilities. We planned a trip to the South of France for a course Susannah decided to take with a master tapestry weaver. When we drove out of Paris alongside hundreds of other frazzled post-confinement families, we expected to find some sun and a break. What we didn't anticipate was a profound lesson: many more people than you imagine, from many walks of life, are giving themselves permission to live fait sur mesure.

The revelations started when we visited architect Le Corbusier's La Tourette, where he broke the design rules of the day to pursue his modernist style based on proportion to the human body to create a nontraditional monastery. When the monks demanded a crucifix at the entrance to the cathedral, he gave it to them but on his own terms: where the massive metal door to the cathedral pivots on a central axis, becoming a vertical beam, it bisects a horizontal beam of light, creating a gigantic ethereal cross the monks file past as they enter the cathedral.

Curiosity awakened, we barreled south through the Ardèche region to our lodging—an aging château—where a cluster of middle-aged people lingered on the steps, talking and sipping glasses of white wine as they watched the sunset. Our host, Christophe d'Indy, ran down the steps to greet us, a twinkle in his eye, and in a charming franglais introduced us to the group. As he gave us a tour of the aging château, Christophe, the great-grandson of the composer Vincent d'Indy, slowly revealed the outlines of his fait-sur-mesure life. The group drinking wine and watching the sunset were his extended family who had moved to the region to live a different life, and he himself worked part-time as a hotelier and part-time as a race car driver. The prerevolution-era château had a pleasant patina, and Christophe was just catching his breath after cleaning up from twenty-four Ferrari-owning guests. But it was clear he loves his life. You could tell by how friendly he was, proudly inviting us back to his region and letting us know we should expect a four-hour drive to Nice (but not without inserting, with a wink, that it would only take him two hours were he to take the same route).

Four hours later, we arrived in sweltering Nice, just in time for lunch with Eric and Rixa Freeze, the couple we mentioned in chapter 11, personal real options. Somehow, when they feel a curiosity to do or learn about something, they find a way to make it happen. They both have PhDs; he's a writer of novels and she's a global teacher of methods for breech births; he free dives to put fish on their table and she started an organization called Breech Without Borders to reverse traditional but harmful practices. They swim in the Mediterranean, ski in the Alps, and live in one of the most expensive areas in the world on a salary far below most people's.

By the time we headed south to Italy for the course run by Lynne Curran and David Swift—the artists we spoke of in chapter 4—our radar for fait sur mesure was on high alert. We already knew they lived a covetable life, visiting their friends dotting the Tuscan hills for bread, flour, fresh cheese, and honey. But living in close proximity to them for a week, we witnessed other relics of their fait-sur-mesure life: studios warmed by teardrop-shaped wood stoves, a garden overflowing with lavender below their moon-watching balcony, and stacked letters from their vast correspondence with friends around the world.[3] David admits that no one can quite figure out how their life works, including their "commercialista," who David described as "a cross between an accountant and a financial adviser. . . . Everyone has one here." When the commercialista asked David how they manage on so little, David said: "In life it's not what you have, it's what you do . . . but we're not sure how we manage either! But today was good and tomorrow will be too and that is enough."[4] During our visit, David shared his longing to someday live near a volcano, and although he is nearing traditional retirement age, he assured us he's just getting started: "Winding down? I'm winding up!"

Take note, fait-sur-mesure types attract others like them. In two days, Lynne and David introduced us to so many made-to-measure lives. Their favorite place to get coffee, Snack Bar Esso, is manned by three proud brothers who run a tidy café inside what looks like a functioning gas station. Gas prices are illuminated on tall Esso signs, but no gas has been pumped there for years. They provide fabulous coffee and pastries, offer delicious small plates for lunch, and stock a fridge with great wines to serve a steady stream of locals. We met a guide who specializes in firefly tours and wolf sightings, and after the sun had set on the field full of chatty Italian families, he led us into the dark forest below St. Francis's monastery, the blackness illuminated by the wild dance of tens of thousands of fireflies. In Arezzo, we met Francesco Mario Rossi, creator, comedian, writer, and curator of Il Museo di se Stesso (the satirical Museum of Itself), which adjoins his fresco-lined apartment with strange contemporary artifacts, including the hilarious portrait of himself in a Renaissance lace ruffle collar.

We met others along the way, including a Roman count who wanders the hillside pensione speaking to guests in his flowery Oxford English; the proprietress of Matrignano, who left a career in fashion to run the family olive press and winery; a Japanese woman who carefully crafts custom leather shoes in a small alleyway near Ponte Vecchio in Florence; and a family that runs a delicious streamside restaurant in the gully below their farm in the middle of nowhere.

It felt like the world was trying to teach us a lesson. While it may appear that there is one way to do things, "it's all made up!" (Thank you, Steve Jobs.) We all can create a life that's fait sur mesure. It isn't a matter of money. In fact, often the rich and famous—who could afford that everything be made custom—are busy copying too. A shopkeeper friend who stocks exquisite, one-of-a-kind tableware recounts how his wealthy customers have asked for a piece identical to the unique one they have seen posted online. He is shocked to find that they refuse a similar object by the same artist because they want the exact one they saw on Instagram on so-and-so's party table.

Failing to live our life fait sur mesure can lead to regret that is emotionally draining and undercuts our performance. Research confirms that people who ruminate on the paths not taken underperform at work.[5] During two short weeks, we learned that people with vast differences in age, career, finances, family, location, and education are able to live fait sur mesure.

Don't get the wrong idea: fait-sur-mesure lives are not about changing all the time or being unreliable. The quirkiness of the way these folks live isn't random or uncertain anymore because . . . it's how they live! They took their extremely personal vision, with all its wondrous creativity and oddity, and then primed for it—thoughtfully measured, planned, and lived it into reality in a very dogged, practical, even rigorous way. There are individuals whose fait-sur-mesure lives are about spontaneity and having uncertainty blow them from here to there, but in each of the cases of the individuals we shared, they were very much planners and hard workers who might not see their lives as anything but under their control. While you are setting up your personal real options and exploring your risk profile, it is the perfect time to remind yourself to add in some fait-sur-mesure elements. Be sure you aren't following someone else's star home.

Reflection and Practice

The thing about fait-sur-mesure lives is that they are contagious. You can't come across individuals living their dreams without catching the bug. But while contagious, a fait-sur-mesure life can be scary to implement. Giving ourselves permission to start scheming, measuring, and adding custom specifications gets easier when we witness the satisfaction they bring. Seriously, the best way to apply this Prime tool is to get so worked up about what you could be doing (to add more of what you love and subtract more of what you don't) that your only option is to start living fait sur mesure right now.

1. *Have the time of your life.* Do you know what that would look or feel like? Start a journal or a note in your smartphone where you can jot down ideas about what the ingredients and "measurements" would be. Fait-sur-mesure lives are born from trial and error. When Sagmeister took his first sabbatical, he assumed he should make no plans, but after just one week he realized that he still needed a detailed schedule to get important things done.

2. *Make a list of people who live fait-sur-mesure lives.* They can be friends, mentors, or even people you don't know. If they are acquaintances, spend more time with them. Interview them about how they crafted such custom lives. Was it hard to give themselves permission? Do they change elements when they get bored? For example, Sagmeister thinks that doing something three times is boring, so he changes it up.

3. *Find what makes you unique.* Fait-sur-mesure characteristics don't have to be huge displays of daring such as taking regular sabbaticals. Even particular wardrobe choices broadcast a willingness to be yourself. One Sunday afternoon, while standing in line for coffee near the OFR bookstore in Paris's trendy Le Marais neighborhood, we witnessed a very nicely dressed and polite gentleman wearing a hand-knit eye patch that served no medical purpose. To each his own! Be playful and curious.

   Some subtle ideas for fait-sur-mesure wardrobes include:

   - Wearing different socks from two of your favorite pairs, which will signal whimsy and curiosity to anyone who notices. In a similar way, wearing one earring from two pairs creates an asymmetrical nudge toward a less fixed mindset.

   - Wearing new color combinations or mixing patterns, which could infuse some energy if it's something you've always wished you did. Or figure out how to be more comfortable in your day-to-day repertoire—add the tailored pajama look if you can get away with it.

   Here are some easy ideas for creating a fait-sur-mesure workplace. After all, being yourself gives others permission to do the same.

   - Decorate your desk or office with personal effects that celebrate your full personality. Don't shy away from quirky or eccentric flourishes.

   - Introduce a ritual or tradition (authentic to you) during break time and invite others. You might lead a mindfulness meditation, share your favorite jokes, or start a snack-share schedule and rotate who's in charge.

4. *Plan a fait-sur-mesure field trip.* Visit someone or someplace that exhibits a lot of fait-sur-mesure characteristics (big cities tend to have ample opportunities) to inspire yourself to embody the idea more.

5. *Teach someone about this tool.* Ask them if they know people living fait-sur-mesure lives that don't fit the "rich, famous, got it made" stereotype. Start by explaining Sagmeister's idea for spreading sabbaticals out over a career and retiring a bit later. It would be a fun conversation starter.

Chapter 17

Don't Force Machinery

When you feel the anxiety that comes with uncertainty, it can be tempting to grab at anything certain to escape the discomfort of the unknown. We instinctively want to figure things out as quickly as possible, but sometimes patience is precisely what is needed for an opportunity to emerge, an answer to surface, the path to become clear. An old idea from medicine, *iatrogenics*, teaches that sometimes the best treatment is doing nothing at all. Time can resolve injury, and uncertainty, sometimes better than action can, and research confirms that taking a little time can increase our willingness to take risks.[1] The maxim "don't force the machinery" comes from a friend's grandfather, a master mechanic, who constantly reminded everyone around him that if a piece of equipment isn't working as expected, forcing it will only damage it. Instead, patience and time are required to resolve the issue. Likewise, when it comes to uncertainty, we run the danger of forcing the machinery by grasping at premature certainty—those suboptimal certainties we latch on to when we can no longer handle waiting—thereby forgoing better possibilities further down the line. We aren't saying that you should always wait. Indeed, we believe that action is the primary way to resolve uncertainty. We are simply saying that there are times when it is important to be patient for the insight or possibility to emerge rather than forcing the machinery.

How do you know whether you should take action or be patient? It is a decision where the head and the heart need to come together, rather than letting the anxiety make the decision for you. For example, after Timberland acquired the company Howies, changing the founding vision to something they could no longer support, David and Clare Hieatt began looking for something new to throw their hearts into. Despite their experience building one of the UK's top clothing brands and the impulse to do something new, David recalls that they just didn't have the why—the "wind in your sails."[2] For two years they waited. David recalls taking long runs with his dog through the lonely hills surrounding Cardigan, feeling depressed and wondering what to do next. Only later did they learn that Cardigan, the very town where they had been living for the last two years, had once been the jeans manufacturing capital of Britain. However, twenty years earlier the factory had closed as jobs moved overseas to cheaper locations, leaving behind economic collapse and skilled workers with no way to ply their trade. At that moment, the head and heart came together. The Hieatts asked themselves: what if they hired these still-skilled workers, honored their craft by calling them grand masters, and made "jeans for life" in a sustainable manner, rather than just making cheap jeans? For David and Clare, patience revealed the "why" for starting Hiut Denim, the wind in their sails that has helped them become the internationally recognized brand and force for good in the clothing industry that they are today.

When the head and heart come together, it is time to act. Before that, it may be wise to avoid forcing the machinery. But you can gently nudge things forward. How? Ask trusted friends or mentors for advice, as they often observe things about you and the situation that you may not. Also ask if removing or stopping something could be as beneficial as taking action. For example, often leaders wonder "What should we do to innovate more?" but rarely ask "What should we stop doing that is blocking innovation?" Sometimes we need to nudge a possibility forward with a small step—a conversation, a book, a course—to start the process of possibility.

And sometimes we just need to get curious. Earlier we mentioned Elizabeth Gilbert's experience of letting herself garden when her book turned out poorly. She says that when we don't feel drawn to anything in particular, good old curiosity is a good first step: "Curiosity is accessible to everyone. Passion can seem intimidatingly out of reach sometimes, a distant tower of flame accessible only to geniuses and to those who are specially touched by God. But curiosity is a milder, quieter, more welcoming, and more democratic entity."[3]

We have learned about the dangers of forcing machinery—and the benefits of patience—firsthand. After graduate school, we stumbled onto the opportunity of a lifetime: the chance to spend three months in Paris on a visiting professorship. What we didn't expect is how those magical three months would affect us. The richness of daily life, the ancient cathedrals covered in lichen, the white facades of the Belle Époque apartments, all of it struck a chord deep inside. When finally we returned home to the January gray of our small town, we felt homesick for France. It was hard to explain, perhaps not entirely rational, but we both wanted to get back to Europe. Nathan started making inquiries and, by great fortune, that fall was invited to give a job talk at University College London.

A few months later, when we checked into our hotel near King's Cross, we took a walk to see how it might feel to live there, peeking into the university buildings, an eclectic mix of modern facades and gargoyle-capped turrets. The next day, Nathan's presentation went well, and after a full day of meetings with the faculty, the professor scheduled for Nathan's final interview suggested they talk at the café across the street. They had barely sat down to their exorbitantly priced millionaire's shortbread cookies when the professor blurted out, "Are you f@$^ing crazy to move here?"

"What?" Nathan asked, confused.

"There's no way you can afford to live here with four kids on the salary we would give you. You would have to live in some tiny flat hours outside of London, and you'd spend all your time doing extra teaching to make ends meet, which means you wouldn't do enough research to get tenure here, but then when we kicked you out, you wouldn't have enough research to get a job anywhere else. You would be totally screwed."

All Nathan could do was take a bite of cookie while his excitement deflated.

The professor continued. "You should just stay where you are, work hard, and publish. Then, only then, should you maybe consider moving somewhere like this." There are times when we face opposition, or quest destroyers, and we should ignore the advice we are being given. But what made this colleague's harsh words harsher was that somewhere inside, Nathan knew he was right.

We flew home somber but with a new resolution. It was time we made the best of what we had. Rather than haphazard family get-togethers, we started inviting Susannah's parents over for regular Monday night dinners. Nathan started taking time at the end of workdays to hike up the canyon. Despite money being tight, we bought the locals-only discounted lift pass and started skiing on Saturdays as a family and hiking those same trails in the summer. We soaked up all the perks of living in a small town, near family, and had fun doing it—knowing that if and when we did leave, we would have fewer regrets.

Years passed, but while we waited for a European life that made sense, we kept tiptoeing toward the dream, taking French classes and lining up more visiting professorships. On our third visit to France, INSEAD's department chair asked Nathan if he would be willing to move to France. We were stunned, wondering if this was the offer we had been waiting for. Nathan replied enthusiastically, and we started to scheme about how it might work to move back just a few months later. But then we didn't hear anything for three months as the department chairs changed, and the new chair informed Nathan that he still didn't have enough publications. We sat tight and continued to live our suburban lives with as much gusto as we could. The next spring, on our fourth visit to France, INSEAD asked if Nathan would make a visit. Two months later they offered Nathan a job, and when they did, the head and the heart came together. It was time!

Sometimes forcing machinery shows up as writing something off too soon. Value judgments can kill ideas when they still have a pulse. Marketing guru Duke Stump has helped companies like Nike and Lime define their image, but he's still susceptible to misjudging a brand. When a recruiter called about a potential job at Lululemon, he adamantly refused. When the recruiter pushed a bit, Stump explained, "Hell no! . . . I have no connection to that brand. There is a proxy battle with the founder, which sounds like a shit show. It's listed as a brand that won't exist in 2015, so why would I go up?" But after continued pleas that he "go up" for the job, Stump conceded. He admits he had expected to walk in and find a "morgue," but instead "I walked in and it was shiny, happy people. I was like, 'Don't you know that Rome is burning? And you are a brand that won't exist?'" But to his surprise, the company had a feeling completely different from that depicted in the external media. After that first day, even though it made no sense on the surface, "it felt right," so he joined the company and commuted from California to Vancouver every week.

In a twist of irony, Stump's close call with his premature certainty about Lululemon enabled him to lead the company through a defining moment. When he joined, many on the board were hoping to expand beyond yoga as a revitalizing effort. There was an urgency, Stump recalls. "A lot of people were like, 'Yoga is so finite. It's limiting. We need to sign big athletes and do running.'" But he encouraged the team to "sit still" and focus on their purpose. By sitting with it a bit and not forcing the machinery, they ultimately concluded that they created the most value by focusing on doing yoga really well. With this insight, they launched a series of campaigns based on their core value, which helped save the company and position it as the world leader in yoga, almost tripling its revenues over the next few years.

Patience, even when it's the right choice, has never been easy. While the famous Stanford marshmallow experiment showed the benefits of delayed gratification, it's not rocket science why individuals capable of waiting can sometimes experience better outcomes. A creative leadership course offered at Kaospilot includes a final module based on the principle that extraordinary results always require patience, courage, disruption, and the ability to lead others on that harrowing journey. Jakob Wolman, a former student, paraphrased the main takeaway: "Something we quickly identified was the need to stay a little longer with the tension, suffer a little more to get the extraordinary outcome."[4]

André Leon Talley, former creative director and editor-at-large of *Vogue*, recounts a miserable Christmas break of waiting through uncertainty. Just at the start of his career and virtually unknown, he had just finished up his one big break, an unpaid internship at the Metropolitan Museum of Art's Costume Institute with legendary fashion editor Diana Vreeland. No jobs or opportunities had materialized, and he had no money and nowhere to stay. Vreeland warned him that if he went home, he'd take a teaching job and never come back: "Stick it out! You belong in New York."[5] Talley had to sleep on the floor of a friend's apartment, and with no money, hungry, he walked the bleak streets, stopping in churches to offer prayers but "grateful to be in New York, even if my future was uncertain."[6] When she returned from the holidays, Vreeland helped Talley find work, writing letters "on my behalf to every important figure in fashion journalism. Like a trumpet, with her booming voice, she built me up to everyone. . . . She never let up speaking on my behalf."[7] Talley landed his first real job as assistant for Andy Warhol's *Interview* magazine, which became a critical platform for his entire career. Had he given up too soon, he would have missed out on that opportunity, just days away, and the slew of other opportunities that followed.

Even when we intuit that our decision is right, waiting till the right moment takes leadership and practice. Kate O'Keeffe, the creator of

Cisco's Hyperinnovation Living Lab and an executive in Boston Consulting Group's Digital Ventures initiative to help corporations create internal startups, describes this patience as an important part of her work creating new startups. Whether her team is interviewing customers, prototyping a solution, or exploring a new business model, waiting for insights and possibilities to emerge, as opposed to jumping to premature conclusions, is a continual challenge. "I often feel like I'm Mel Gibson in the movie *Braveheart*, when he plays William Wallace leading the Scots in the war for independence, and he's holding them back until the right moment to attack. I just keep saying, 'HOLD . . . HOLD . . . HOLD' to keep them from charging ahead too early."[8]

The old adage that patience is a virtue can apply in times of uncertainty. Alert and proactive patience, not simply biding your time, is the key. Rainer Maria Rilke's *Letters to a Young Poet* is famous because the book includes generous wisdom about living well, and not surprisingly, patience is a main theme. Rilke writes, "I want to beg you, as much as I can, dear sir, to be patient toward all that is unsolved in your heart and try to love the questions themselves like locked rooms and like books that are written in a very foreign tongue. Do not seek the answers which cannot be given you because you would not be able to live them. And the point is, to live everything. Live the questions now. Perhaps you will then gradually, without noticing it, live alone some distant day into the answer."[9] Rilke's advice is clear: take action on the question, don't force the machinery on the answer.

Reflection and Practice

It's tempting to escape the anxiety of uncertainty by forcing machinery. We have all had that moment when we forced machinery and broke it. Being able to push gently, or wait for the right thing or the right moment, requires intense emotional hygiene and the conviction that what you're waiting for is worthwhile and possible. Both of these are discussed at length in section 4. Read on for insights and exercises for enduring uncertainty a bit longer.

1. *Seek uncertainty balancers.* Described in chapter 12, uncertainty balancers are small things that help you offset the uncertainty of

the unknown. You can apply a similar principle while you wait for insights to emerge, that is, immerse yourself in small comforts that balance the anxiety of waiting. For example, as we waited to see if living in Europe would ever emerge as a possibility, we did little things like regular reading on the couch, had family activities like Saturday hikes, and created new traditions such as having pancakes every Sunday to create comfort to balance the anxiety of the unknown.

2. *Throw yourself into the question.* Rilke and others are clear that patience doesn't mean inaction. Live the question, explore it, turn it over in your mind. Throw yourself more fully into your current situation. Are there things you will regret not having done (exploring new locations, careers, etc.)?

3. *Nurture your curiosity.* In her remarkable discussion of this idea, Elizabeth Gilbert shares the story of a playwright who suffered an enormous setback that spiraled him into a horrible depression that lasted years. When his young daughters asked him to help decorate their bikes, something about their small, humble request caught his attention. He ended up spending hours hand-painting stars and other embellishments on their bikes and those of several of their friends. It pulled him out of his funk when nothing else had.[10]

4. *Revisit your uncertainty thermometer.* Taking an audit of uncertainties you are currently facing can reveal how close you are to the panic zone, which is where you might be tempted to opt for the next suboptimal thing that comes along. Becoming aware of these breaking points before they happen can lead to smart action that will diffuse your angst and increase how long you can wait for the possibility you want to emerge.

Section Three

Do

Notice that the tools we are sharing to inspire and inform action in the face of uncertainty keep asking you to reconsider the way things are. Philosopher John O'Donohue lyrically argued: "Possibilities are always more interesting than facts. We shouldn't frown on facts, but our world is congested with them. . . . They are possibilities that have already been actualized. But for every fact that becomes a fact, there are seven, eight, maybe five hundred possibilities hanging around in the background that didn't make it to the place where they could be elected and realized as the actual fact."[1] When we meet uncertainty from this expanded sense of possibility, doing becomes an imaginative, generative, discovery-driven action.

Max Richter, a modern composer at the intersection of electronic and classical music, intuitively understood this when he "recomposed" Vivaldi's *The Four Seasons*, the most famous violin concertos in the history of music. "I took the opening motif, which I always thought was a dazzling moment in the Vivaldi, but in the original it's only four bars. I thought, 'Well, why don't I just treat this like a loop, like something you might hear in dance music, and just loop it and intensify it, and cut and paste. . . . And, you know, my piece doesn't erase the Vivaldi original. It's a conversation from a viewpoint. I think this is just *one way* to engage with it."[2] If the familiar *Four Seasons* can inspire Richter's new music, adored by millions, then perhaps we too can create new possibilities despite all-too-familiar patterns in our own lives.

As you implement the Do tools described in the following table, remember that what happens in the future depends on the "conversations" you are willing to have, then give yourself permission to boldly engage with what's already been done to create new possibilities. Anything and everything can be recomposed.

Tool	Description
Activate and Unlock	Despite the human obsession with managing and reducing risk, some things are better when you stop trying to control them. Look for ways to activate and unlock the essence of the uncertainty you are facing.
Values versus Goals	How can you set yourself up so you never fail? When you navigate uncertainty based on your values instead of mercurial goals, you free yourself from anxiety-producing outcomes over which you have no control and lay the groundwork for success, no matter what happens.
Cognitive Flexibility	Successful innovators don't persist at all costs. Instead, they adapt their worldview as they go, adopting an "attitude of wisdom" that allows them to become cognitively flexible and ready for changing circumstances.
Learning in Fog	Navigating uncertainty can feel like trying to find your way through a dense fog. Using the right learning strategies helps blow away the fog and guide you to new opportunities.
10,000 Shots	The notion of unqualified genius is a fiction. Fields like acting, photography, and entrepreneurship show us that before we can succeed, we must try, try, try again.
Bricolage	Innovators don't wait for the perfect circumstance to take action. Instead they use whatever they have at hand to get started, which, in a twist of fate, often helps them discover yet more possibilities.
Small Steps	We don't have to do everything at once to succeed. Most victories are the culmination of a slow climb up the mountain, one step and one experiment at a time.
Pivot	When dealing with uncertainty, it is inevitable that you will need to change direction. Give yourself permission to adapt.

Chapter 18

Activate and Unlock

When Nathan started this research years ago, he wanted to explore how innovators manage uncertainty. But when he talked to innovators, although they expressed enthusiasm about uncertainty, they disliked the word *manage*. It was only when we came across the work of Roberto Burle Marx that we stumbled upon the right word. Burle Marx was one of the leading modernist landscape architects, whose pivotal insight occurred when he was attending art school in Berlin. He was visiting an exhibit on plants from his native Brazil, and as he wandered through the iridescent tattoo flowers and giant water lilies bursting from their constricting containers, the question arose: What if the real power lies not in trying to manage and control something, the way the narrow pots were doing, but instead in trying to unlock and activate its inherent potential? Burle Marx applied this principle to design over three thousand inspiring landscapes, including the undulating black-and-white stones of the Copacabana boardwalk in Rio de Janeiro. Inspired by him, we set about exploring what other things, including uncertainty, might be better when activated and unlocked rather than managed. We found a surprisingly large number.

In the domain of education, Maria Montessori, the first female graduate of the University of Rome's medical school, became curious about children with special needs, whom society had consigned to asylums where caretakers controlled their behavior through medication. She wondered, What if these children have inherent capabilities that could be unlocked with more holistic courses engaging their senses and their minds? Her approach proved so successful that these children, whom society had abandoned, learned to read and write well enough to pass the standard state exams. She then repeated her experiment with low-income children (at that time considered incapable of high-level mental work) and found that when engaging their natural cycles of interest, they preferred learning to toys and displayed equally high levels of achievement. Montessori's approach, focused on unlocking children's inherent love of learning, has since spread to over 25,000 schools in 145 countries. Montessori, who has been nominated three times for the Nobel Peace Prize for her work, observed, "I did not invent a method of education, I simply gave some little children a chance to live."[1]

Within the business world, we found similar examples. Years ago, when Microsoft conducted a global software survey, it revealed that the most frequently installed software in the world wasn't Microsoft Windows, but a video game made by a handful of people in Texas. Gabe Newell, a leader on the Windows team, concluded that if eight people in the middle of nowhere could beat the might, money, and reach of Microsoft, perhaps the business world was doing something wrong. So he quit and cofounded Valve, a software company whose advantage is in trying to unlock and activate people's inherent intelligence, creativity, and intuition. Valve employees do not have titles or positions, and no one tells them what to do. Instead, the employee handbook instructs them that they have a desk with wheels, and they should move it to where they create the most value. The company's belief is that it "spent the last decade going out of its way to recruit the most intelligent, innovative, talented people on Earth; telling them to sit at a desk and do what they're told obliterates 99 percent of their value."[2]

Research seems to support these anecdotes. For example, a study by researchers at Harvard Business School found that when companies in the photography and paint industry implemented quality management systems like ISO 9000, they succeeded in managing for better quality, but actually decreased their ability to innovate and create new growth.[3] Likewise, a recent field experiment, also done at Harvard, showed that participants at a hackathon who held more frequent meetings (e.g., stand-up meetings) increased their coordination but decreased their innovativeness.[4] By contrast, a separate research project studying the world's top culinary teams observed that the most innovative ones purposely inject more uncertainty into the process to activate and unlock new ideas.[5] Scholars doing work on uncertainty talk about "endogenous uncertainty," or the idea that new opportunities can actually be created by choosing to increase uncertainty, rather than the more common approach of reducing uncertainty.[6] For example, whereas Blockbuster tried to use proven strategies to respond to changing technologies and failed, Netflix actually increased the uncertainty by exploring multiple new options, which contributed to its becoming one of the world's most valuable companies.

Admittedly, "activating and unlocking" can seem like a somewhat ambiguous concept. Consider that museum designer Adrien Gardère describes it as "releasing" the possibilities that are already there, saying in the context of his own work re-imagining an existing museum: "That is what I love to do, is take what is there and use it, not having to do anything more than use what is there."[7] In other words, the possibilities are already latent in the thing you are unlocking "like the seed of a tree, it has the whole of a tree, . . . Relieving and releasing [what is already there] is work I find far more exciting than doing my smudge and saying 'that's mine.'" For example, when Gardère was called in to redesign the Roman Museum of Narbonne, in France, where centuries of carved stones had been used and reused over centuries of construction and destruction, he asked himself, How do I release them, how do I let them become what they already inherently have inside them? Rather than create one more boring exhibit with tiny plaques labeling lifeless stones, he designed an interactive wall with a robotic arm that lets museum guests rearrange the museum stones in new combinations, just as those stones have been reused over the centuries with each passing civilization.

If Gardère's approach sounds a bit too abstract, consider the similarity to how Ralph Hamers, former CEO of ING, motivated the transformation of a sleepy brick-and-mortar bank into a global digital one. Hamers recounted, "I went back to our DNA of what had made ING successful over a century . . . There were two things: innovation and simplicity. . . . I just had to touch [that core identity] to activate it, and everyone recognized it."[8] By the way, Hamers used the word "activate" unprompted. But he pointed to it as part of the essence of the bank's successful change.

Ultimately, the real question is, What would it mean to activate and unlock, rather than to manage and control, the uncertainty in your own life? David Whyte eloquently describes having such a moment while working as a marine biologist. "Busyness was an integral part of my identity that year . . . besieged by what seemed like unremitting and unending deadlines." One day, with reluctance, he agreed to lunch with a stranger, who asked his advice about restoring a ten-thousand-year-old salmon run blocked by a tidal gate. Whyte recalls, "I was shocked by . . .

the sudden image of the forlorn salmon unable to enter the stream," guided by generations of chemical memory, to precisely this gate where they would wait and die. "His words had the strange effect of touching me at a level far beyond his immediate practical need."[9]

After lunch, instead of returning to the office, Whyte drove home and pulled out a sheet of blank paper to reflect on what was asking to be activated and unlocked:

> At this stage it is so easy to want to turn away from our own faculties of attention and turn something else on: the radio, the television, the lawn mower, to want someone else's voice, someone else's work, anything but . . . this invitation to the depths, this challenge to get below the surface . . . for all people who really want to know what is eating at them, what is asking to be addressed, what lies beneath the surface of busyness.

On the blank page, he wrote the names of salmon, and then the lines "For too many nights now I have not imagined the salmon, threading the dark streams of reflected stars." He continued writing until, by the end, he came to the realization that "my job was not to abstract the life of the oceans and parcel it up into educational soundbites, but to make it real for myself and for others in language against which our normal defenses have no power. Writing, in other words." Over years, Whyte transitioned from biologist to writer and consultant, working with individuals and large organizations. Looking back on the experience, he, like Max Richter, describes it happening as a "conversation" between his existing life and all the possibilities, not as a sudden leap. But he warns against ignoring the invitation to this conversation: "In building a work life, people who follow rules, written or unwritten, too closely and in an unimaginative way are often suffocated by those same rules and die by them, quite often unnoticed and very often unmourned."[10]

Reflection and Practice

We can't activate ideas we don't care about. Much like finding adjacent possibles, activation and unlocking happens for those who are puzzling over, dreaming of, and envisioning what's aching to be unleashed. And it won't work if we force the machinery. It's more of a coaxing energy that trusts something worthwhile is there.

What should I activate?

- *Where do you have curiosities, interest, or talent?* What is the need you are trying to meet? Is there a project you set aside that might be ready to be unlocked? Or, as discussed in chapter 17, are you trying to force activation in the wrong direction?

- *Where do you imagine change?* Tyler Mitchell is an African American photographer and filmmaker. He recounts, "Growing up with Tumblr, I would often come across images of sensual, young, attractive white models running around being free and having so much fun. . . . I seldom saw that freedom for Black people in images—or at least in the photography I knew. My work responds to this lack." He activated and unlocked a reality by creating it. "I feel an urgency to visualize Black people as free, expressive, effortless, and sensitive. I aim to visualize what a Black utopia looks like or could look like."[11] Mitchell's work is "gut-punching in its optimism" and in how it unlocks possibilities for others.[12]

- *What are you doing anyway?* Can you elevate a mundane activity? Anything important that has lost its impact (relationships, cooking, sex life) is waiting to be activated! Author Priya Parker puzzled over the difference between the productive conflict negotiations in her professional life and the unproductive gatherings in her personal life. She began to wonder: Rather than plan another "off the rack" birthday party, could she encourage people to activate and unlock gatherings? She says that the more obvious the purpose of a gathering (wedding, birthday, etc.) is, the more likely it is that you'll fall into the same format you've always used. Parker gives guidelines for reinventing such events, energizing participants, and creating meaning in her book, *The Art of Gathering.*

How do I unlock something?

Managing uncertainty is about controlling, reducing, and containing uncertainty. Activating and unlocking is about allowing, encouraging, and exploring uncertainty.

- *Create space to explore.* How can you activate something if it is tied down and controlled? You have to create time and space to explore. Valve gives employees freedom to explore how to create value. Likewise, Netflix founder Reed Hastings and INSEAD professor Erin Meyer have written about the company's culture of "no rules," which is vital for trying new things and adapting quickly. The same applies in your personal life: give yourself the space to explore. The idea for the hit Broadway musical *Hamilton* was sparked when Lin-Manuel Miranda read Ron Chernow's biography of Alexander Hamilton on vacation and wrote a rap about the historical figure. He spent a year rewriting that single song before it expanded into other songs and eventually the musical, which has won dozens of awards.

- *Stop busyness.* Whyte recounts how, before he realized he needed to change course, his days were obscured by perpetual busyness. One day he charged into a meeting room at work and asked, "Has anyone seen David?" His colleagues laughed at what they thought was a joke: he was the only David working there. But Whyte recognized the symbolic meaning of the slip—how we can literally lose ourselves in tasks.[13] In this spirit, Olivier Blum, chief strategy and sustainability officer at global equipment firm Schneider Electric, urged senior executives to find a way to "free up your energy" when the company was facing the need for digital transformation. He pushed them to scrutinize commitments, meetings, and tasks to create room for creativity, insight, and innovation.[14]

- *Inject uncertainty.* As mentioned, research suggests that innovators often purposefully inject uncertainty into an activity to increase their ability to innovate. What would it look like to inject uncertainty into your own life? Would it mean to try something new, talk to someone new, or break your routine? Recall CEO Piet Coelewij, who took up a completely new sport—kickboxing—to increase his willingness to take on uncertainty in his career. As thinker and poet Wendell Berry advises those who want to create a meaningful life, "So, friends, every day do something that won't compute."

- *Trust it's there and that you won't mess it up.* There might be dead ends and false starts, but the thing that wants to be activated or unlocked isn't going anywhere. Like Adrien Gardère describes, it's already *inherent* (from the Latin meaning "to cling, adhere, or stick to") in the thing. You do have to invest the energy to explore and get curious, but you don't need to become a genius to invent it; you only have to activate it. Let that reduce your stress and increase your ability to listen.

- *Drop your ego.* Often our egos create restricting beliefs that work against our ability to activate and unlock. For example, psychologist Shefali Tsabary describes how parents' egos have led to the controlling and overscheduling of their children, which actually works against the parents' goals to unlock and activate their kids' potential. Tsabary argues that we have to "unfold, and undo" this worldview and then kids "will spontaneously reach for the fullest expression of themselves and find everything they require for this to happen."[15] Likewise, in what ways have our egos led us to seek control rather than activation? What projects have we said yes to that we don't really care about, or what ways of living have we adopted that limit our ability to activate and unlock?

What will it take and look like?

- *Be open to the essence of the thing being different from what is easiest, fastest, or flashiest.* What is activated and unlocked may not be ideal or perfect. It may take time and be different than expected. Think of organic apples—they look dull and small compared with the shiny, pesticide-coated ones, but they taste so good!

Sometimes we don't want to deal with what wants to be unlocked and activated. Our friend Pádraig Ó Tuama, the Irish poet, spoke about how he dreamed of joining a monastery in New York City. After years of preparation he flew to New York, but "within five minutes of being inside the monastery I knew I wasn't a fit." Discouraged, he describes how he "got lost on the subway most days. I walked the city alone. And I kept meandering towards a gay bar. I hadn't ever been inside a gay bar alone before. This was early 2001. I was 25, curious, frightened."

Finally, one afternoon he went into the bar and bought a lemonade. "I must have been shaking. I got talking with the man behind the bar—he had an Irish grandparent. 'What's got you in New York?' he asked.

What the hell, I confessed it all: priesthood; New York City; four years of dreaming; all broken in an instant; surprise—the bad kind; a whole life in front of me now; no plans left; everybody was right: I was an aimless wanderer."

Having grown up in a strict religious environment that rejected homosexuality, Ó Tuama had never allowed himself to ask to wonder if he was gay until the bartender, in a kind and empathetic tone, asked, "Have you ever been in love?"

Ó Tuama recounts his shock. "Nothing had prepared me for his question. Up until that point, I'd believed such love was neither possible nor permissible. The barman could see my surprise. He was in no rush. I'm guessing I cried, but I can't really remember. . . . I don't remember going back to the monastery."[16]

Today Ó Tuama is a conflict mediator, poet, speaker, thought leader, teacher, storyteller, and theologian as well as openly gay. You would struggle to find a more loving, empathetic person or a kinder friend. He spends his time exploring the questions, paradigms, and systems that harm and trap people, whether national struggles like the Irish conflict or individual ones like self-hatred. He is both much happier and more impactful, activated and unlocked to be himself, pursuing his true calling in life, rather than forcing himself to be the New York City priest he believed he was supposed to be.

Chapter 19

Values versus Goals

For most of his career, Nathan has studied possibility in terms of radical outcomes, such as SpaceX creating reusable rockets. He has championed innovators like Elon Musk, CEO of SpaceX, believing their accomplishments worthy of study and imitation. But after hundreds of interviews with remarkable individuals who have received very little recognition, Nathan has begun to doubt this view. While it would be easy to promise that the tools in this book guarantee outsize success (something many books do), that might actually be counterproductive. By focusing on external metrics like fame and money, we would be exposing you even more to the downsides of uncertainty—the anxiety and pressure of trying to achieve a specific outcome over which you have limited control. In contrast, if we encourage you to focus on something over which you do have control—your values rather than your goals—then we could nurture your ability to face uncertainty by making you failure-proof!

Focusing on values rather than goals can feel counterintuitive for those of us steeped in the Western dogma of self-actualization. While we aren't arguing that all goals are inherently bad, so often our explicit or implicit goals are tied to arbitrary success outcomes like money and recognition. To illustrate their arbitrary nature, consider those who achieved objectively great things but received little recognition during their lifetimes: Ada Lovelace laid the foundations of modern computing but remains relatively unknown, Vincent van Gogh sold one painting during a lifetime of constant rejection, and Nikola Tesla invented the wireless communications underpinning your social network but died penniless. (Tesla's name would be largely unknown but for the car company named after his electric engine.) And how many others made significant steps forward only to have been completely forgotten? Some unknown Roman—or Romans?—invented stronger concrete two thousand years ago than we can make today, and unlike our modern concrete, it grows more durable in seawater.

What about individuals who don't do anything "noteworthy" for the masses but make a difference in their immediate circle? Every person reading this book is doing so because a teacher, likely paid an abysmal wage, taught them how to read, opening up a whole world of possibility. Others may point to a peer, leader, coach, or mentor who changed the way they saw the world. What about parents who receive almost no recognition for the sacrifices they make but enable their children to reach new heights through mundane and exhausting efforts? It is all these daily and repetitive acts added up that make the world go round, not the "great" heroes on which chance has shone the spotlight.

Add to this that the spotlight isn't all it's cracked up to be. Robert Waldinger is the director of the most robust research on happiness, the Harvard Study of Adult Development, which has followed more than seven hundred people, from across social classes, for over eighty years. Although 80 percent of young people list becoming rich as a life goal and 50 percent list becoming famous, Waldinger observes "the lessons [of the research] aren't about wealth or fame or working harder and harder. The clearest message that we get from this seventy-five-year study is this: good relationships keep us happier and healthier. Period."[1] He goes on to explain that wealth and fame, as much as conflict and loneliness, actually lead to declines in cognitive, emotional, and physical health, whereas loving, connected, supportive relationships improve happiness, health, and memory and even buffer disappointment. As corroborating evidence, Karl Pillemer, sociologist and gerontologist at Cornell University, interviewed one thousand elderly Americans and reported that "no one—not a single person out of a thousand—said that to be happy you should try to work as hard as you can to make money to buy the things that you want. No one—not a single person—said it's important to be at least as wealthy as the people around you, and if you have more than they do it's real success. No one—not a single person—said you should choose your work based on your desired future earning power."[2]

Alain de Botton, philosopher and founder of the School of Life, argues that this problem starts with the "beautiful but dangerous" idea that anyone can achieve anything. In his own words, "If you really believe in a world where you believe you can do anything, and you only have done a bit, my goodness, how crushed you will feel. The possibilities for humiliation are so much greater now. . . . Leading a good life isn't good enough; you need to be extraordinary, become Mark Zuckerberg, become somebody else. This is the kind of torture we have imposed on ourselves."[3] De Botton concludes, "How have we made a life where the statistical odds . . . the 99 percent surety that you will lead [an ordinary life] . . . has come to seem like a humiliation and the wrong sort of life? This is setting yourself up for disaster."

What would happen if everyone, from executives in large companies and startups to schoolteachers and garbage collectors, thought about value more broadly? Would we be more satisfied with the tasks we are doing? Would we take more risks? Would we celebrate and value the thankless jobs spontaneously, seeing them for how they enable us? None of this is easy. Nathan has struggled with this relevance ladder his entire career, always wanting his work to have greater reach, be more impactful, and be better known. In reality, this outcome-based "success" lasts for a brief season even when it comes. One of PayPal's founders, who made hundreds of millions from the company, famously slept under his desk in his next startup because he worked so many hours, wanting the venture to be bigger than PayPal. Was it? No. Even if it had been, would that have been enough to satisfy him? Most likely not. And what happens when you have sacrificed everything to the project's success and it isn't a success?

By now you know we admire David Heinemeier Hansson, creator of Ruby on Rails and Basecamp, but what we love more than his startups is his perspective on work. He rejects the view that we need to sacrifice everything to achieve a goal. "I've been working on internet startups, companies, apps for the last twenty years and have done so in a way that it never consumed my life."[4] Heinemeier Hansson is brash when dismissing outcome-based goals when you are facing uncertainty: "First of all, goals are bullshit. Second, they are oppressive. Third, [they don't] even work. Whether you meet $10 million or not does not happen because you set that as a goal." He argues that focusing on goals only creates the illusion of control—while also increasing anxiety and the likelihood that we make trade-offs about the things we care most about.

By contrast, if we pursue a project based on our values, rather than on goals, we are better able to face uncertainty and our future outcomes will be more satisfying because we can achieve that value—we can succeed, no matter what happens to the project. Heinemeier Hansson explains that when he selects a new startup project, he focuses on values like learning from the experience, writing good software, treating his employees well, and acting ethically in his interactions with the market. He explains, "I would rather set my approach up so that [I'm thinking about] 'OK, did the market like it or not?' Do you know what? If they didn't, I will still look back on the path—the two years and millions of dollars we spent developing this thing—and feel great about it." By focusing on what he can control, Hansson creates a world where he cannot fail. "That is the way to deal with the fact that putting something into the world can be an inherently frightening, disconcerting, disappointing thing to do," he says.

The irony is that extraordinary outcomes often come to those who are doing their work based on values, or the "why." A growing body of empirical research underscores the importance of knowing the purpose behind a task. In a study of call center employees raising money for student scholarships, when employees spent just five minutes talking to a student who had benefited from a scholarship, they spent twice as much time on the phone and raised almost three times as much money.[5] Similarly, in a study of volunteer lifeguards, those who were told stories about saving a life volunteered 40 percent more hours than volunteers who read stories about the personal benefits of being a lifeguard.[6]

Likewise, when founders and entrepreneurs are motivated by a personal "why," success often follows. Entrepreneur David Hieatt explains:

> Most brands think they have a sales problem. What they actually have is a culture problem in disguise. Their brand to the outside world looks the part. But on the inside, it's empty. The folks on the inside don't feel it. And so, therefore, the customers don't feel it either. . . . As an entrepreneur, your job is to attach meaning to the time [employees and customers] give you. The brands we love working for change things. And, as it turns out, change is something we are happy to give our time to. . . . Stress is doing something you don't care about with time that you do.[7]

The benefits of believing in the work you do are even more noticeable in the lives of educators, artists, and makers who choose careers based on values from the outset. Before we started writing this book, we felt an intense craving to find people living and working from their integrity. We felt discouraged by seeing teenagers trapped by the dogma of passion—the stressful idea that if they could find the one thing they cared about and sacrificed everything to it, they would be the next Steve Jobs. We could see both the anxiety it created and the fallacy it imposed. We were searching for people doing work in earnest ways (wholehearted, authentic, diligent, passionate, and mindful). The project took us to a literary festival in Liverpool; a walking tour through England's Lake District; bakeries and restaurants in Paris; the magical world of a tapestry weaver and toy maker in Tuscany; a silversmith, a goldsmith, and basket makers in the UK; a Mexican restaurant with a poet and photographer/philosopher in San Antonio, Texas; a city planner in Melbourne; and an EMT/film producer/writer in Sydney. We met enough people working in this earnest way to convince us of its possibility for all of us. When we work at anything for the sake of doing it well, according to our values, it produces enduring distinction and greatness no matter how mundane or underrated the work is in the public's fickle eye.

Although we may live in a world that sings the praises of a winner-take-all mindset, the heroes in our stories, and in our lives, don't take it all for themselves. That's what villains do. Instead, heroes create opportunities not just for themselves but for others as well. In closing, we like the way one of our "earnest" friends, Palestinian American poet Naomi Shihab Nye, turns the traditional notion of fame on its head. In her poem "Famous" she writes, "I want to be famous to shuffling men / who smile while crossing streets, / sticky children in grocery lines, / famous as the one who smiled back. / I want to be famous in the way a pulley is famous, / or a buttonhole, not because it did anything spectacular, / but because it never forgot what it could do."[8] The "fame" that Nye is reminding us of is a purer version of distinction available to us all.

Reflection and Practice

When you face uncertainty based on your values, not arbitrary goals, you can't fail. That will put you at ease to do your best work. As a bonus, your values will lead you to the uncertainty that's worth taking on, and your outcomes will ultimately be more satisfying, and maybe even more successful, because they are being fueled by your "why." Here are some ways to think through your values.

1. *Revisit your uncertainty manifesto.* Remember the Uncertainty Manifesto tool from chapter 9? If you have yet to create your own statement, now is a good time to define your values and philosophy.

2. *Write a letter.* Jump-start a values mindset by writing a letter or email to someone who inspired you. Remind them, or let them know for the first time, how their care or attention changed you.

3. *Define fame.* Make a list of ways that you are already "famous" in the vein Nye describes or in ways that you would like to be famous—the quickest to forgive, the most considerate officemate, the most empathic boss, the most thoughtful gift-giver, the one with the dauntless glass-half-full perspective, etc.

4. *Focus on "must."* Elle Luna, a former designer at IDEO, has written and spoken widely about the difference between "should" and "must." Where musts are the things connected to your real values, shoulds are the layers of things that are just a part of life. Luna suggests that when making a decision, you label a chair for each category. Sit in each, writing down the list of things that fit under that category—the shoulds and musts of the decision. Anything that feels congruent with the "must" chair becomes a compass for guiding your project forward.[9]

5. *Imagine your audience.* When working toward a deadline or project, remind yourself often of the personal values that will infuse it with purpose. When we write to an imagined audience of today's unrecognized van Goghs, Teslas, Lovelaces, or other unsung heroes to encourage them in pursuing their earnest work, we more authentically tell the upside of uncertainty. Helping to activate and unlock readers so they can face uncertainty fully and courageously is why we are writing this book.

Chapter 20

Cognitive Flexibility

When a lightning bolt started the Mann Gulch fire in Montana on August 4, 1949, the fifteen smokejumpers who dropped from their plane thought they could put it out by the next morning. After a quick dinner, they headed down to the canyon, but to their surprise the fire had jumped the ridge in the rising wind, blocking the downhill escape to the river with a thirty-foot wall of flame. As they fled up the steep seventy-six-degree ridge, team supervisor Wagner Dodge lit a small fire in the dry grass and yelled for the others to drop their tools and lie down in the ashes. The instructions ran counter to their training to always keep their tools and so they ignored Dodge. But the flames chasing them at six hundred feet per second quickly caught them, melting their watches at the time of death, 5:56 p.m. The blaze proved so large that it took 450 firefighters five more days to put it out.[1]

Looking back on this tragedy, organization theorist Karl Weick reflected that "people, including those who are smokejumpers, act as if events cohere in time and space and that change unfolds in an orderly manner . . . [then an] episode occurs when people suddenly and deeply feel that the universe is no longer a rational, orderly system. What makes such an episode so shattering is that both the sense of what is occurring and the means to rebuild that sense collapse together."[2]

In such uncertain circumstances, the solution, according to Weick, is to adopt an "attitude of wisdom." He says, "In a fluid world, wise people know that they don't fully understand what is happening right now, because they have never seen precisely this event before."[3] A wise person thus believes in what they know just enough to take action, but doubts what they know just enough to take other voices into account. By contrast, "the overconfident shun curiosity because they feel they know most of what there is to know. The overcautious shun curiosity for fear it will only deepen their uncertainties."

Mike Cassidy, who has created more than a billion dollars in value across five startups, vividly illustrates this attitude of wisdom in practice. Cassidy has never been much of a gamer, but he joined forces with Thresh, the world champion of first-person-shooter video games *Doom* and *Quake*, to create Ultimate Arena, a service where players contribute money to play and then winner takes all. Cassidy and Thresh raised venture capital, built the site, and Thresh attracted droves of gamers. Even after the site had half a million users, Cassidy sensed something was awry. Digging into the data revealed what the flood of new users hid: an incredibly high churn rate as players quickly abandoned the site. When Cassidy shared the data with the team, to his surprise, many of them fought back against changing direction. Given the long-term unsustainability, Cassidy had to force the change, inviting the resisters to leave and rebuilding the team to pursue a new direction, a company called Xfire, which sold to Vivendi for over $100 million.

Looking back on his experience, Cassidy tried to make sense of why he could see the need to change while others could not. For one, Cassidy had a broad, multidisciplinary background. He studied jazz at the Berklee College of Music before earning bachelor's and master's degrees in aerospace engineering at the Massachusetts Institute of Technology, followed by an MBA at Harvard. For Cassidy, there were "always many ways to see the world, and many solutions." As he looked back on the team at Ultimate Arena, ironically, the obstacles to change were passion and talent—many of the folks who struggled to change were talented engineers but refused to acknowledge different perspectives on the situation. If they had, they might have seen the imperative to shift. In Nathan's interview with Cassidy, he summarized, "The thing that scares me most is someone who is convinced they are right, because they will never change."[4]

Inspired by the interview, Nathan put this idea to the test in the emerging solar photovoltaic industry. As entrepreneurs from all backgrounds jumped in, investors faced a challenging puzzle: Who should they invest in? The PhD who spent a lifetime in science or the internet entrepreneur with several successes under their belt but little scientific expertise? The research revealed that being a scientist in and of itself wasn't good or bad, but that founders who had spent a lifetime in one industry tended to get stuck in proving they were right, falling behind the evolving frontier of the industry. Those startup teams that had a greater breadth of experience across industries or entrepreneurial experience were much quicker to adapt to the changing environment and had greater success. Nathan concluded that cognitive flexibility—the ability to update your mental maps as the data changes—could be vital to success in uncertain environments.[5]

Interestingly, a separate study of "near misses" looking at prominent scientists who just barely missed the Nobel Prize–winning breakthrough for silencing ribonucleic acid (RNA), makes similar observations but in the inverse. Interviews with the scientists, all of whom were leading researchers in the topic, revealed that they failed to recognize anomalies in their own data, resisted trying solutions outside the established paradigm, and failed to connect to people outside their discipline who held the keys to the ultimate solution.[6] In other words, they didn't adopt an attitude of wisdom or have the cognitive flexibility to update their mental maps.

What does this mean for you and me? When we face uncertainty, if we can adopt an attitude of wisdom and nurture the cognitive flexibility to integrate new data, we will be more agile, adaptable, and successful. Rather than digging our heels in on one particular possibility, we can treat it the way a curious, open-minded scientist treats a hypothesis, adapting to the data rather than adapting the data to their ego. Merce Cunningham, the late leading innovator in modern dance, illustrated the spirit of cognitive flexibility in his composition process. "When I'm working on a new piece, I'm always convinced that there's something that I'm missing, as though I can't quite see around the corner," he said. "I know that there's something else that I'm not getting at, which I would be interested in; that this is not the only way to do it."[7]

Likewise, Martin van den Brink, chief technology officer of ASML, the leading semiconductor equipment firm, provides an excellent example of cognitive flexibility in a very different setting. He faced immense uncertainty in leading a decade-long, multibillion-dollar breakthrough to make semiconductors using extreme ultraviolet light. Along the way van den Brink faced opposition and encouragement, obstacles and successes. As he reflected on the twisting path to breakthrough, he told us, "I am never sure of my choice. I can make a decision today and I can challenge myself an hour later and feel comfortable." For van den Brink, "people who can't handle the truth can't admit a mistake, and so they go blindfolded off the cliff." He argues that it is much more interesting to "look at the cliff and find different ways you can approach it . . . it is OK to be wrong if it can be translated into another opportunity. So I never pretend I will be right. I just say, 'This is what I think, tell me the flaw in my thinking.'"[8]

Reflection and Practice

How can you improve your cognitive flexibility? You may need to approach it differently based on your natural inclination toward confidence, optimism, and openness to new experience. Nathan learned this firsthand while teaching a course in startup investing where, in partnership with the Kickstart Fund, students performed research on whether to invest in startup pitches. To his surprise, despite a robust curriculum on investing, students tended to bifurcate into two camps: pessimists who saw nothing but risks and optimists who saw nothing but opportunity. Nathan realized that his job was to help them learn to be *realists*: capable of recognizing both opportunities and risks and then exploring whether risks could be creatively addressed, rather than letting the risks kill the investment outright. Here are some ways you can do that too.

1. *Become a realist.* If you had to categorize yourself, what camp would you put yourself in: optimist or pessimist? If you are in the optimist camp, you might need to consider being a bit more open to contrary opinions, realizing that the existence of risks doesn't mean you should not pursue an idea. In fact, investor Jerry Neumann argues that risks are a good thing, because they protect an idea from quick imitation by a more powerful adversary.[9] Successful entrepreneurs tackle risks, addressing them one by one. If you are in the pessimist camp, you need to be very diligent about seeking out yea-sayers, since listening to the negative voices exclusively will dissuade you from continuing. To become a realist, you need to see risks simply as hypotheses to be tested, not foreboding "do not enter" signs.

2. *Talk about your idea.* Choose an idea you have been working on (e.g., business idea, career change, relocation, relationship) and consider if you have been open to other opinions or viewpoints. Make sure you hear from enthusiasts and skeptics. Use

what skeptics tell you to inspire new ways to see your project, rather than letting it stop you. Use enthusiasts as fuel for moving forward.

3. *Listen to opposing views.* Develop your ability to learn from other perspectives, even contrasting views, by listening to them. Read broadly, ask lots of questions, and talk to others with different ideas. When we hear what others think, we open ourselves up to changing our views—no matter what those views are. Derek Black was the heir apparent of the first internet hate site when he met Matthew Stevenson, an orthodox Jew, at college. Stevenson started inviting Black to Shabbat dinners and to hang out with friends at the nearby bay. Over time, their conversations evolved into friendship, and Black came to doubt the hateful ideology he had inherited.[10]

4. *Develop a T-shaped perspective.* Increasingly, engineering schools seek to train people to be "T-shaped," having depth in one area and breadth across areas (or at least the ability to connect to other disciplines and perspectives to integrate them). Although knowledge forms the foundation of a T-shaped perspective, becoming T-shaped begins with curiosity and empathy. Simply wanting to know about another discipline, wanting to see connections, and being curious enough to watch a documentary or listen to a lecture can be enough to nurture a depth-and-breadth perspective.

Chapter 21

Learning in Fog

Martin van den Brink, who led one of the most challenging break-throughs in semiconductor manufacturing, says navigating uncertainty is like driving a car in difficult conditions: "It is foggy and dark. [There are] a few folks with red lights ahead of you, and you are driving as fast as you can. But as you start to get more successful, you are in front. There are no more lights in front, and you have no clue what to do."[1] How do you navigate through the fog?

The fields of evolutionary biology, strategy, and innovation sometimes use the analogy of an "opportunity landscape" hidden by fog to describe uncertain situations. Imagine a 3D topographical map full of hills and valleys. With no knowledge of the landscape shrouded in the mist, how could you know whether you are standing next to a cliff—a dangerous area—or next to a bigger hill, an even more interesting opportunity? Research suggests that the best way through the fog is to adopt a set of learning techniques—fast cycles, simple rules, and switching approaches—to learn as quickly as possible so that you don't spend all your time hesitating on a hilltop or bumbling blindly through the gloom.

Fast Cycles

Startup accelerators are a great environment to get clues about how to learn quickly under uncertainty. Founders face dozens of unknowns, from which market to tackle to how to negotiate a contract, and accelerators are a new type of organization created to support them. Unlike startup incubators, which provide an office for an indeterminate period, accelerators accept a group of startups (a class) for a fixed period (typically three months), give them "ramen money" (enough money to survive on ramen noodles) in exchange for equity, and then coach them until a final demo day, when they pitch to external investors for funding. For example, Y Combinator hosts a dinner each week for participants, where successful entrepreneurs describe their lessons learned as well as introduce accepted entrepreneurs to mentors and customers who challenge their assumptions. Today there are several thousand startup accelerators, and graduated companies include Airbnb, Dropbox, and GitHub.

A recent academic study of the eight leading accelerators asked, What is the best way to design an accelerator to help the founders learn as quickly as possible?[2] Should you standardize or customize the program for each startup, compress or pace interactions with mentors, guard secrets or require founders to share with each other? The researchers found that the greatest challenge founders face is the trap we described in chapter 17 of forcing the machinery (settling for suboptimal certainty) in the face of so many unknowns.

Great accelerators counteract this tendency by forcing entrepreneurs to do things they wouldn't do on their own. They force founders to meet with a torrent of mentors and customers—as many as two hundred in the first month, so they get exposed to more of the opportunity landscape before locking into their initial hunch. Initially, many founders are anxious to describe their idea for fear it will be stolen. Great accelerators force them to talk to people because they recognize, as Debbie Sterling, founder of GoldieBlox, a company created to foster engineering skills for girls, explains: "I don't think it's ever really too early to start sharing even just a rough idea or a sketch on paper. I really don't. I have not yet had an experience where a half-baked idea of mine got stolen by somebody else or executed any better than I would've."[3] Sharing her idea with a waiter at a restaurant led to an introduction to the waiter's aunt, an editor at the *Atlantic*, who wrote an important article about GoldieBlox that helped launch the business.

The best startup accelerators also force their entrepreneurs to present to each other, sharing their progress. Once again, many founders are reluctant to share with other founders for fear that their ideas will be stolen, but they consistently discover that the benefits of discovering how to solve a shared problem or seeing new ways to approach a challenge outweigh any imagined risks.

Lastly, great startup accelerators force their startups to meet with a broad array of people, rather than customizing the conversations to a narrow group of "relevant" ones. For example, one founder creating software for social causes balked when the accelerator arranged a meeting with *Playboy*'s VP of marketing. To his surprise, the *Playboy* VP was also an active churchgoer and had fabulous ideas. Afterward, the founder gushed, "That was the best meeting I had all summer."[4] Sometimes the best insights come from far afield. As entrepreneur David Hieatt explains, "If we go looking for answers where everyone else does, we soon think as everyone else does. . . . Originality requires some element of oddness."[5]

Simple Rules

Research suggests that simple rules—fast and flexible heuristics based on past experience—can also help you learn your way through the fog. Rather than relying on overcomplicated plans or just shooting from the hip, you can use simple rules to improve your decision making by combining lessons from past experience with the flexibility to adapt. If we look closely, we can see simple rules at work everywhere in the world. Although ant brains are forty thousand times smaller than human brains, a simple rule of "look for work" allows millions of ants to develop complex divisions of labor, create intricate supply chains, and independently change jobs.[6] A simple rule at Intel—allocate fabrication space based on profit per wafer—led middle managers to transform the company from making memory to making microprocessors without guidance from senior leaders.[7] Likewise, after Amazon presold over a million DVDs of *Mamma Mia* for $30, when a competitor announced it would sell the same DVD for $10, the simple rule of "customers first" helped executives make the decision to price match (a $20 million loss of revenue) in "less than 60 seconds," without guidance from Jeff Bezos.[8]

Researchers at Stanford, Nathan among them, have done extensive research on how entrepreneurs develop simple rules in uncertain environments. They found that more successful entrepreneurs use past experience to develop rules about what to focus on (for example, develop low-cost semiconductors for video game makers rather than attracting new customers) and how to do it (for example, hold weekly meetings with marketing and engineering to integrate new customer insights). As teams learn how to work together, the most effective ones develop more sophisticated heuristics about the timing, order, and priority of different opportunities, such as how to prioritize which geographies to enter. By contrast, less effective entrepreneurs don't take the time to think about and communicate simple rules, and instead repeat past mistakes again and again.[9]

Startup investor David Hornik says that when it comes to uncertainty, "people who rely upon heuristics to make decisions, as opposed to exhaustive information, will be much better at dealing with uncertainty, because you didn't have to worry about the fact that information is shifting, because heuristics shift with new information." Hornik uses a simple rule he calls "human-driven decision making" to make startup investments. "I'm not investing because you are an expert. I'm not investing because I have a theory. I am investing because you have demonstrated you are the sort of person I would like to invest in: you are motivated by passion, not money, and you are creative when facing uncertainty."[10]

Switching Approaches

Finally, it helps to recognize that there are different learning strategies and that you may need to change yours to match the problem you face. Consider the race to create consumer drones, those flying machines piloted by amateurs buzzing overhead. The entrepreneurs who created this new industry faced three major challenges: what the best architecture is, what drones can be used for, and how to create drones ready to fly out of the box. Stanford researchers studying the industry compared 3DR, founded by former *Wired* editor Chris Anderson, and DJI, founded by Frank Wang when he was a graduate student. To solve the comparatively simple problem of the best architecture, 3DR's reliance on crowdsourcing, or turning a problem over to a large group of people, proved most effective. A user in an obscure part of the crowd proposed a quadrotor design from the 1950s that rapidly outpaced Wang's iterative approach based on his original helicopter design.

But when it came to the more complex problem of finding a use for drones, after falling behind with his helicopter design, Wang decided to switch his approach to learning how to solve the challenge. Wang engaged in parallel experimentation, talking to many users at once, such as firefighters, sports enthusiasts, and farmers, until he met a pilot who described how much money film studios pay for bad aerial footage. Drones could serve this market but doing so depended on creating a high-quality gimbal, a sophisticated device to shoot steady video. To solve this problem, Wang changed strategies again, assembling a multi-disciplinary team with software, mechanical, and electrical engineers, then engaging in rapid cycles of experimentation to create a gimbal that ended up increasing revenues to over $100 million. By contrast, 3DR stuck with the community-based approach that had worked for dis-covering the quadrotor. But while the community members spotted the need for a gimbal, they could never adequately coordinate to make one.

When entrepreneurs tackled the final big challenge, designing a ready-to-fly drone, once again the 3DR community struggled to coor-dinate, whereas Wang's team adopted a strategy of switching between big-picture architecture and individual components. "We duct-tape and zip-tie the thing together to show it kind of works, and then just make literally twenty prototypes on a weekly basis, constantly building a new prototype, constantly replacing the zip ties with better parts," explained an engineer.[11] After hundreds of rapid cycles, DJI created a ready-to-fly drone that captured 77 percent of the drone market, making Wang a bil-lionaire and leaving 3DR in the dust. The Stanford researchers concluded that simple problems can be tackled by people working independently, complex problems require cooperation, and integrated problems require both. More generally, their findings show the importance of being able to switch your approach to learning by asking, "What challenge do I face, and what learning strategy could help me figure it out faster?"

Reflection and Practice

Learning in fog requires adopting fast learning cycles, developing simple rules, and changing your learning strategy as the situation demands. Here's how you can get started.

1. *Create your own accelerator.* What would it be like to create your own accelerator experience, such as by forcing yourself to talk to as many people as possible, as quickly as possible, about your idea? When Robin Chase was searching for the right way to

describe Zipcar, the vehicle-sharing startup she cofounded, she wrote ideas down on index cards and tested them with everyone she met. She soon discovered the secret to convincing people to try the service was in the words she used to describe it: wheels when you want them![12]

2. *Develop simple rules—fast and frugal heuristics—based on your past experience.* You can have simple rules for almost any area of life. Create or adjust simple rules based on what *you* want to do. Thoughtfully develop your own rules but keep them flexible. They can also turn out to be uncertainty balancers, as they free up mental energy. For example, a benevolent humanitarian's simple rule might be to give fifteen minutes to everyone asking for it, or a shrewd art collector's simple rule might be to follow head, heart, and price tag.

Here are a few examples of simple rules to get your imagination started. For staffing: hire slow, fire fast. For eating: have desserts on weekends but not weekdays. For your budget: make coffee at home instead of buying a cup every day. For your social life: spend time with people who make you feel alive. For vacations: visit new places balanced with returning to old favorites. For your relationship with your partner: always (or never, depending on what works for you) resolve a disagreement before bed.

Most importantly, adopt the rules that work for you. In one of the more hilarious illustrations, when Gertrude Stein—novelist and mentor to Ernest Hemingway, F. Scott Fitzgerald, Henri Matisse, and others—discovered her beloved dog, Basket, had passed away, a friend suggested getting a dog of the exact same breed and calling it Basket. Pablo Picasso took the opposite view, arguing that getting the same dog would only remind them of the one they'd lost. Two conflicting simple rules. What did Stein do? For a while she tried to combine them, to "have the same and not to have the same." But in the end Stein decided she wanted the same dog, and she did call him Basket. "I cannot say that the confusion between the old and the new has yet taken place," she said.[13]

3. *Match the learning technique to the problem.* If you face a technical problem, seek out the advice of experts. If you face a customer demand problem, talk to users. If you want to challenge your thinking, talk to contrarians. If you want to broaden your

thinking, talk to those outside your discipline. If you tend to read books rather than engage in conversation, then do the uncomfortable thing and get out and talk to people. Change up your style depending on the problem.

4. *Prioritize taking action over finding the best way.* Many times, our projects depend less on figuring out the best way to do them and more on just getting started. Each step we take reveals more of the opportunity landscape. Although we can see the success of DJI in monetary terms, it's worthwhile to remember that 3DR is not a failure—it continues to serve other market needs, including the community of drone enthusiasts.

Chapter 22

10,000 Shots

The executive team of Match.com, the well-known dating site, sat in the darkened offsite room watching the video of SpaceX attempting to land the world's first reusable rocket on a barge tossing in the open ocean. Just as the rocket seemed about to touch down safely, it tilted too far left and then, overcorrecting, swung the other way, crashing in an explosion of fire and smoke. When the clip ended, Match.com CEO Sam Yagan asked his assembled team: "What did we just see here?"[1] For a moment the silence hung heavy, and then the chief marketing officer raised her hand and said, "It's a failed rocket landing." Yagan paused for a moment, thinking to himself, *I'm so glad she said the word "failed."* It would help him teach the lesson for which he had called the offsite in the first place: you can't achieve great things without failure.

Yagan turned the lights back up, thanked the CMO, and then asked, "Is it at all conceivable that you could go to Mars without failing along the way?" The CMO smiled, recognizing where this was going, and replied, "No, of course you would fail." Turning to his team, Yagan came to the crux of what was holding them back. "By definition, grand achievements cannot be achieved without failure. If you can do it without failing, it is not that hard. Therefore, you must fail to achieve great things." The lesson must have stuck, because after that, the Match.com teams tried and failed seventeen times to create a new business model until they discovered Tinder, which after many more experiments and iterations disrupted the parent company, attracting six times as many users and becoming the new paradigm in the field.

That failure is part of doing uncertain things is only half of the story, however. The other half is that because we hate to fail, we too often avoid the very uncertain situations where great things could happen.

Even when we dip our toes into the water, we are so keenly sensitive to anything going wrong that we back away quickly at the first sign of it. But there are some people who get used to trying again and again, as it's baked into their jobs. It was on a hike with actor Dallas Roberts that we realized how problematic a failure-avoidant reaction can be. Climbing through a thick stand of trees above a beautiful green plain, our conversation turned to navigating the uncertainty that comes with doing new things. After listening carefully, Roberts remarked, "Maybe people just need to try more. You know, for most actors, for every role they land, they've tried for 100 roles they never received."[2]

How many times have you tried more than twice for something, let alone 100 times? "You have to be willing to be bad, willing to embarrass yourself," Roberts reflected. He told us about an example that inspired him: "In the old days when *National Geographic* sent someone out on a photo shoot, they sent them with enough film for ten thousand shots and instructions to shoot every frame. Even though the magazine would only end up using a handful, it took those ten thousand shots to get the few great ones they published." Inspired by his comments to try more often, we actually looked it up, and it turns out that National Geographic typically asked photographers to take more like twenty thousand to sixty thousand shots—for a dozen photos that would be published. Amazing!

The lesson is that most of us need to try more than we are used to when we face uncertainty. In his book *Originals*, about people who pioneered new ideas, organizational psychologist Adam Grant argues that most of us are afraid to try for fear of looking stupid. The vast majority of people—85 percent—reported that they remained silent rather than speaking up about their most important idea.[3] By contrast, Grant says, "if you look across fields, the greatest originals are the ones who fail the most, because they're the ones who try the most." He points out that Darwin's first theory of evolution—that evolution would happen within a lifetime—was wrong; we now know that evolution occurs over many lifetimes. Darwin's journals reveal, however, that rather than giving up, he kept trying to improve his ideas, resulting in one of the most foundational theories in modern science. And among classical composers, Grant argues, one of the best predictors of success is the sheer volume of compositions. "The more output you churn out, the more variety you get and the better your chances of stumbling on something truly original. Even the three icons of classical music—Bach, Beethoven, Mozart—had to generate hundreds and hundreds of compositions to come up with a much smaller number of masterpieces."[4]

Along the way, there may be many failures. Let's look again at the reusable rocket company SpaceX, which failed many, many times along the path to transforming the space industry. Notably, its first Falcon 1 rocket exploded thirty-three seconds after takeoff, the second launch in 2007 failed to reach orbit, the first launch with a NASA payload crashed into the ocean, and the first four attempts to land at sea ended in explosions. There is a long list of other explosions, failures, and mistakes. But CEO Elon Musk never expected to succeed without failing. In fact, in an interview with Musk, he told us that he didn't take money from friends or investors early on because "I thought it would fail!"[5]

Likewise, although Amazon is known for its business successes, it has had many failures, including the Fire Phone, the Dash Button, and the Amazon Tap. "I've made billions of dollars of failures at Amazon, literally," Bezos admits. "None of those things are fun, but they also don't matter." Why? Because companies (and people) "eventually get into a desperate position" when they stop experimenting. "If you're going to take bold bets, they're going to be experiments, and if they're experiments, you don't know ahead of time if they're going to work. Experiments are by their very nature prone to failure."[6]

There are many other examples of people who had to try many times before their effort found firm footing. Children's author Dr. Seuss's first book was rejected by twenty-seven publishers when he bumped into a friend from college, Mike McClintock, who just that morning had started a job at Vanguard Press in the children's section. They signed a contract by the afternoon.[7]

Likewise, Jack Ma, founder of Alibaba, the e-commerce platform that is one of the most successful Chinese companies in history, reports, "I failed a key primary school test two times, I failed the middle school test three times, I failed the college entrance exam two times." On his math exam he scored 1 out of 120 points. When he applied for jobs after school, the police force rejected him with the comment "You're no good," and the local Kentucky Fried Chicken hired twenty-three of its twenty-four applicants, rejecting only Ma. He applied to Harvard ten times and was never admitted, his first two ventures failed, and he made many mistakes at Alibaba. "I call Alibaba '1,001 mistakes,'" Ma says, laughing. Looking back on his experience, he advises that "if you don't give up, you still have a chance. Giving up is the greatest failure."[8]

As a final example, take note that even though we remember Thomas Edison as a brilliant inventor, he too made many mistakes along the way. He spent a fortune on dozens of failed inventions like the automatic vote recorder, the electric pen, the tinfoil phonograph, his talking doll, an ore milling company, his Home Service Club (intended to be the Netflix of phonographs), and the home projection kinetoscope. What set Edison apart was his willingness to try again. "He [knew] that if one idea or one product doesn't do well, he [had] others . . . that can make up for it," said biographer Leonard DeGraaf.[9] Ironically, as we think about *National Geographic* photographers taking ten thousand shots for a handful of great photos, Edison famously stated, "I have not failed ten thousand times—I've successfully found ten thousand ways that will not work."[10]

A ten-thousand-shots framework could set us all free. As psychologist Angela Duckworth explains, *grit* is a blend of passion and perseverance—hard work more than talent—and those who are gritty have a better chance of achieving things they set out to do, because they don't give up.[11] They keep trying, regardless of their current level, grades, or pedigree, or of what people have told them.

Reflection and Practice

The way we think about genius is distorted. Genius is born of practice and many hours of work (ten thousand of them, according to writer Malcolm Gladwell).[12] The heroes we celebrate practice a lot and try things many different ways. That's how you get your best work—even if your first attempt is good, allowing yourself additional tries enriches and expands the final product. Below are some ideas to consider along the way.

1. Evolutionary psychologists trace our fear of rejection to our hunter-gatherer past. Exclusion from the tribe would have been a death sentence, so we learned to fear rejection—to conform—to remain in the tribe, and survive.[13] Today our context has changed; now learning to do new things and adapt in our dynamic environment is a key to success. We can reprogram these inherited responses to uncertainty and failure, though, which we discuss at length in chapter 26.

2. We are programmed to think that having to try hard or many times is a sign of weakness (see Carol Dweck's research on growth versus fixed mindsets).[14] When you are rejected from something or told to go back to the drawing board, try to reframe it as "I may not have succeeded as I imagined just yet, but I have a chance to get better!" Trying hard, in different ways and many, many times, increases our grit and also our intelligence, evolution, optimization, and refinement.

3. What would it look like if you allowed yourself more tries—even ten thousand of them? Most likely you would need to start earlier, invest less in each try, and allow yourself to continue on when things don't work out. Interestingly, many disciplines have this very advice at the heart of their narratives about their craft. For example, if you peruse the books about writing (two we like are *Bird by Bird* by Anne Lamott and *Writing the Australian Crawl* by William Stafford), the advice is usually the same: your first effort is always terrible, but the key is to keep trying, tackling your writing bit by bit rather than as a monolithic accomplishment. This advice applies in most pursuits, projects, or values.

4. What have you given up on too early? Is there something you put down that you should revisit? A project, friendship, talent, or skill that calls out to you but that you've judged to be out of reach too soon? Have you let a sense of rejection dissuade you from something you are meant to do? If so, maybe it's time to pick it up again.

Chapter 23

Bricolage

Sometimes we wait to start taking action because we feel we don't have the resources we need. But there is an abundance of evidence to suggest that successful innovators do just the opposite, getting started with what they have rather than waiting till the conditions are perfect. *Bricolage* is a French word coming from the medieval verb for "to fiddle or tinker"; sociologists use it to describe how innovators use what they have on hand to do something. Bricolage is closely related to one of the most prominent explanations of how entrepreneurs succeed, a process called *effectuation*, the basic principles being that you: (1) pilot the plane (you can make your own opportunities by influencing the future), (2) use the bird in the hand (like bricolage, make do with what resources you have), (3) make lemonade out of lemons (do what you can with surprises), and (4) embrace the crazy quilt (find value in having a variety of partnerships).[1] Although bricolage and effectuation differ in minor ways (some claim that bricolage is a resource logic and effectuation a decision-making logic), they basically say the same thing: make the most of what you have and just get started!

To illustrate, consider the race between US and Danish companies to create the sustainable wind energy industry.[2] Danish companies adopted a "get started with what we have" approach, cobbling together wind turbines from gears pillaged from trucks and wood panels to quickly deploy prototypes in the field and jumpstart a cycle of trial-and-error iteration. Moreover, they did it in the spirit of collaboration, with engineers meeting up to help each other solve problems, sitting down with customers to learn what worked, and even warmly cooperating with regulators to make sure their turbines were safe. Rather than keep their advances secret, the Danes started conferences and forums to share information and designs with each other. Surprisingly quickly, the crude wind turbines evolved into ever-more-sophisticated turbines that capture energy from the steady winds blowing off the North Sea.

In contrast to Denmark's bricolage approach to building wind turbines, US firms adopted a high-tech, science-based approach, relying on the latest theoretical thinking in aeronautics and structural dynamics in hopes of creating breakthroughs in the lab that, they assumed, would leapfrog the Danes' simpler methods. Many US engineers looked down on the scrappy Danish wind industry. "I felt their approach was too easy or not challenging enough," recalls one of the pioneering US engineers. Fearing their ideas might be stolen, US engineers avoided collaboration, and there was a spirit of disdain for the nuts and bolts of installing and operating turbines, which meant there was almost no feedback from customers to the labs: What could the field have to tell science anyway?

In the end, even though the US companies did make several breakthroughs, the Danish turbines were often already ahead or caught up so quickly that the breakthroughs were on par. But there was one crucial difference between the US and Danish wind turbines: the Danish designs were much cheaper and more reliable than US ones. Through bricolage—by using what they had on hand and trial-and-error efforts— the Danish companies solved one of the most challenging technical puzzles of their era and dominated the emerging wind energy industry. On reflection, the same US engineer who had denigrated the Danes and their bricolage concluded, "We trusted our engineering tools too much, and felt that they could solve the hard problems. . . . We felt bright and able . . . to solve anything. We thought, in a typical American fashion, that there would be inevitable breakthroughs that would make the 'pedestrian' Danish approach obsolete overnight."[3]

Even in big, disruptive leaps in innovation, when you peel back the accumulated layers of history, you often see a remarkable amount of bricolage underneath. When Bell Labs invented the transistor in 1947, many recognized its potential to transform electronics constrained by bulky, unreliable vacuum tubes. But in those early days, transistors were too weak to substitute for the vacuum tubes powering the large televisions and radios Americans wanted to buy. Nonetheless, RCA Victor, one of the dominant players in TVs and radios, recognized the disruptive potential of the transistor and so authorized a landmark $100 million investment in R&D to one day replace vacuum tubes with transistors. But in another corner of the world, a scrappy, young Japanese company named TTK, a newcomer to the industry, adopted a very different approach. Instead of pouring money into R&D, they decided to use the transistor to make a small, portable radio. The transistors were so weak that the radios were poor quality compared to RCA's (the sound was tinny and weak), but people with small budgets and teenagers who wanted to get out of the house to listen to rock and roll loved them. TTK sold tens of thousands of radios, improving them with each production run until their transistors became so good, the company realized they could use them to make TVs. RCA was already making big color televisions for the mainstream market, and TTK could only make tiny, black-and-white TVs, but these proved immensely popular for people who couldn't afford or didn't have a place for big TVs. Once again, TTK sold tens of thousands, improving with each round of bricolage and learning by doing until the once-tiny company, now named Sony, disrupted RCA's main market with cheaper, more reliable color televisions and radios. Although RCA had started with far more money, they never really caught up to Sony's bricolage approach.[4]

Over and over, research has underscored the power of bricolage. One of the more colorful accounts describes a farmer capturing seemingly useless methane, burning it to create electricity that he sold to the local utility, then discovering that he could use the heat to warm water for a hydroponic vegetable business and to raise fish.[5] Bricolage can also save the day in more high tech domains: the Apollo 13 astronauts only made it home safely after their oxygen tanks exploded because they used bricolage to make a round filter fit a square hole![6]

Anyone can tap the power of bricolage. It has even proven helpful in situations with more poverty and scarcity than most of us can imagine. Marlon Parker founded RLabs in the Cape Flats area of Cape Town, South Africa, a community where less than 5 percent of residents have a high school degree and youth unemployment exceeds 50 percent.[7] In a community many residents described as "hopeless," Parker used bricolage to build a community-training organization: "Most of the people that we were working with were gang members. . . . It was just not a very appealing group of people . . . so nobody wanted to give us any money."

Like in our discussion of reimagining resources in chapter 15, Parker asked, "What do we have in abundance?" He realized that with so many people out of work, people had an abundance of free time, which they could use to teach or learn. Parker scrounged an old computer from the attic of a local business and then recruited fourteen locals willing

Quality Ingredients

In speaking of bricolage—making do with what you have—we caution that there are times when the quality of your ingredients plays an important role in creating the possibilities you dream of. This idea is vividly illustrated in Virginia Woolf's damning feminist critique, "A Room of One's Own," in which she lays out the immense obstacles facing women writers over the ages. The essay compares, for example, a meal she ate with the scholars at a men's college—fish in a luxurious cream sauce, partridge accompanied by a "retinue of sauces and salads," potatoes delicately sliced thinner than coins, sprouts "foliated as rosebuds," rich roast beef, and a pudding for the gods, all of it accompanied by ever-flowing white and red wines—and a dinner at a women's college with a lowly budget, a coarse meal of beef and greens followed by stringy prunes, accompanied not by wines but by water. Her takeaway is that "the lamp of the spine does not light on beef and prunes."[a]

Concluding that "a woman must have money and a room of her own if she is to write fiction," Woolf makes the point that sometimes we need quality inputs to reach our highest possibility. We all face constraints, some more than others, and bricolage is about taking action despite those constraints. This doesn't mean the inputs need to cost a great deal. Beautiful music and inspiring words can be accessed for free. But part of navigating uncertainty may be asking in what areas of your life you need to maintain the quality of your inputs to create possibilities. Some inputs may be as simple as painting your walls or decorating your space. Nico Alary and Sarah Mouchot did save money on their apartment when creating Holybelly, but they did not compromise on the quality of the ingredients or the happy atmosphere at the restaurant. One of our colleagues, featured in chapter 26, doesn't make a great deal of money as a therapist, but he observed that when he finally allowed himself to splurge on a ski pass for the resort near his home, he suddenly found he leaped out of bed, had more energy, and felt a spark he had not felt before. In sum, there are times to prioritize things or comforts that light the lamp of brilliance within you.

a. Virginia Woolf, *A Room of One's Own/Three Guineas* (Vintage Classics, 2016).

to teach each other in an unused storage space in an effort to create an environment where people could feel hope. Parker encouraged people to share their stories and then teach each other what limited computer skills they had. One by one, as people learned basic IT skills from each other—and gave each other hope that the future could be better—they started to land jobs.

Momentum built and word started to spread. Visitors began appearing at RLabs asking how they could recreate their success in another community. Little did they know it was a difficult proposition: most social ventures fail because what made it work in one place doesn't work in another. But RLabs has managed to defy this common curse, spreading to dozens of cities, creating 90,000 jobs, and inspiring hope, all by applying bricolage. What does it look like? Whenever Parker helps open a new RLabs hub, he asks the founder to write down what they need and then ask, "Is it really needed?" He explains,

> The idea is that we say, 'Always look for alternatives. Do you really need to buy what you say you need to buy? Is there another way to do it? . . . If not, do you know someone who has it?' And so on. It guides people along the journey of nudging them to use small budgets and really utilize what and who is around. It's also a feeling of victory for the person whenever they find a solution—to sense that you solved a problem.[8]

The company has proven that bricolage works even in the most desperate circumstances. Yusuf Ssessanga, a chicken farmer and the founder of an RLabs group in Tanzania, explains, "[They taught me to] start from where you are and use the resources you have; that's how things happen . . . [by] looking at what we have. . . . It's inspired—you can do things on your own. It gives you dignity. It's the opposite of being in need, of being a victim."[9]

Reflection and Practice

Let's take inspiration from chicken farmer and RLabs participant Ssessanga. There may come a day when you get access to all the resources you imagine you need, but until then, getting started with what you have and learning as you go can be rewarding and even fun. Bricolage can even be used to make something out of nothing.

Charlotte Cory, a London-based writer and artist, was tasked by the BBC to create a bicentennial celebration of the birth of the writer Charlotte Brontë. As she considered different approaches, Cory had the idea: What if Brontë visited the Sir John Soane's Museum—a residence that has not changed since Brontë's lifetime—and we could hold the exhibit there, in a space that looks and feels like her century and where she could have actually spent time. Cory began searching the ancient visitor logs for Brontë's signature. "With mounting excitement, I combed the columns of signatures, knowing that maybe, maybe on the next page I might possibly find [hers]."[10] But after many hours, there was nothing. "I cannot describe the disappointment with which I finally closed the tantalizing tomes and admitted defeat." Discouraged, Cory was headed for home when she had a new idea: "[M]y heart leaped. It looks as if Charlotte Brontë did not visit the Soane, but why not bring her here for her bicentenary? She did not come, but she should have . . . so why not bring her to London again and give her another chance to enjoy the best of what the city has to offer? What better two-hundredth birthday present for a writer who has stood the test of time than a visit at long last to this timeless place?"[11]

Bricolage can help you achieve your goals, sometimes even seemingly out of nothing. Here are some approaches to help you get started.

1. Ask yourself if there is a creative way to get started on your task now. You may not have the resources for an entire project, but what could you do today with the resources you do have? For example, Nathan encourages his students to draw pictures of their ideas and show them to customers to get feedback before they spend a cent. Likewise, how could you start learning today? Many resources are available online or in libraries for free.

2. Can you put yourself in a position where you can start learning by doing, rather than just thinking about your project? Learning by doing is incredibly powerful. One chef we interviewed, who has worked in some of the greatest Michelin-starred restaurants, got his start volunteering at a local restaurant to see if he liked being a chef. We learn the most by trying, so find a low-cost way to try.

3. One of Nathan's colleagues teaches entrepreneurship in some of the poorest countries in the world. Class starts with a trading game where students try to exchange a rock for something better, then trade that for something yet better. After many trades, one entrepreneur turned a rock into a chicken that laid eggs he could sell. Many of us are fortunate to have more valuable things we can trade into something else. Like the chef in the previous exercise, could you trade your time to start learning today?

4. Cory's bricolage example is liberating because she created something out of nothing. Inspired by her Brontë exhibit, we asked ourselves, Could we invent something for a similar effect? We landed on the idea of writing imaginary endorsements for this book, such as "The book Steve Jobs would love if he had read it," and "The book that inspired Eliza Hamilton to cofound her pioneering orphanage." Maybe a similar creative activity could kick-start your imagination.

Chapter 24

Small Steps

Once something becomes successful, in retrospect it can seem like an overnight victory. When *Pokémon Go* attracted half a billion downloads in just two months, earning millions of dollars a day through in-app purchases and advertising, most people thought it was an instant success. But the origin of *Pokémon Go* actually extends back decades. Founder John Hanke started creating multiplayer games in 1994, at the time experimenting with online maps and photos, a project that Google bought in 2004, turning it into Google Earth. Once at Google, Hanke worked on Google Street View, and then created multiplayer games linked to maps. When a 2014 April Fool's joke went viral—a video in which Google announced positions for Pokémon Masters—Hanke wondered: Could he combine Pokémon with his maps games? In 2016 Hanke launched *Pokémon Go* and although by 2020 the company was making $1 billion a year, it had taken twenty years to get there.[1] The truth is that, as was the case with *Pokémon Go*, big breakthroughs are often through small experiments, one after another, day by day, not by big leaps.

A recent study conducted at Stanford underscores the value of small steps. The researchers compared eight startups (two matched cases in each industry) and asked whether it is more effective for entrepreneurs to tackle the tasks required to build a startup all at once or one at a time.[2] For example, they compared competitors Zaarly and Paintzen, which were in a race to create online marketplaces. Zaarly seemed to have everything going for it, winning first place at Los Angeles's Startup Weekend, raising $15 million in funding, and gaining endorsements from Bill Gates, former eBay and Hewlett Packard CEO Meg Whitman, and tech investor Ashton Kutcher. In just eleven weeks, Zaarly claimed to have successfully assembled an engineering team, built robust technology, opened two offices, filed several patents, and launched to the market. By contrast, Paintzen, seemed only to be getting started, chasing a narrower market in painting, and had only just started testing an estimation tool. They didn't have painters or customers, let alone a launch to the market. Instead they planned to tackle these things later, one at a time, after they had nailed the estimation tool. If you had to invest, where would you put your money? It might surprise you that, in the end, Zaarly's team failed to get any traction, burning out because they were spread too thin. "We were doing a lot of things poorly," its CEO admits. "We saw a lot of glimpses of [success], but there was no way to guarantee more of it without just really, really tightening focus."[3] By contrast, by taking small steps one at a time, Paintzen built such a strong platform that they beat out well-funded competitors like EasyPaint and Amazon Home Services.

Taking Small Steps Like a Great Chef

The Stanford researchers concluded that the best way to pursue a new project in an uncertain environment is to take small steps, switching between different demands rather than trying to do everything at once. They suggest focusing on the most critical area (and using backstops for the others) until it is good enough—though not necessarily perfect—and then switching to the next most critical area. It is a bit like preparing a meal. A great chef doesn't try to stir every pot at the exact same time, nor finish one dish to perfection and then put it aside to spoil while perfecting the next dish. Instead, they juggle the tasks in a series of small steps. The most critical tasks are on the front burner, the less critical items are on the back burner, and the chef rotates them when the one in front is good enough (as opposed to finished), and so on, weaving together a meal.

Juggling small steps helped Aashi Vel and Steph Lawrence to build the successful culinary startup Traveling Spoon, which connects travelers with local hosts. The inspiration for Traveling Spoon began on a trip to Mexico, when Vel recalls seeing "through a window a woman in her kitchen, making dinner," and feeling the keen longing to be "sharing a homemade meal with this local Mexican woman, hearing her stories and learning about her culture."[4] Vel and Lawrence joined forces to create a new platform to host authentic cultural experiences. But they debated the best way forward. A recently launched competitor in Paris doing the same thing seemed to be pulling ahead of them by doing everything at once.

Nonetheless, Vel and Lawrence decided to proceed one small step at a time. For example, after talking to as many people as possible, they realized that great hosts would be the key to drawing users and fueling future growth. "We spent two years in just [India and a few other Asian countries], really understanding what it is that [hosts] wanted," Lawrence recalls. Along the way they discovered that some of their assumptions turned out to be wrong. "We thought we would give women in rural villages the opportunity to make money doing what they love . . . [but] we found very quickly that because we required that our hosts speak English and have access to the internet, that put them into a middle or upper income bracket."[5]

Focusing and taking small steps helped them develop simple rules (like "choose hosts who speak English and can access the internet") and using backstops for the noncritical areas helped them save time and money. "We were so glad that we didn't spend tens of thousands of dollars building something because we just didn't know [what was best]. . . . We can't decide at stage one what travelers would need," Lawrence reflects.[6]

Once they reached a learning plateau where their understanding of hosts was "good enough," like great chefs, Vel and Lawrence switched to the next most critical activity, in this case figuring out the right geographies to focus on. After spending time exploring this next small step, they developed simple rules like "avoid partier locations" and ideas about how to best recruit hosts. Vel and Lawrence continued working sequentially, tackling one activity at a time until it was good enough, absorbing the most important lessons, and then turning their attention to the next big issue. Ultimately Traveling Spoon grew to become a profitable, sustainable company, hosting food experiences in more than 180 cities in 60 countries. By contrast, the Paris-based food tourism startup that tried to do everything at once failed, their founders concluding that they had never been able to really get traction because they were doing too much at the same time.

Although Traveling Spoon and Paintzen are in vastly different markets, the lesson remains unchanged: You do not have to do it all at once. Taking small steps helps you make more progress and learn more effectively. You don't have to reach perfection either. Instead you can pause at a plateau, rather than waiting for a peak, which allows you to effectively switch focus to other important elements. Although we are attracted to stories of overnight success, more often the slow, incremental path up the mountain leads to better outcomes.

Use Experiments to Take Small Steps

Thinking of each small step as an experiment can help you move forward, blowing away the fog on the opportunity landscape and creating more confidence with each step. As Ken Moore, chief innovation officer at Mastercard, describes it, small experiments help you "move from a huge number of assumptions [about the unknown], to do work to turn those into knowns."[7]

For example, when Nathan's students wanted to create a baby monitor using wireless pulse oximetry to monitor an infant's oxygen levels and warn parents about breathing problems in the night, they faced a forest of unknowns. Hardware is complex and expensive, big players dominate the distribution channels, and they were inexperienced undergraduates. Rather than try to tackle every uncertainty at once, Nathan encouraged them to focus exclusively on the most important unknown: Would customers want it? After initial conversations with parents proved promising, they created a video that was "nothing more than smoke and mirrors showing what the product would do." It got picked up by media outlets, leading to tens of thousands of inquiries from urgent parents writing, "Just sell it to me now."[8]

With the uncertainty around customer demand resolved, they turned their attention to the next unresolved uncertainty: Can we build it? Even though the team had limited engineering skills, they realized they could still develop a prototype. With only $2,000 they managed to build a functional prototype, proving that the idea worked, but also revealing an important design flaw—they needed to change from an easily dislodged ankle monitor to a snug sock. With the technical uncertainty resolved, the next big unknown was what price they could charge customers. To explore this question, they called thirty baby stores to ask what prices parents pay for baby monitors, which for the time was good enough. Later, when they wanted to get a more precise understanding of the optimal price, they ran an A/B test on their website offering that customers could "Reserve Now" at different prices.

At some point along the way, the team discovered that if the device had an alarm, it would require an expensive FDA approval process. Rather than give up, they asked a different question: Would parents still buy a baby monitor providing great data but without an alarm? To experiment about this unknown, they printed out pictures of their product and three competitors' products and stood outside of baby stores asking parents, "Which one would you buy?" They were happily surprised to discover many parents wanted their product the most.

The team faced much competition, including teams founded by alumni of Google, IDEO, and MIT. But in founder Kurt Workman's words, "We had experimented . . . and we knew better than our competitors that what parents wanted most was not the data, but to know everything was OK." Through hundreds of small steps, the team succeeded in commercializing the Owlet baby monitor, rising to number one in their category and going public at a billion-dollar valuation.

Anyone Can Experiment, Not Just "Innovators"

Experimenting can seem like something only innovators can do, but we would argue that it is the other way around: being willing to experiment is what creates an innovator. Back in 2001, an undistinguished university graduate was struggling to stay positive in his first job, making cold calls to sell data storage, until one day he asked himself: "What if I tried something completely different for forty-eight hours?" Instead of making calls during the day like everyone else, he started making calls morning and evenings, and rather than following the script, he decided to just ask questions to customers. During his liberated daytime, he studied the technical details of the data storage so he sounded more like an engineer than a salesperson. By catching clients during off hours when they were less stressed and asking them questions, in the next quarter he outsold the competitor's entire office. That lowly employee, Tim Ferriss, today a popular author, reflects on that experience arguing that "success, however you define it, is achievable if you collect the right field-tested beliefs and habits."[9]

Get Moving, Keep Moving

Albert Szent-Györgyi recounted how during World War I a group of Hungarian soldiers became lost in a blizzard in the Alps. To everyone's surprise, they made it out alive, stumbling into camp days later. When their lieutenant asked how they found their way back, the soldiers credited the map they had found in their packs. But when the lieutenant inspected the map, it was of the Pyrenees, not the Alps![10] The story has since been retold many times to teach an important, enduring lesson: getting started is more important than having all the information. As Charles Gorintin, cofounder of one of Europe's fastest-growing insurance companies explains it, "We encourage our leaders to make a decision with seventy percent of the data because making a decision is often more powerful than delaying a decision. Even if you make the wrong decision, if you just get started, you have time to figure out the mistake and fix it."[11]

Creatives and innovators consistently harp on the importance of just getting started and then creating an environment that helps you persist. Cartoonist Scott Adams recounts how he hated his job and commute, so he created a routine of rising at 4 a.m. to draw, which eventually led to the wildly popular comic strip *Dilbert*.[12] Author Brad Modlin purposely didn't sign up for internet service at home so that at night he could focus on writing.[13] Creative Jessica Abel argues that the idea of "the starving artist in the garret, the heroic paint-spattered painter with a whisky in hand . . . [is] super destructive in terms of how people think creativity is supposed to work. Creativity comes out of coming back to the 'thing' over and over again—by confronting yourself with it, letting yourself sit with it, and then moving forward bit by bit. That's how things get finished."[14]

Hard Work

Experimenting is hard, but don't let that stop you from getting started. Annemarie O'Sullivan is a former competitive swimmer who was working as a coordinator in a local hospital when she took a course on basket weaving. Just feeling the willow branches in her hands "felt like swimming again, it was just so natural. I just wanted to do this."[15] Despite recognizing her calling, she persisted in her hospital job in which she felt ever-decreasing interest. Months later, she was crabby and frustrated, and her husband Tom, observed, "You seem really calm and happy when you are weaving." Annemarie snapped at him, "Of course I am! Can't you see this is what I want to do?"

Tom replied calmly, "You can." Annemarie was thunderstruck. They were in the middle of two careers, with two young boys in tow. Could it be possible? But Tom, a thoughtful and generous companion, sat down and together they came up with a plan. Tom started a landscaping business that would cover living expenses. "It wasn't my passion," Tom admits, "but it let Annemarie start weaving." From there, it was a series of "tiny, tiny steps," she recalls. "It was a lot of hard work," and "you have to be prepared for things to go wrong." But the basket orders started to trickle in until one day a huge order came in from a chic San Francisco boutique. Tom suggested that he close down the landscaping business and join her full-time. Today they work together and their baskets, using traditional methods and heirloom varieties of willow, have been featured in museum exhibitions, galleries, and the *New York Times*.

Reflection and Practice

Wes Anderson is one of the most distinctive and influential filmmakers of our time. His career started because he was willing to run experiments. He recalls how in the beginning he had no more to go on than questions. "Maybe it should be like this . . . I think maybe this is the lens? And this is the shot? And this is the angle? This is the feeling?"[16] Success came one step at a time. Some experiments worked and some failed. His first big break, a thirteen-minute short with friends Luke and Owen Wilson, won critical acclaim. But when they were funded to create a feature-length movie based on the short, the resulting film *Bottle Rocket* flopped. Anderson describes the experience as a Cinderella story in reverse, with an emphasis on turning back into an ordinary pumpkin at the end. Still, Anderson continued experimenting, ultimately creating films that have won scores of awards.

Despite his success, he continues to experiment. When asked to curate an exhibit at Vienna's Kunsthistorisches Museum, he and partner Juman Malouf designed a room full of the empty carrying cases for precious things (without the things themselves) such as cases for Italian crowns and archaic instruments, as well as a room containing only emerald green objects. It was not an easy exhibit to develop. When they asked curators for a list of emerald green objects, the curators just rolled their eyes. Some reviewers panned the exhibit, but many found it enlightening, allowing them to appreciate objects that had been locked away in warehouses for decades. Afterward, Anderson reflected that "should our experiment fail . . . we are, nevertheless, confident it will, at the very least, serve the purpose of ruling out certain hypotheses, thereby advancing the methods of art history through the scientific process of trial and error. (In this case, mostly error.)"[17]

We might be more willing to experiment if we realize, like Anderson, that even failed experiments teach us important lessons. Moreover, virtually everything can be transformed into an experiment, even complex, expensive things. SpaceX has a prototype of the Falcon rocket laid out so teams can experiment with changes in advance. IDEO likes to test building layout changes with cardboard mockups before knocking down walls for remodels. To get started on your experiment, here are some questions to ask yourself.

1. What decision, project, or idea could you transform into an experiment? How could you break it down into a smaller, faster test?

2. What is the deal-breaker assumption that needs to be tested? Take that hypothesis and find out whether it holds or not using a low-cost experiment. For example, Jennifer Hyman and Jenny Fleiss identified the most critical questions that could undercut the idea for their company, Rent the Runway: are women highly motivated to rent a designer dress for one-tenth the price of buying it, and will they return it in good condition? To test this question, they broke the unknown down into something they could test with a fast, low-cost experiment: they borrowed dresses and set up a rental room in a Harvard dorm before a big dance. Hyman and Fleiss observed that 34 percent of women who visited the booth rented a dress and 96 percent returned it in good condition. This seemed encouraging, so they repeated the experiment several times, first by allowing women to see the dresses at the kiosk but not try them on, and later by skipping the kiosk and simply sending an email offering dresses for rent. Each

experiment helped them discover the opportunity and today, hundreds of experiments later, their company Rent the Runway has over $100 million in revenue.[18]

3. If you want to change jobs, how could you turn it into an experiment that would give you a better idea of what the new opportunity would be like? Can you volunteer part-time to explore the new job? Can you save some vacation days and do a week-long internship in the new position? Could you set up an option to return to your existing job while you try something new? How about just taking people who work in that organization or job for coffee?

4. Want to change the course of your life? How would you do it as an experiment? It may help to revisit chapter 7 on regret minimization, including the idea of transforming "one-way door" situations into "two-way door" options.

Chapter 25

Pivot

Pivoting, or changing course, is often something people and organizations feel ashamed to do. Nathan recalls the moment when, standing in the back of the room, he watched the chief digital officer at the front of the room, slide clicker in hand, apologizing that the digital team was changing the product road map based on what they discovered in early market tests. A few heads in the audience turned, revealing skeptical smirks. Seeing this, Nathan yelled out, "Woo-hoo" and started clapping. Then he declared, "This means your team is on the right track. If you are doing new things, you should expect to change course along the way." The assembled group smiled at his antics, but that was part of the message he was there to teach: in a world of uncertainty, inevitably some part of what you imagine will need to be changed.

Famed innovation professor Clayton Christensen estimated that 93 percent of startups have to change their strategy. Consider Max Levchin's long, twisting journey to co-create PayPal. When Levchin dropped in on a cryptology lecture at Stanford University, there were only six people in the room, one of them a hedge fund manager named Peter Thiel. The two agreed to team up, founding a startup called Fieldlink, which created software libraries for the coming wave of application developers who would need to facilitate handheld device access to IT networks. Levchin recalls thinking, "Any minute now, there'll be millions of people begging for security on their handheld devices. [But] it just wasn't happening."[1]

So they pivoted—in business terms, changing direction based on what you have learned—from creating software libraries to creating the actual software itself. A few people expressed interest, but no customers materialized. So they pivoted again, changing their name to Confinity and offering an electronic wallet. Once again, no customers materialized so they pivoted to sending money between Palm Pilots. This idea at least attracted an investor. But although they managed to attract a few thousand users, growth was slow. Levchin suggested setting up a way to send money to people via their email address, in case they didn't have a Palm Pilot. Unexpectedly, users started flocking to the email payment part of the business, including users from a "sketchy" new online platform called eBay. Levchin recalls how at first they resisted, but when the number of users for email payments reached over 1.5 million (compared with their 12,000 Palm Pilot users), they pivoted again, changing their name to Pay-Pal.[2] Looking back on those days, Reid Hoffmann, PayPal's first chief operating officer (and who later founded LinkedIn) recalls, "I couldn't have drawn a road map. We discovered our future as it happened."[3]

Pivoting is something almost every company has to do, whether they are easily adaptable software startups or hard-science companies like Fluidigm, which shrunk a chemical testing laboratory down to the size of a chip. On the journey from idea to company success, Fluidigm founder Gajus Worthington had to lead this highly technical, complex company through three major changes: from microfabricated plumbing chips to a microfluidic device for biotech applications, then to a microfluidic chip applicable across many industries, and finally to being a commercial manufacturer. Each change required immense organizational and personal change. Looking back, Worthington observes that "people who are able to adapt have an allegiance to learning, to self-improvement, to the mission of the company."[4]

Pivoting isn't about abandoning course but instead about using what you learned to adjust your course. As entrepreneur Eric Ries, who popularized the term *pivot* in this context, put it, "pivoting redeems failure" by using what you learned to make adjustments based on what you have learned to be more successful.[5] Although PayPal has pursued many ventures, it has always evolved around security and payments. Likewise, Fluidigm tried many ways to miniaturize laboratory procedures. The lesson is that it is normal to have to change course when navigating uncertainty.

Personal Pivots

The most important pivots are the ones that enable personal transformation. In spite of the exhausting or awkward phases they may demand, these pivots result in individuals living the fullest expression of themselves. Christophe Vasseur recalls the transcendent summer evening in Provence, the sun low on the fields of wheat and lavender, when his father's friend took them to a special restaurant. Down a tiny dusty road, at the end of a stone path in an old barn, Clément Bruno had set a service for twenty people. There were no signs for Chez Bruno and no menu, but the owner welcomed these strangers with "open arms and a singing voice."[6] As the summer afternoon faded into dusk, Bruno brought out one delicious dish after another. "A sublime ravioli with fresh herbs, seasoned with just a touch of olive oil," followed by "a few crayfish flambéed with cognac and deglazed with champagne . . . because they're so light!" Vasseur remembers.

The experience changed him permanently. "Never again did I experience such an encounter. More than a festive dinner, it was a lesson in life. At the time I was sixteen, and [Bruno's] words, his passion, and his belief opened a path." Vasseur continued his education, working for ten years in the fashion industry in Asia and Europe until "[I] was tired of the suits and ties that I encountered every day." He decided it was finally time to explore his curiosity and registered for a course in bread making. "I remember my first contact with bread dough. I felt like I was in communion, in conversation with it."

Vasseur recognized the desire to change his career, but he wondered how he could support himself during the change. He reached out to a business school in Paris and found an adjunct teaching position that would cover his rent. Then he started taking baking classes. "My professional transition would be long and fraught with difficulties," Vasseur remembers. It was less glamorous off the fast track, and making ends meet proved difficult. He persevered, following his curiosity about traditional baking techniques, trying out recipes for four years while teaching at the business school before he felt ready to start his own bakery.

"Rollerblades on my feet, I combed the streets of Paris. I stopped at all bakeries that attracted me," Vasseur recounts. "At the intersection of Rue de Marseille and Rue Yves Toudic, there was not a soul on the horizon; just wholesale leather shops and this bakery on the corner, giving the impression of always having been there." When he inquired about buying the bakery, he discovered that the baker had gone bankrupt three times in the last seven years, there were five competing bakeries within a one-thousand-foot radius, and the street had almost no foot traffic. "I was indeed the only one to see a future in this bakery," Vasseur admits. Despite the obstacles, and to his amazement, the bank accepted his offer to buy the bakery out of bankruptcy.

Vasseur renamed the bakery Du Pain et des Idées (Bread and Ideas). He kept the historic glass ceilings and beveled mirrors, then decorated with antique baking tins and generous baskets to hold the bread. Vasseur remembers he had to "work like a madman" to get it off the ground, all while continuing to experiment. One project involved reviving an abandoned "drop firing" technique, where the bread bakes as the oven cools. Vasseur named the loaf *le pain des amis* (bread of friends). A few weeks later, an older gentleman walked into the bakery. He explained that his wife had picked up some *pain des amis*, and that "when he opened the bag, he found himself as a seven-year-old in his grandfather's bakery." The older man "started to cry upon rediscovering the buried impressions of his childhood, and the memory of a loved one who had suddenly left this world." Vasseur himself shed tears. "He gave me the confirmation that I was on the right track and that I should persevere." Although Du Pain et des Idées has gone on to become one of the most famous bakeries in Paris, "more than any other accolade, his message touched me deeply," Vasseur says.

Looking back, he admits that at sixteen, he wasn't ready. "I had not clearly formulated the dream of becoming a baker," and he hadn't developed the strong convictions necessary to "make this professional universe my own and turn it into an art." But when the time did come, Vasseur was willing to pivot and so effected a massive change through a series of small, incremental steps. Looking back on his journey, Vasseur reminds us, "It is normal to fail, to not do it right the first time, just like a child learning to walk. If it doesn't work, it won't kill us; but we can perish from not having tried." For those who are on the fence, he counsels, "It's never too late to go toward one's passion, to embrace it, to throw oneself headlong into it. Never too late to be ruled by your heart, to listen to what your nature is telling you. Never too late to change your way of consuming and working."

Today Vasseur runs both the bakery and a baking school in the south. Moreover, three decades after that magical dinner in Provence, Vasseur received a letter from Clément Bruno, inviting him back to Chez Bruno. The now-Michelin-starred chef had seen Vasseur on a cooking show, and after a joyful reunion in the south of France, Chez Bruno became a client, serving *pain des amis* at the very restaurant that had originally sparked Vasseur's passion so many years ago.

Reflection and Practice

Pivoting is an essential part of navigating uncertainty. There is rarely one clear path that stretches forward without a bend or fog or obstacle. And even when a path or obstacle may feel certain, it can change, sometimes quickly. Krista Tippett, who was living in West Berlin as a *New York Times* journalist in the late 1980s, recounts visiting a friend in East Germany who had just finished reading Margaret Atwood's novel *The Handmaid's Tale*.[7] "To imagine that a hundred years from now," she said—risking censure if the microphones in that apartment captured her glee—"the GDR will just be a thing of the past, like that!" Tippett recalls feeling pity for her friend. "Such was the sense of totality and finality in that historical moment that I could not imagine the beyond of it, even in a century." But then only three years later, the Berlin Wall fell after a "bumbling bureaucrat" mistakenly announced that East Germans would be allowed to apply for a passport. "What people heard was possibility. And what followed, as en masse the population of the entire city stepped out of their apartments and began to walk towards the checkpoints of the Wall, was the final unraveling of fear. The Wall had never had a chance against this mass of humanity."

Tippett's experience reminds us that big changes are possible, even when they seem impossible. Pivots are a tool to help that change along, whether they be small course corrections or a 180-degree about-face. Pivots build on what we learned from the past, redeeming what the overly critical might call a failure, by reseeing it as a valuable lesson for taking the next step. Pivots also help make changes feel safer because they aren't wild leaps into an abyss. Like in basketball, where a player must keep one foot planted to make a fair pass of the ball, a pivot is a shift rooted in a place that you are moving away from but still grounded in. Recall that Vasseur didn't just quit his job one day and start a bakery the next. Instead, he took classes while continuing to work in fashion, then took a teaching position at a local business school while taking baking classes full time, and finally made the step to become a baker.

Here are a few ways to think about pivots in your life.

1. Although it might feel that change is not possible, for a moment consider whether there are situations at work or in your personal life that might work better if you tweaked them. Are certain problems or longings showing up repetitively and begging you to pivot? How could you try an experiment as the first step toward a simple pivot?

2. Are you doing things against your conscience to belong to or continue a tradition that you know needs to change? Could a pivot with this tradition (taking a break, exploring other ideas, talking to people involved) give you more courage to act with integrity?

3. Could pivoting be about eliminating something that's no longer necessary in your life? In a study where young children and chimps had to perform a series of steps to get candy, chimps learned to skip the unnecessary steps, whereas children kept them because they had been taught to follow instructions. Where do you need to pivot from the instructions for life that you inherited?

4. It might help to recall a time in the past when you pivoted or someone you admire who did. What did you learn from that experience? Or perhaps you could share your experience with someone else who wants to make a change.

Section Four

Sustain

J ust as food and drink sustain our bodies, the Sustain section provides tools to nourish and comfort you through the downsides of uncertainty. Regret, anxiety, grief, self-doubt, and even embarrassment can be powerful obstacles to navigating uncertainty well. Remember, there will be obstacles whether you chose the particular uncertainty or not. The verb *sustain* has five important variations that illustrate what these tools involve:

1. To strengthen or support physically or mentally

2. To bear (the weight of an object) without breaking or falling

3. To undergo or suffer (something unpleasant, especially an injury)

4. To cause to continue for an extended period or without interruption

5. To uphold, affirm, or confirm the justice or validity of

As the symbol for sustain, we adopt Paris's coat of arms: a boat floating above turbulent water, often accompanied by the Latin motto *fluctuat nec mergitur*, "tossed but not sinking." The image of this boat appears all over Paris—lampposts, schools, bridges, archways, sewer covers. It is a moving reminder that in the face of plague, siege, war, genocide, starvation, bigotry, and cruelty, Paris always emerges beautiful, liberating, and inspiring. Despite it all, and perhaps because of it all, Paris remains the City of Light.

Entrepreneur Alexandre Thumerelle, founder of the beloved Ofr bookstore, expounded on this undimmable character of Paris when Covid-19 closed its famous cafés and silenced the busy streets. "In Paris, everything is possible. Even without money, especially without money . . . we come to challenge ourselves, to question ourselves, to try out a thousand different things. . . . We take our heads out of the sand and build movies, books, boutiques, cafés, concerts that we dream of. We create magazines, TV channels, art festivals. A quenchless Paris, across all the ages, what a miracle!"[1] Sustain is about not giving up on our dreams, our values, or ourselves.

There is an important difference between this section and the others: Sustain tools are most helpful in a moment of crisis. To make their implementation easier for you to remember, we have sorted them into three categories (emotional hygiene, reality check, magic); each category has its own chapter, and each chapter contains several tools. To further encourage their application, we paired these categories of tools with roles for you to inhabit (doula, counselor, artist).

Tool	Description
Emotional hygiene: Consistent and skillful care of our emotional selves. Practice being your own doula, a caretaker who assists you in delivering the possibility you are striving for.	
Riding the Waves	Emotions come in waves, with highs and lows. Know that the cycle is natural—everyone feels it. If you're at a low point, better times are coming!
Hope Is Active	Hope isn't something that happens; it is an active choice to believe our dreams into being, even if we feel they are on shaky ground.
Connection and Community	We are sustained by enriching communities. Surround yourself with others who understand your situation or can build your optimism. Connect with people you can learn from.
Comforts	Our senses bypass the thinking brain and bring immediate comfort. Use them to create a haven at home or at work and to ground you when you are distressed.
Reality check: Using the reasoning mind to unpack the real situation. Practice being your own wise counselor, finding solutions or options that are realistic and valuing the lessons you can learn.	
Embrace Being Human	Surrender to the reality that humans have instinctual fear—it has helped our species survive. Then move into a more meaningful attitude toward anxiety and uncertainty.
Learned Optimism	Decatastrophize setbacks by seeing them as temporary, isolated to the circumstance, and not entirely your fault. Celebrate your victories and dispute the negative beliefs to find more energy to try again.
Frustration Management	It's OK to let yourself feel frustrated by a setback for a period of time but then use reframing techniques to defang the setback. After all, setbacks are an inevitable part of uncertainty and possibility.
Sorting Knowns versus Unknowns	Identifying what you know and what you don't know can decrease your anxiety and provide some knowns to fill in the gaps. You might be able to use analogies to make sense of the unknowns to give you some firmer footing.
Alternatives and Probabilities	Too often we think in binary terms, obsessing about success versus failure. In reality, life has many more possible outcomes than we can imagine. Seeing the broader set of options and thinking in terms of probabilities can help decrease your stress about the unknown.

Tool	Description
Creative Competition	Don't lose sight of the benefit of competition: It gets you doing your best work. What can you learn from competitors? How can they inspire you? Creative collaboration is even better, and it's a way out of the competition dilemma.
Worst-Case Scenario	Obsessing about the worst-case scenarios can be disabling. Sometimes unpacking the worst-case scenario and walking it through to its final implications can reveal that the "monster under the bed" isn't quite as terrible as we feared.
The Optimization Myth	There isn't one best way to do anything. Don't get so obsessed with what you imagine the optimal outcome to be. You might miss out on the way it was really meant to happen.

Magic: The leaps of insight, connection, and serendipity that change and inspire us. We don't control magic, but we can make more room for it. Paying attention like an artist increases our chances for serendipity and inspiration.

Picaresque	Few people live the life they planned. Go along for the ride of your life. Don't take things too seriously or personally. Cultivate your garden and discover the magic that is already there.
As If	Living as if something was already true is a technique philosophers and political activists use to invoke action and change. Living as if possibilities exist can increase the chances that they will come to be and helps us endure while we wait for them.
Helping Others	Empathy, compassion, and service all reward the giver and the receiver. When people are kind during times of struggle or stress, they experience less distress and more hope themselves.
Memento Mori	From the Latin for "Remember, you must die," this practice is an ancient form of meditation on the certainty that your time is limited, which can help infuse the days you do have with more vibrant living and joy.
Techs You Live By	If technology is "any phenomenon put to use," what technologies are you using and why? Being intentional about adding philosophy, art, poetry, music, and other such "high techs" creates more room for magic.

Chapter 26

Emotional Hygiene

It can be tempting to think of emotions as unfortunate evolutionary by-products, signs of weakness to be avoided. But emotions play an important role, in life and in uncertainty, that should not be ignored. As Emiliana Simon-Thomas, PhD and science director of Berkeley's Greater Good Science Center, writes "[Emotions] provide us with quintessential information about what's important and what to do next and how to do it and who to do it with."[1] Uncertainty comes with emotions, and becoming aware of those emotions, learning how to observe and validate them without impulsively acting from the pain or worry, is a vital part of sustaining yourself.

How do we become better at navigating the emotions that come with uncertainty? Psychologist Paul Ekman is known for his groundbreaking work developing a "science" of emotions.[2] Together with his daughter, Dr. Eve Ekman, he created an "atlas" that categorizes every human emotion into one of five universal categories: anger, disgust, enjoyment, fear, and sadness. They designed the framework to create awareness of the mechanics behind emotions, including triggers, reactions, intensity, and the negative consequences of unconscious responses. The framework underscores the tangible algorithms behind intangible emotions, and the importance of paying attention to them, rather than ignoring them.

Historically, our ancestors paid limited attention to physical hygiene, which shortened their lives and increased their physical suffering. When simple things like washing hands and other physical hygiene practices were finally introduced, it doubled humans' life expectancy. But just as our physical bodies require hygiene, our emotional bodies do as well. Yet today we still pay limited attention to our emotional care, which undoubtably prolongs our emotional suffering. Guy Winch, an author and psychologist who received his PhD in clinical psychology at NYU, argues that by ignoring emotional hygiene, we often make our situation worse rather than better. Winch illustrates this dynamic with the example of a woman who, after twenty years of marriage and a messy divorce, finally gets up the courage to go on a first date. Ten minutes after meeting her date at an upscale bar, he stands up and announces, "I'm not interested." Devastated, the woman calls a friend, who says, "Well, what do you expect? You have big hips, you have nothing interesting to say. Why would a handsome, successful man like that ever go out with a loser like you?" Shocked? Of course, no friend would say such a thing. Winch reveals, "It's what the woman said to herself."[3]

It doesn't make sense to hurt ourselves emotionally, but that is precisely what most of us do in the face of emotional wounds. As Winch points out, "You wouldn't get a cut on your arm and decide, 'Oh! I know—I'm going to take a knife and see how much deeper I can make it.'" When it comes to dealing with uncertainty, though, we critique our lack of courage, criticize mistakes, and feel shame for taking a risk that doesn't work out. Winch says this kind of thinking can be debilitating. "If your mind tries to convince you you're incapable of something, and you believe it, then . . . you'll begin to feel helpless and you'll stop trying too soon, or you won't even try at all. . . . You see, that's why so many people function below their actual potential. Because somewhere along the way, sometimes a single failure convinced them that they couldn't succeed, and they believed it."[4]

We are not psychologists, and we wholeheartedly encourage seeking help from a professional when emotional wounds warrant expertise. But we have observed how robust emotional hygiene enables creatives, entrepreneurs, and pathbreakers to sustain their uncertainty journeys. To help you remember this urgent task of emotional hygiene, we suggest you become your own *uncertainty doula*. Doulas are nonmedical individuals who provide physical, emotional, and informational support during a significant experience, most often childbirth. Doulas come from an ancient tradition—stone carvings from prehistoric times depict them at work—but modern research underscores their effectiveness in childbirth, demonstrating they can help reduce anxiety, labor time, and additional medical interventions while improving mother-baby bonding.[5] Even though they are not licensed medical professionals, they are so effective that the World Health Organization has recommended that every birth mother have one. Doulas advocate for and remind their patients of their most important hopes and fears, guiding them toward their best outcomes when things get stressful or change unexpectedly.

Sadly, we weren't familiar with doulas when Susannah gave birth to our four kids. We were commiserating about how we wish there were doulas for uncertainty, for bringing possibility to life, when we wondered: What if there were individuals who were willing to give continual support for transilience, for transforming uncertainty into possibility? Then we thought: Why couldn't you be your own doula, providing yourself the support, confidence, warnings, and wisdom to bring your possibilities to life?

When we went back to the interviews we had done, we realized this is something that many innovators have learned to do for themselves. For example, despite David Heinemeier Hansson's extensive experience creating new businesses, he admits that he still feels stress and anxiety when doing something new. Rather than attacking himself, he has become practiced at acknowledging these emotions, recognizing they are human and normal, and using certain techniques to lessen their negative effects.[6] Meanwhile, others we interviewed invited people into their lives to act as doulas. Mentors, life coaches, therapists, partners, and friends can all act as these special assistants, helping guide you to your best outcome.

Imagine having someone there to sustain you, remind you what's most important, and guide you to your best outcomes during a period of pain. Someone who would help you bring your life . . . to life! They would talk you through the most vulnerable moments, when you might hurt yourself more, and help you see the other side of the stories you tell yourself and pick the one that empowers you rather than disables you. It's a powerful idea, and one that can be implemented immediately. Without a doula (an emotional, physical, informational advocate) your unaddressed emotional obstacles make transilience harder. Whether you manage to act as your own uncertainty doula or invite others to fill that role, the point is to bring about the calmer and happier "births" of your pursuits and dreams.

Riding the Waves

Part of what makes childbirth doulas so effective is their prior experience with the stages of labor. They understand the natural cycles of anxiety, frustration, pain, and exhaustion that accompany the anticipation, joy, and awe of that momentous event. The emotions that accompany uncertainty also follow cyclical patterns, with both highs and lows that occur repeatedly. Entrepreneurs almost universally describe their experience as being like riding a roller coaster, with incredible highs and incredible lows, sometimes in the same day. An uncertainty doula would remind you that the waves of emotion are a normal part of the journey, give permission to feel the accompanying emotions, and suggest how to sustain yourself through the journey.

Recognizing this cycle helped Luca Belpietro recover from the unexpected loss of his lifelong dream mere months after he finally reached it. From his earliest memories, Luca dreamed of living in Africa. At the age of four he camped alone in his family's vineyard in Italy, snuggled up next to the dogs, trying to prove he was ready to go on safari. After high school he lived with farmers on Lake Naivasha in Kenya, and in university he wrote his thesis on the idea of sustainable ecotourism, "seeding the concept for a new model for conservation" based on a symbiosis of tourism, wildlife support, and community-driven decision-making.

To fund this dream, he cofounded a financial services firm, where he worked for ten years until 1995, when he and his now-wife, Antonella, moved to Kenya's Chyulu Hills. Rising over the plain beneath Mount Kilimanjaro and providing water to over seven million people, this green and vibrant landscape is the majestic setting that inspired Ernest Hemingway's *Green Hills of Africa*. But when the Belpietros arrived, "there was no infrastructure, no buildings, no communications, no water, not even a road, absolutely nothing." They lived in a tent for two years, building a lodge alongside the Maasai tribespeople. It took years of hard work, setbacks, and immense courage to build Campi ya Kanzi and to earn the trust of the local tribe. But slowly they succeeded in creating a sustainable ecotourism lodge to support the local community.[7]

Then one night, faulty wiring sparked a fire that burned the entire camp to the ground. Looking out over the smoking ruins of decades of work "was absolutely heartbreaking," Luca remembers. "There was nothing left, we lost literally everything." The grief and discouragement defied words. Antonella was back in Italy with their small children and asked him to consider moving back. They had given Campi ya Kanzi everything they had. Couldn't it be time to switch gears and throw their effort and attention to the family vineyard?

For Luca the decision rested on recognizing that he was in the lowest low of an emotional wave. Whereas in university his dream had only been an ambition, now he *knew* it was possible. Realizing this helped him find the courage to restart. When he let the Maasai know of his intention to rebuild, they admitted they had been watching to see how he would respond. Recognizing his courage, they offered the land rent-free and worked with him without wages until they had rebuilt. Likewise, seeing the strength of his commitment inspired a friend to donate $100,000. Slowly, Luca rebuilt what is now one of the leading examples of long-term, sustainable, community-based ecotourism. Looking back on that day, he points to his framed quote by General Douglas MacArthur: "Youth is not a period of time. It is a state of mind, a result of the will, a quality of the imagination, a victory of courage over timidity, and the taste for adventure over the love of comfort."[8]

In addition to acknowledging that highs and lows are a normal part of the journey, being your own uncertainty doula includes foreseeing trouble spots, gearing up for the hard "contractions" where you might lose your sense of purpose, and applying the right care for the moment. Research has identified emotional roller coasters in almost every change journey. There is the emotional expat experience of honeymoon, followed by disillusionment, followed by adaptation, for example. We experienced this personally after we arrived in France and baguettes, castles, chocolates, and food markets turned into school bullies, impatient bakers, gloomy winters, and confusing systems (pick something out, pay at the cashier, then go back to pick up what you bought). Organization change experts talk about the emotional cycle of transformation: an initial high, followed by a period of disillusionment that requires encouraging activities, then proof points of success, and finally communication until the organization transitions to a new normal. Creatives, artists, and designers talk about the thrill of starting a new project, followed by a dark forest with cycles of inspiration and doubt, of grueling work and flow, until they emerge victorious near the completion of the project. Recognizing that these cycles of joy and pain are normal and universal can help, but they need to be met with appropriate emotional hygiene, which helps transform our pain and distress into manageable obstacles we can overcome on our way to possibility.

Even the Covid-19 pandemic created an emotional cycle, which many psychologists compared to the Kübler-Ross stages of grief because of the multifaceted loss it created. As defined by psychologist Elisabeth Kübler-Ross, the stages are denial, anger, bargaining, depression, and acceptance.[9] Because any emotional wave can be navigated more smoothly with appropriate emotional hygiene, sociologist and therapist

Martha Beck came up with specific ideas to counteract the ill effects of each grief stage: denial needs accurate information and communication with others, anger and depression need emotional support, and bargaining and acceptance need access to creativity about what is possible. Beck promises that with "each round of turbulence [you] will find yourself higher and higher. A mind that's been blown open can do anything. A closed mind can't progress."[10]

Know that the emotional lows are the hardest part, and it is these times when we most need to care for ourselves. A low can feel like being lost in a hopeless murk. When Nathan was thinking about a career change, he wrote,

> I keep trying to clear out my head. I go through waves of feeling like, 'Hey, it will all be OK. If you want to switch careers, you could have a great opportunity to do that soon, just keep plugging' and then swinging to the franticness of uncertainty [of,] 'How could this not be what I want to do? . . . How could I have not seen this more clearly earlier, what should I do NOW, how do I salvage the situation?' It is suffocating. So what is the truth? Am I on some great path that is going to open up some great opportunities, or am I walking down the wrong road?

Finally, doulas remind clients of their nonnegotiables in tense moments. You can do the same thing by going back to your story, your values, or the adjacent possible you are working toward. Some cycles are so significant that they are transformational, changing who we are. Beck compares these to a caterpillar that literally becomes a "soup of cells" before transforming into winged creatures that fly. She reminds us that "any transition serious enough to alter your definition of self will require not just small adjustments in your way of living and thinking but a full-on metamorphosis."[11]

Reflection and Practice

As serial innovator Kate O'Keeffe observes about being at a low point, "Sometimes you just have to wait, you just have to lower your expectations and make it through. Surviving is good enough."[12] Part of surviving involves being kind to yourself when you need it, as well as using your support networks, drawing on all your uncertainty balancers, and practicing other Emotional Hygiene tools while you wait for your next moment of clarity or elation. Here are some ways to do that.

1. If you're feeling like you might be at a low point, take a moment and ask yourself, "Am I possibly in an emotional wave?" If the answer is yes, ask yourself, "Have I felt this emotion cycle before, or perhaps witnessed it in someone else?" If so, how did it play out? What worked and where did you or they get stuck?

2. Consider the stages and time frame of the current wave: How did you feel last week? Last month? Where might this current wave be heading in the future? Remember, doulas help you foresee trouble spots, gear up for the hard "contractions" where you might lose your sense of purpose, and apply the right care for the moment. Think about how you might do that for yourself now.

3. Given where you are in the emotional wave, what would be the right tactic to apply? For example, in the trough of emotional waves, it is critical to remember your story—your reason for making a change—and to encourage yourself. When we hit an emotional low in the winter after moving to France, we had to remind ourselves every day of the reasons we moved and that one day things would get better. In the meantime, we had a lot of pastries for breakfast, hot chocolate at night, and small fun activities to buoy our spirits.

4. During any change process, it might be worth reading a brief article about some of the more influential change models, such as Kurt Lewin's Unfreeze-Change-Refreeze model (which we mentioned in chapter 5), or becoming more familiar with Kübler-Ross' Change Curve, based on her model of the five stages of grief, to better understand the natural behaviors that you or others may exhibit. Explore the recommendations for the right emotional hygiene steps at each point in the journey.

Hope Is Active

Sometimes uncertainty introduces problems and pain that seem to have no purpose. In these circumstances we can get stuck in rumination or grief—but finding a tiny thread of possibility beyond the sadness can provide the spark that leads to transilience. Hope is a good thread to look for as it can be a sort of bridge to possibility. Journalist and thought leader Krista Tippett explains, "Hope for me is distinct from idealism or optimism. It has nothing to do with wishful thinking. It is a muscle, a practice, a choice: to live open-eyed and wholehearted in the world as it is and not as we wish it to be."[13] In other words, it's not about hoping to avoid loss, but about persistence, growth, and kindness in the face of loss.

When Jos Skeates met Alison, he was a "poor art student with a bad haircut" and she was dating "an African prince who drove a Porsche around London." Today Jos laughs: "I wrote her letters every day. He didn't have a chance."[14] Jos and Alison dated for a few years while he, already a master goldsmith belonging to London's Goldsmiths' Company, which has a royal charter, finished his training at art school Central Saint Martins and Alison worked as a rising executive at Compaq. But after they married and started a family, they decided to take the leap into entrepreneurship, joining forces to launch their own boutique in London's cool Clerkenwell neighborhood. They dreamed of showcasing new jewelers alongside Jos's exquisite designs. Their talent quickly attracted clients from all over the world, and they began to envision a new kind of luxury group, democratizing access for the most creative emerging artists. Together they took on investment and started opening stores, first in Notting Hill and then Chiswick.

Then a series of disasters struck. First, a yearlong construction project killed the crucial foot traffic for their Notting Hill boutique as workmen pushed wheelbarrows full of mud across their front doorstep. Next came the 2008 financial crisis, which emptied their customers' budgets for jewelry. "For a six-month period, we were running out of road," Jos recounts. "I remember waking up one New Year's Day . . . [and] we owed a third of a million, had no money in the bank, and the money was due."

Meanwhile, Alison had been sick frequently, but they just chalked it up to stress. When a friend visited, though, she took one look at Alison and announced, "Get in the car, I'm taking you in." She sat Alison down in front of the family physician and said, "I think she has leukemia." The doctor agreed that something was very wrong, and Alison was rushed straight to the accident and emergency department. The friend called Jos, busy with the pre-Christmas rush and desperately trying to keep the business afloat, and said, "You need to come right away." Not understanding, Jos replied, "Let me finish these earrings." But the friend insisted, "No, put down the earrings. Come right now." Tests confirmed the grim diagnosis. Jos remembers taking to the London streets to run numbly through the dark, his mind gnawing at his troubles.

Yet there was a point of clarity amid the uncertainty. Sometimes when cancer strikes, partners split, realizing they would rather spend their remaining time with someone else. But Jos recalls that conversation with Alison, as she lay in her hospital bed, and the realization they both shared, looking into each other's eyes: "You are the one."

What then? Amid this immense uncertainty and tragedy, Alison told Jos, "We have to be hopeful because there are no guarantees." When they talked to their daughters, they told them, "Hopeful is our word." But hope, as Alison said, "is not a passive thing, where you just wait and see. Hope is active. It is participatory—we will take this view on life." She admits that it took all her energy and required that she remind herself over and over, "I have everything to live for."

As part of maintaining hope, they purposefully adopted a light-hearted tone. When Jos walked their two young girls to the hospital, he tried to make it more fun by pretending they had to dodge sharks hidden en route. Just before they arrived at Alison's room, Jos would text her so she could take off the oxygen mask and receive them with a warm smile. They even embraced a bit of gallows humor to ease the tension—one of the techniques we described in chapter 12—with Jos joking to the whole family, "Don't worry, if mom dies, I'm going to marry Taylor Swift." (Swift was the girls' idol at the time.) They would all laugh together at the absurdity of their situation.

Fortunately, after months of struggle, Alison recovered. But the business failed. They knew that Alison's recovery was the most important thing and are glad for the way they prioritized her recovery. Still, the failure of their business remains a bitter memory. Even though Jos managed to repay all their suppliers and they were voted London's best jeweler of the year, he laments: "I still feel shame for putting the company down."

Not surprisingly, their resolve to embody active hope helped them reenvision their business together. Jos and Alison still had all the talent they needed to recreate the luxury group, but maybe, they realized, scaling up wasn't the impact they wanted to have. The jewelry industry has a good deal of waste and high risks of unethical sourcing from locations where people are exploited. Together, Jos and Alison decided they wanted to lead the way in creating a sustainable artisanship, forming

London's first B Corp in the jewelry sector and becoming spokespersons for sustainable business. At their store, EC One, Jos trains cohorts of new jewelers, teaching them how to engage in and spread sustainable practices throughout the industry.

But their greatest contribution might simply be their example, their warm laughter together, and the lesson they have to teach all who endure uncertainty—that being hopeful is a deliberate and sustaining choice. Although not easy to do, it is a muscle we can build and develop. And it can help us face the emotions that come with the unknown.

Reflection and Practice

1. Consider an experience that caused you suffering in the past. How did you make it through that experience? Did hope as described above factor into your resilience? How could you use what you learned the next time you face an obstacle?

2. Hope can be an agreement with yourself, or others, like it was between Jos and Alison Skeates. Consider making an agreement about what hope means for you and how you plan to practice it.

3. Consider signing up for the twenty-session Hope Is a Muscle course hosted on the On Being Wisdom app, with teachings and reflections from Krista Tippett, to find—in her words—"a home and community of accompaniment for becoming more fluent in our humanity—a place to progressively deepen our presence to ourselves and each other and the world, from the inside out and back again."[15]

Connection and Community

We have all experienced the thrill and relief of finding a like-minded community for our ideas and projects. It can be a sort of homecoming to team up with others after you have been carrying a torch for something by yourself. Often, we forget that part of building robust hope is honoring and holding space for its opposite—the fears and doubts we have about our abilities, the validity of our ideas, or the way we are pursuing them. This is made easier when we can count on the emotional hygiene that's strengthened by talking with "our people." Although it sounds obvious, when threatened or anxious, most people tend to turn inward, afraid that how they feel reveals a flaw in their ability or character. It doesn't—you are just human. Part of being your own doula, then, is not only coaching yourself to find and share with a community that sustains you but talking to yourself with awareness and kindness.

Sustaining yourself by talking with others happens when you share with the right people. By "right people," we acknowledge that as the leader of an organization or as a parent, you may have one kind of conversation with those you lead and another with the people who care for you, personally or professionally, or who share your situation. Talking with others in the same community or situation helps normalize both the uncertainty you are feeling and the frustrations and doubts you have as part of the journey to possibility.

Recall that actors may win one out of 100 parts they audition for, and photographers publish perhaps one out of 10,000 shots. "It's a bit like walking into a casino with a bucket of quarters, and you have to lose 100 times before you get one win," jokes actor Dallas Roberts.[16] When he taught us this lesson, he emphasized the stabilizing influence of his community of fellow actors, which we mentioned in chapter 12. "Seventy percent of my email comes from a group of seventeen other actors, and we just all help each other."

Community helps us sustain ourselves and learn from the uncertainty, not just resist it. At the unconventional business school Kaospilot, first-term students are put in charge of marketing and producing Denmark's largest cultural festival. Suddenly, they are tasked with a host of complex action items: design cinematography, build toilets, rescue a failed catering order, optimize ticket sales. One moment they may be using a hammer to pitch in on the bleachers, which were delivered late, and the next negotiating with one of the artists on a contract. "We tell students that we cannot guarantee that they will learn everything in the curriculum. In fact, we will only deliver 80 percent of objectives. But we can guarantee that you will learn 110 percent. It's very confusing for them at first," head of school Christer Windeløv-Lidzélius explains. "It all comes down to dialogue, it all comes down to talking. Talking about it is what helps you learn."[17]

For situations when we can't talk to others, there are ways of talking to ourselves that can help. Mindfulness coach Daron Larson helps leaders at companies, hospitals, and even prisons navigate personal and professional challenges. He warns that when we step into the unknown, "it's easy to view unwanted emotions as additional opponents. We instinctively attempt to defend ourselves against frustration, fear, and vulnerability. But when we feed them with our resistance, they get stronger." Instead of trying to sweep our emotions under the rug, he advises, we can talk to ourselves, saying, "This is what it feels like to feel X—scared, annoyed, bored, angry." For example, "when you notice that you're feeling nervous in anticipation of a pitch meeting, you might say to yourself, 'This is how it feels to be nervous about pitching an idea I care about,'" Larson explains. Or "when you find yourself bogged down by a lack of clarity, try to ease up on finding a solution. . . . Say to yourself, 'This is how it feels to not have an answer right now.'" Larson says that talking to yourself this way helps you simply notice the emotions rather than fighting them, which creates a more empathetic response and ultimately weakens their debilitating effects.

Reflection and Practice

Too often we let circumstance create our community, making friends with whoever crosses our path. Instead, consciously create your community: invite people whose values you admire or with similar experiences to dinner or coffee.

1. *Create a community around a value.* Finding a supportive community in France has proved challenging for us. We do embrace the expat and school community, but we also launched an exploratory odyssey called the Earnest Project to find people doing beautiful work for the joy of it. We interviewed artists, makers, entrepreneurs, and others. Many of those people, and friends we've brought along for the ride, have become part of a growing global community.

2. *Create a community around similar experiences.* Often the best people to talk to and process with are people going through

the same things you are. Writers join a writing group as much to share their feelings as to share their work. Could you find a group aligned around your uncertainty? Or create one? You could even host a conversation about *The Upside of Uncertainty* with friends. There are discussion materials and videos available at www.theupsideofuncertainty.com.

3. *Create a community within your team or organization.* If you are a leader of a team or organization, consider how acknowledging emotional hygiene could strengthen your organization, both by making them aware of the need for emotional hygiene and being a support. Constantijn van Oranje, crown prince of the Netherlands, regularly works with other leaders in his role of encouraging innovation. He observes that often "CEOs are themselves not used to uncertainty, so they try to hide from it instead of embracing it, and making it their strength."[18] He flips the fear of uncertainty, arguing that it can become a strength. "If you enter uncertainty, there is a pride that you're doing new stuff." As van Oranje argues, "even when you feel confident, you have to be empathetic towards the anxiety of others, and then you have to show there is a way out."

Comforts

Being your own doula also means having comforts on hand that sustain you. Similar to uncertainty balancers, which are meant to be ongoing practices that offer continual sustenance, comforts are like a secret arsenal we can use at a moment's notice as an extra dose to sustain our floundering boat. There are many sources of comfort when it is needed. One of the most important is a place, particularly a home, where we can seek comfort and reassurance. In *The Poetics of Space*, philosopher Gaston Bachelard says that home is like a forge where creativity and dreams are created. "The house protects the dreamer. The houses that are important to us are the ones that allow us to dream in peace," he wrote.

But before you start scheming that you can't be comforted or creative without the ideal space, challenge what you really need to create that space. For the Travellers, an ancient culture of Irish nomads, home could be an old lay-by or an empty field filled with memory and pride.[19] Nick Ashley, son and business partner of designer Laura Ashley, whose company once had five hundred shops worldwide, remembers their home being redone every year as an example for stylists. When his mother died, the company lost its heart and soul. Nick realized that although he lost the curated home, he actually wanted something different. "My idea of heaven is to pick my own food, cook it, eat it, sit by the fire, and then go to bed on a wonderful mattress. I mean, come on, you can't argue with that."[20] Even famed designer Kenzō Takada, whose house had a swimming pool in the living room, argued that atmosphere was all that really mattered. "When I go into other people's homes, the first thing I look at is the atmosphere."[21] We can create that atmosphere anywhere, even in a tiny apartment, with care and thought.

In addition, a good doula reminds you to think about what, how, and where you eat. The myriad ways we experience food—its aromas, flavors, textures, and memories—can too easily be taken for granted. Mary Frances Kennedy Fisher was a brilliant food writer who described eating well as one of the "arts of life." Her essays weave together gorgeous descriptions of memorable meals and the stories surrounding them with an underlying claim about how food sustains us on a deeper level. In *The Gastronomical Me* she endearingly writes,

> People ask me: Why do you write about food, and eating and drinking? Why don't you write about the struggle for power and security, about love, the way others do? . . . The easiest answer is to say that, like most other humans, I am hungry. But there is more than that. It seems to me that our three basic needs for food, security, and love are so mixed and mingled and entwined that we cannot straightly think of one without the others. So it happens that when I write of hunger, I am really writing about love and the hunger for it.[22]

Sensory comforts are sustaining and are meant to be—our senses have evolved to steer us toward safety, nourishment, and pleasure or to warn us from their opposites. Take note of the comforts that sustain you. These comforts can become sources of healing in our daily lives, refueling us for the journey through uncertainty.

Reflection and Practice

When we tell ourselves we can't dream or envision our dreams until we have, own, or live in _____ (fill in the blank), we forgo the peace and imagination that are available to us in the places we already are. Taking a cue from Takada, how could you focus on the atmosphere of your home (defined as the mood or tone) to foster more well-being? We can take simple steps toward more sustaining atmospheres by keeping our spaces clean and tidy (at least make your bed!), hanging pictures or artwork that makes us happy (or even pages torn from magazines or inexpensive prints), and lighting candles or using incense to create pleasant environments. The *hygge* craze (Danish for cozy comfort) proved that sustaining comforts don't need to be elaborate or expensive to bring contentment. We can and should introduce them so that we have a routine of comforts available to us when things are hard.

1. What is your idea of heaven? Seriously consider it. We spend so much time being sold images of what will make us happy that we can overlook what really gives us comfort. Nathan often falls into the trap of thinking that a spot on the French Riviera would make him happy. But when he asked himself what really gives him comfort, it turns out lying on the couch to read might be his heaven as much as, or more than, the crowded, expensive Côte d'Azur.

2. Make a list of favorite things for times when you lose clarity and need a quick go-to reminder of what you love. You can also create a spot (maybe a drawer or an envelope) with meaningful reminders that *you* are loved. Nathan keeps a container topped by a ceramic owl near his computer monitor. Inside he has placed a fragment of a mosaic tile found in Rome and a love note from Susannah. Seeing that wise owl, and recalling the tokens tucked inside, brings perspective when he struggles.

3. Christine Runyan is a clinical psychologist and professor at the University of Massachusetts Medical School. Her empirical work validates that uncertainty causes us stress. Runyan advocates mindful awareness as an antidote to stressful situations and recommends sensory experiences as one of the best ways to bypass

the thinking brain and calm the nervous system, bringing "safety and pleasantness."[23]

Runyan highlights how *savoring* even regular sensory experiences allows us to go deeper into their healing properties; finding the "wonderment" in ordinary things increases the pleasantness of even neutral things. She describes how this can work using two very simple exercises: (1) grounding postures: sitting in a chair with your feet flat on the floor, your heels pressing slightly down beneath you, can bring you back to your present moment, and (2) imaged sensory experiences: close your eyes and imagine the steps of cutting a slice of lemon, holding it up to your nose, and then placing it on your tongue. What happened when you read that? The imaginative act is so powerful that our brain responds by causing us to salivate. We can calm our panicked and stressed brains by savoring powerful sensory responses, even imagined ones, at every moment.

We asked a licensed therapist to share some of the sustaining guidance he gives clients facing uncertainty (see the sidebar "Returning to Center: A Therapist's View on Navigating Uncertainty") to anchor the tools we have observed. Emotional hygiene takes courageous effort but is a critical first step in the Sustain phase of uncertainty possibility. Like Paris's symbolic boat being tossed on the waves but not sinking, emotional hygiene calms the rough waters of the unknown.

Returning to Center

A Therapist's View on Navigating Uncertainty

BY JORDAN K. HARMON, LCSW

As a therapist specializing in personality disorders and addiction, I often have clients who have been given over five diagnoses and have experienced multiple traumas and consecutive "treatment failures." Intense shame, fear of rejection, and chronic suicidal thoughts are their baseline experience. For them, the storm-tossed waves of uncertainty are not just temporary experiences but tend to make up the internal and external ground of their daily lives. The evidence-based approaches I use for my clients draw heavily from Buddhist mindfulness practices that teach us that suffering is inextricably tied to human existence. Often, our attempts to avoid or escape pain and suffering only compound it. Whether you experience chronic mental health struggles like my clients or not, the inevitability of suffering will rock your boat and threaten to capsize you. Mindfulness practices and acceptance strategies can help you to center and connect with yourself, others, and life itself in the midst of any uncertainty you are facing. For definitions of terms, see table 26-1.

Mindfulness and Emotion Regulation

Mindfulness is often defined as paying attention in the present moment in a nonjudgmental way. It is less about directly reducing pain in our lives and more about changing our relationship to that pain. We can attend to our pains in a different way—being compassionate and curious rather than clinging, avoiding, or escaping in maladaptive ways. Cultivating this kind of nonjudgmental awareness can help us to both prevent difficult experiences and sustain through them.

Imagine an individual, Mia, who struggles with severe emotional dysregulation. She swings from intense emotions to a complete shutdown of feeling, leading to dysfunction and misery. When in her *emotional mind*, she is controlled by her emotions and does whatever they urge her to do. When in her *logical mind*, she is numb to feelings (pleasant or painful) and operates from

(continued)

task to task, losing sense of a bigger purpose. Swinging from one extreme to the other leads to more misery and coping through increasingly harmful ways.

Mia begins to practice mindfulness, and it's uncomfortable. Noticing difficult emotions and thoughts without acting on them feels new. As she practices, she starts to experience the growth of a kind of psycho-spiritual muscle. She learns to access the positives of both emotional mind and logical mind. In dialectical behavior therapy, we call this balanced state of being *wise mind*. When Mia swings back into emotional mind, rather than reacting to urges to lash out at loved ones, she is able to invite in logic—causes and consequences. When Mia swings back into logical mind, she is able to invite her emotions to the surface rather than staying disconnected from her humanity. Mindfulness helps her notice her experience nonjudgmentally and with curiosity. In her wise mind, Mia sits in the calm at the center of the storm.

Mindfulness Leads to the Middle Path

The example above demonstrates how mindfulness skills and ways of being can help people with severe emotional dysregulation. Even when our struggles are not as severe, the stress we face can push us to extreme responses (emotional or logical) and away from a more effective middle path. We all tend to default to one pole or the other and cope accordingly.

Consider the following dialectical poles and ask yourself these questions: "When experiencing the distress of uncertainty and psychological pains, where do I default to? What small adjustment can I make to move toward the middle of these apparent opposites?"

None of us will be perfectly balanced while attempting to walk a middle path between apparent opposites. Small adjustments in ways of thinking and acting are easier when we open up to our experience in the present with curiosity and compassion.

Reality Acceptance

Along with balancing opposites, another important aspect of mindfulness is reality acceptance. There may be times in our lives when extreme distress calls for distraction and avoidance so that we can stay above water. However, if our main coping mechanism is avoidance, we will continue a cycle of

TABLE 26-1

Quality	Description
Acceptance	Believing things are what they are and there's nothing you can do about it
Being	Feeling completely relaxed and living only for the present
Change	Believing things are not what they should be and they must change to be what you want
Dependence	Acting helpless when you are not
Doing	Being completely active and busy at all times
Emotion	Running hot, urging toward action, not being in control, not necessarily matching feelings to the facts of the situation
Independence	Not expecting or accepting help from another person
Logic	Running cool, focusing on facts/tasks/rules, being unaware of emotions and values of yourself and others, being computer-like
Overindulgence	Giving yourself whatever you want—even if it causes you more stress later
Self-denial	Not allowing yourself any pleasure, treat, or break

rejecting reality and compounding suffering. Most of the time, our reality is best coped with through centering in acceptance first.

Acceptance of reality does not mean approving of reality or resigning oneself to it. It means opening one's whole self (mind, body, spirit) to life as it is in the moment. There are many ways we reject reality, and one key word that can alert us to when we are doing this is *should*: "I should exercise more." "I should spend more time with my family." "I should not lose my temper." "My partner should eat better." "My coworkers shouldn't send me so many unnecessary emails."

We often use "should" when we relate to the world we want to inhabit. The problem with a should orientation is that it centers our change strategies in shame, fear, and unhelpful judgment. But we can't just get rid of should altogether—that would be rejecting reality as well! We can accept the fact that we naturally have should thoughts and mindfully notice them as part of our reality. When we look deeper at our shoulds, they can alert us to our values, and a space opens up for "could" or possibility. Valued and effective change naturally grows out of our finding a deep connection with reality.

(continued)

Here's an example. "I should spend more time with friends or family" becomes "I have a lot of work that is important to me *and* I notice some guilt about not spending more time with loved ones. Could I find a way to be present with my loved ones and honor the importance and reality of my work commitments?"

Mindfulness and Acceptance as Compassion

At the end of the day, love, or compassion, is the ultimate answer to how we can sustain ourselves through the emotional difficulty caused by uncertainty. Broken into its Latin roots, compassion means *suffering with* or *feeling with*. I consider nonjudgmental attention to be a synonym for compassion. When we give our compassionate and curious attention to something, we are attending to it with openness—we are suffering with (and allowing) whatever is present, right here, right now.

Opening up to the experience of our reality in the moment and truly being with it can often be painful. Our natural tendency to avoid pain also leads us to avoid life and is called *experiential avoidance*. Experiential avoidance may feel like helpful coping in the short term, but it typically leaves us more vulnerable to the waves of pain and uncertainty the next time around. Mindfulness and acceptance strategies aren't just helpful ways to cope with difficulties. They are portals to waking up to and centering in our fundamental reality in the moment. And this reality is always changing under our feet. Heraclitis was spot-on—the only constant in life is change.

Chapter 27

Reality Check

Awareness and care of our emotional state is more sustaining when paired with a balanced look at what's really going on. Reality check is about using your reasoning mind to cut through the gloom of negative or naive stories to enable change and growth toward your values. Jordan K. Harmon's discussion in chapter 26 of reality acceptance—not approval or resignation—as it is in this moment highlights how important these tools are. While Harmon's reality acceptance comes from a mindfulness lens, the Sustain Reality Check tools are an actionable set of ways to find the reality that is hopeful, helpful, and motivating.

In her book *The Future of Happiness*, Amy Blankson writes that "the human brain receives eleven million bits of information every single second but can only process fifty bits at any given time. Allowing our brains to perseverate on the stresses, hassles, and complaints in our environment decreases the capacity for our brains to seek out other salient, equally true, and potentially more useful information."[1] If, by contrast, we can simply "see and lean into the positive information in our environment," then as research suggests, the results are "three times the levels of creativity, 31% more productivity, and 23% less stress."[2] Reality Check tools aid us in shoveling away the obfuscating snow of uncertainty that has fallen on our clarity and courage.

Just like we encourage practicing emotional hygiene from the lens of an empathic and skillful doula, we suggest inhabiting the role of a *wise counselor* to help you dispute pessimistic beliefs and see the facts with clear eyes. Nathan remembers an eye-opening experience while finishing a master's degree in the liberal arts. Realizing he needed to change career paths, he went to see a university career counselor. Gray-haired and almost retired, the counselor leaned back in his chair, twirling a pen absentmindedly as Nathan poured his heart out: we had a baby on the way, he felt unprepared for a job, he felt old compared to the undergrads—how could he possibly change careers? As Nathan's anxiety reached a fever pitch, the counselor suddenly interrupted. In a kind but weary voice he said simply, "I don't want this to come off wrong, but I have socks in my drawer older than you."

Nathan froze, stunned. The counselor quickly clarified, "What I'm trying to tell you is that life is long, it's full of opportunities, and you are going to figure it out, even if you don't feel that way now. You have time." That last phrase struck a chord because the one thing Nathan did not believe he had was time. But somehow, the socks comment rang true. The counselor then leaned forward in his chair, put pen to paper, and started to talk through some of the many options Nathan could pursue. Nathan left seeing the world completely differently.

A wise counselor offers a broader vision by reminding you of all your options and warning you about common pitfalls or ineffective coping. Their neutral stance and willingness to walk you through challenges brings hope and calm that a solution will reveal itself. Their wisdom lies in their ability to help you uncover your authentic self. What if you could take cues from a wise counselor and incorporate some of their skills when facing uncertainty? You would be optimistic, rational, and calm as you challenge yourself to see things in new and different ways. At the very least, from that place of awareness you would take more time and attempt to decatastrophize the situation you are in.

Embrace Being Human

As a species, we are wired so that uncertainty creates anxiety. It's a fact confirmed by numerous neuroscientific studies.[3] Rather than trying to avoid or suppress that anxiety, just accept it as normal. The first step of a reality check is accepting that you are human, and uncertainty makes humans feel anxious, discouraged, and sad. If you feel this way, hooray! You are alive. As serial entrepreneur David Heinemeier Hansson said, "That is just a hardwired human thing. [The goal is] *not staying* in that anxious, paranoid, frightened moment for as long."[4] A helpful reality check normalizes these instinctual responses, even the ones we face repeatedly due to our careers or activities.

A reality check also provides steps for dealing with anxiety. The polyvagal theory, based on the dominant vagal nerve in our body, argues that we can adopt steps to overcome our natural fight-or-flight reaction. Anxiety is a signal to slow down, get curious, and ask questions. This gives us time to observe our hardwired biological reactions of fight or flight and make wiser choices. Another framework, described in terms of *avoidance* versus *active* coping, suggests that worry is a natural response to anxiety because it feels like we are doing something. However, worry only makes our anxiety worse, because we aren't really dealing with the stressor; a more productive response of active coping includes both reframing how you see the anxiety and making a plan to address it directly. For example, rather than worrying about if your presentation will be finished in time, visualize the nature of what needs to be done and how you can succeed, breaking it down into manageable steps you can take action on immediately.

In a recent dialogue with high school students, novelist Zadie Smith shared the anxiety inherent in the uncertainty of her work: "Most of the time while I'm writing, I have a very vague idea of why I'm doing what I'm doing. I have to give myself a kind of pep talk every day."[5] When our daughter, familiar with our project, asked Smith whether she has a practice for facing uncertainty, Smith replied,

> That's the key, I think, the question of being comfortable. The thing I don't do with the uncertainty is try and pin it down, or eradicate it, or run away from it. . . . I am always trying to retain something that I feel is genuine in the world: a sense of not knowing, of being extremely uncertain, of being very afraid. I think a lot of people are very afraid most of the time, trying to disguise it most of the time. . . . Even the simple things that your grandmother would have told you, the fact that adults continue to feel like children throughout their lives, [are things] they don't tell their children. But these things which I know . . . are existentially true and so it's worth somebody remembering that. And that is the tiny corner of writing that I think of myself as being concerned with.

Everyone, even the wise and talented, feels confused, lost, and uncertain. When we surrender to the experience of being human, we realize we are in great company with everyone else daring to do and create great things.

Reflection and Practice

1. *Anxiety triggers.* One step to facing anxiety is to recognize what triggers it and thus, by anticipating it or recognizing when it happens, lessen its sting. For example, Nathan is easily overwhelmed by having many tasks to do, while Susannah fears for the safety of those she loves. Having identified common triggers, we are better equipped to diminish the anxiety before it overwhelms us, normalizing it and leaning on past experiences of how things have worked out. Often when Nathan feels the anxiety of whether he can meet a deadline, he remembers, "This is what I do, remember?" and it can calm him down.

2. *Anxiety cycles.* When does anxiety tend to hit you? Night or morning? At certain points in the creative cycle? If you find anxiety occurring at regular points, like late at night, it might be more biological than real. During these times, you may just need to defer judgment. For example, Nathan has learned that before he publishes anything, he has a rush of anxiety that what he has written is terrible. Recognizing this, he always pushes through and submits to publication rather than holding back. Susannah has a different anxiety that surfaces whenever things are going really well or if there is an exciting change on the horizon—a sense of foreboding that something is going to fall apart. Brené Brown calls this experience "foreboding joy," explaining that joy is an emotion that requires vulnerability because, every moment is fleeting (which we will discuss in the Magic tool Memento Mori in chapter 28), there will be suffering, and we can't hold onto that joy forever. Her advice? Savor the joyful moment with gratitude, which allows you to fully enjoy it and not sabotage it with the fear of something that hasn't happened.

3. *Neutral confidence.* Sometimes we can make decisions based on emotional highs or depressing lows. But the decisions that endure are made neither from the high or the low, but from a sense of neutral confidence. Aim to tackle your big decisions from that state of mind.

Learned Optimism

We tend to think of ourselves as optimists or pessimists. But Martin Seligman, a leading researcher in psychology and a pioneer of positive psychology, argues that optimism and pessimism are actually learned explanatory styles that we develop over time, not inherent orientations that are a fixed part of our personality. Furthermore, over a battery of empirical studies, Seligman confirmed that people who developed a more optimistic, explanatory style resisted *learned helplessness*—that is, when we no longer try to change an adverse situation because we believe we are powerless—and found ways to change their situation for the better. For this reason, Seligman argues optimism can be learned and can help us face uncertainty.[6]

Seligman's insight arose from his early work exploring learned helplessness. For example, when dogs were given a shock in a closed room, and then later were given the chance to escape another shock by leaping over a small barrier, most did not try to.[7] In fact, experimenters had to carry the dogs over the barrier several times before they learned that they could help themselves.

When Seligman started to investigate learned helplessness in people, he found a similar pattern but with one curious exception: people with an optimistic orientation resisted learned helplessness and found a way to change their situation. Intrigued, Seligman decided to investigate further, and to the research team's surprise, they discovered that optimists hadn't necessarily been born that way, but instead had learned to view the world a way that helped them overcome challenges. Specifically, optimists tended to view problems as (1) temporary, (2) limited to specific situations, and (3) having several causes for what happened, so they could avoid blaming themselves alone. As a result, optimists were able to decatastrophize a situation, finding specific steps within their control as responses, and even experience "energization" to search for further change. By contrast, pessimists tended to view problems as permanent, impacting every aspect of their lives, so they blamed themselves exclusively for what went wrong. As a result, pessimists tend to sink into rumination and negative self-talk, which increases the feeling of dejection and passivity.[8] The good news is we can use the same techniques as optimists do to decatastrophize situations we encounter by reframing them as temporary, limited, and not entirely our fault.

While the Hope Is Active tool in chapter 26 is about emotion, practicing *learned optimism* is about cognition: the idea that you can analyze and challenge your thoughts, especially negative ones. We might have been born with an instinct tending toward one explanatory style, but Seligman's research has shown that just by becoming aware of our beliefs and learning to dispute them, we can develop a more optimistic approach. Studies of groups taught learned optimism showed a 50 percent decrease in anxiety among students, a 35 percent increase in salespeople's effectiveness, and increased function for children suffering brain injuries—not because the children had implemented learned optimism but because their caretakers had.[9]

According to Seligman, the key to developing learned optimism is to begin disputing the negative beliefs when something negative happens. Without interrogating them, we might misinterpret them as fact ("I am a bad mom" or "I will never be healthy" or "I am not a good student"). These debilitating thoughts sabotage our efforts to overcome the obstacles that are creating our belief in them. For example, if you speak up about an idea you have and no one responds, the voice inside a pessimist might say, "Oh, it was a dumb idea and I'm stupid." Instead, Seligman proposes, argue with the negative belief: "perhaps the context was wrong, perhaps it went over their heads, perhaps others were impressed but didn't know how to share it—or perhaps it was a dumb idea, but who cares! Great thinkers have many mediocre ideas mixed in with great ones. Seligman says that as we dispute beliefs, we increase the energy to make change.[10]

The key is to take any setback, disappointment, or anxiety and argue with it until your view shifts from the setback being permanent, pervasive, and unchangeable to being temporary, isolated, and changeable. Working with a trusted friend or adviser can be tremendously helpful in disputing beliefs, because it allows you to externalize the ones you are holding as facts and get another perspective. Sustaining ourselves through uncertainty requires challenging our beliefs and seeing the things that happen to us with learned optimism.

Reflection and Practice

1. What are your negative beliefs about a situation, or even yourself? Externalize them by writing them down or sharing them with a friend. Could you dispute these negative beliefs by asking whether they are simply untrue, partially true, contextual, or whether they might even point to one of your strengths?

2. If the negative belief feels true, reframe the situation from being permanent, pervasive, and unchangeable to being temporary, isolated, and changeable. For example, when Nathan experienced some setbacks with his dissertation, at first, he regarded himself as a failure (permanent, pervasive, and unchangeable). He learned to challenge that belief and see the context as temporary, isolated, and changeable. To do it, he started his teaching career while finishing the dissertation, took time to learn the craft of publishing, setting aside his dissertation, since it triggered an immense sense of failure. Ultimately he self-published a journal paper out of his dissertation and went on to win multiple "best dissertation" awards and publish many papers from what he once thought was a failure.

Frustration Management

Ben Feringa didn't mince words: "If you deal with uncertainty, you will fail."[11] But directly after saying this, he added—with a wry smile that revealed how many setbacks he'd faced en route to creating the molecular machines for which he won a Nobel Prize in 2016—that you have to "get resilient at handling the frustration that comes with uncertainty." His own formula for doing that, after letting himself feel the frustration for a couple days, is to ask, "What can I learn from it? What is the next step that I can be working on?"[12] Whether he realized it or not, focusing on what he learns, in spite of any "failure," is one of a group of *frustration management frames* that can be applied when things don't turn out as planned. Akin to the Reframe tools, these frames are lenses to help you gain a different perspective about the things that frustrate you and derive meaning even from failed attempts. Let's take a look at what each one can do.

- *Learning frame.* Like Feringa, ask "What can I learn?" This is one of the most common responses entrepreneurs give when asked about failures. There is *always* something to be learned, even if it is only what *not* to do in the future. Try to focus on the proactive lessons that help you take positive action on the next go-round (e.g., "I'm going to get better insurance coverage") and avoid negative, self-critical ones (e.g., "Only an idiot would not have taken out an insurance policy"). Improvement and innovation come about from trial *and* error. Error is not negotiable. What we learn in one round can set us up for success in the next. When Lew Cirne founded Wily Technology, he was a great technologist and early-stage company founder, but as the company grew, he struggled. Peter Fenton, his lead investor recounts, "I encouraged Lew to bring in an experienced CEO and to learn from them how to do it."[13] Cirne turned over the reins, and although Wily succeeded, he regretted giving up control. However, using what he learned from watching Wily scale, Cirne founded a second company, New Relic, leading it through the growth phase himself to twelve times the revenue of Wily.

- *Game frame.* Consider failure as just part of the game of life. Frustration and loss are a part of the game just as much as winning is, so don't take them personally. Sometimes things work out and sometimes they don't. Tesla CEO Elon Musk literally describes his startups as games: "It's like playing progressive poker games, where you start off at the small table and you get to the medium table, and over time you're able to get to the high-stakes table."[14] By the way, Musk combines the game frame with a learning frame, emphasizing what he learns from each business so that if one fails, he would still have an advantage in the other. Yes, losing hurts, but you can only win if you are willing to play.

- *Gratitude frame.* Focus on what you still have. When baseball legend Lou Gehrig was struck with amyotrophic lateral sclerosis at the height of his career, he gave an instructive farewell speech that illustrates this frame: "Fans, for the past two weeks you have been reading about the bad break I got. Yet today I consider myself the luckiest man on the face of this earth. . . . I might have been given a bad break, but I've got an awful lot to live for."[15] Gehrig's perspective helped himself and others focus on the marvelous gift of being alive. As it turns out, this was a perspective employed by the ancient Stoics as the recipe for happiness: all we have is on loan from fate—how lucky we are, then, to have what we have.

- *Values frame.* As discussed in chapter 19, when you work according to your values, you succeed no matter the outcome. When Apple threatened to squash his new software business Hey.com with exorbitant fees, Heinemeier Hansson was anxious. But because his team had set up the business to achieve values—building great software, treating people well, and introducing a more ethical business model—he remained calm. Even if Apple ruined the business and they lost millions of dollars of investment, Heinemeier Hansson would still feel satisfaction that he achieved his core values. Regarding being attacked by one of the world's most powerful companies, he said, "Those are the cards we were dealt, and if we lose, then we are fine."[16] But as it turned out, working by values "gave us freedom to go all in," and they set about posting widely about Apple's bullying antics. The unexpected media attention served as a rallying cry for the underdog, and turned Hey.com's harrowing situation into "the greatest launch campaign we could have imagined."[17]

- *Timing frame.* Embrace a more generous sense of timing. Often we get stuck thinking that because our project didn't succeed today, it never will. Timing is finicky and complex. Maybe we have underestimated how much time something will take, or maybe it's just not the right moment. After Susannah started her second business, Pronk, a clothing line inspired by her art history research, she eventually decided to put that pursuit on hold to focus on our four young children, and she doesn't regret it. Other times, you might be too far ahead of your audience or customers. Designer and artist Birgitta de Vos recalls that when she started promoting secondhand denim as a more sustainable option in the 1990s, people turned up their noses; today, of course, secondhand denim has long been championed.[18] Recall the wisdom shared by Håkan Nordkvist, head of sustainability innovation at IKEA, "It's hard because you put your soul into something. Sometimes you have to put it into a drawer and come back to it if it is the right thing. We do live in an external environment independent of your idea. If it doesn't happen today, it could always happen tomorrow."[19]

- *Evolution frame.* Consider the evolution of your project and suspend a final judgment. Sometimes a setback or a failure is simply part of the awkward "ugly" phase when moving from one state to another. Organizations often make the mistake of interpreting the decreased performance immediately after a transformation as a negative signal, when it is actually just part of readjusting to a new normal. The same is true for people. The parent raising a teenager must sustain their belief that one day this difficult adolescent will become an admirable adult. Likewise, when we start a new project, restart school, or change careers, it can be tempting to judge our early performance as subpar (often unfairly in comparison with those who have already evolved in that role), when really we are experiencing evolution to a better state. As the key phrase in a growth mindset—"not yet"—suggests, it isn't that we will never be able to do something, but simply that we are still working toward it.

- *Hero frame.* Heroes are made because they don't give up. Several years ago, while Australian filmmaker and paramedic Benjamin Gilmour was on a trip to the Khyber Pass, Pakistani authorities impounded his motorcycle. Despite the setback, Gilmour continued on foot. Along the way he met a Pashtun boy, the son in a long line of weapons manufacturers, who wanted to become a poet rather than make guns. Inspired by this story, Gilmour made a well-received film, *Son of a Lion,* which premiered at Cannes. When he returned to Pakistan years later to make another film, at the last moment the funding got pulled and most of the cast and crew left. With lead actor Sam Smith, the remaining team rewrote the script and shot the film *Jirga,* about an Australian soldier who goes back to Afghanistan to right a wrong. The film became Australia's submission to the 2019 Oscars. When we asked Gilmour what kept him going in the face of so many obstacles, he smiled warmly and replied: "Most people see obstacles and they interpret it as a sign to stop. I've learned to see obstacles as the sign I was heading in the right direction. . . . Every story we love, from Luke Skywalker to Harry Potter, is about the hero who goes through obstacles. Everyone loves the hero. But the obstacles are what makes the hero. . . . The only way to become the hero is to go through the obstacles!"[20]

In sum, as Feringa observed, it's normal to feel disappointment. Allowing yourself to feel the frustration is an important part of emotional hygiene, but if you can quickly move on to reframing the frustration with these optimistic frames, you will have more energy to dive back in. Even if you are suspicious of reframing, and feel inclined to cling to the harsher story, ask yourself, "Which view of the world will help me move forward?"

Reflection and Practice

1. Look back over the frustration management frames and notice ones that you intuitively use or want to try. Quickly jot down some takeaways that you can come back to when a frustration or sense of failure resurfaces. As the parents of teenagers and young adults, we use the evolution frame on a regular basis to remind ourselves that parenting kids into adulthood has awkward phases. It is unfair to expect a flawless transition! The evolution frame reminds us that, like any home remodel project, before you can get to that gorgeous kitchen with exposed beams and gleaming countertops, you have to knock down walls, expose leaky pipes, and build new structures. It is going to be raw and vulnerable, and you might doubt why you undertook the project when you are tired or overwhelmed. Evolution has strange and awkwardness built into it, but if you can sustain yourself through it, you will live to see the glorious transformation!

2. Please do take advantage of the gratitude frame. Gratitude is powerful for snuffing out despair if we earnestly seek to make a list of even the smallest things we enjoy. When we aren't seeing anything to be grateful for, that's when we need it most! Make a gratitude journal and you will see why Oprah claims hers is "the most important thing she's ever done."[21]

Sorting Knowns versus Unknowns

Another nasty quality of uncertainty is that, like an oil spill, it can easily spread and contaminate perfectly functioning aspects of our lives. We begin to see uncertainty everywhere and in everything, making it difficult to get a handle on what is really going on. One tactic to combat this tendency is to sit down and separate what you know from what you don't know. Unlike cognitive flexibility, which is about considering that you may not have the right answer, information, or method to tackle something, this is about taking comfort in the things you do know and then using analogies or experts to fill in the gaps. It also reminds us that sometimes there are unknowns that no one knows! Sorting obstacles into these three categories helps us recognize where we can do something and where we can't.

The ability to separate known from unknown is an important technique for entrepreneurs, and one that investors often look for. Venture capital investor David Hornik explicitly looks for this ability when deciding which entrepreneurs to fund: "I keep asking questions until they say 'I don't know,' because . . . I learn two things. One, that they can admit they don't know, and secondly, I learn how they respond to not knowing. . . . A great entrepreneur will say 'I don't know, but'—and there is always a 'but'—and then they will give you the information they do know and how it would translate into the situation that is unknowable." For example, an entrepreneur might respond to a question about a big incumbent threatening their business by talking about how Dropbox responded to the threat of Google Drive. As Hornik explains, "Entrepreneurs who can do that are problem solvers and they are people who can deal with uncertainty."[22]

Parsing out what you know from what you don't is harder in the face of anxiety. But simply sitting down and jotting down what you do know can work like an uncertainty balancer, giving you some comfort that not everything is up in the air. You know some things and can rely on them. And for the things you don't know, there are techniques you can use to get insight to reduce your anxiety. One such tool is a 2x2 matrix of known versus unknown, called the blind spot matrix in engineering and the Johari window in psychology (see figure 27-1). One axis maps out if something is known or unknown to you, and the other maps if it is known or unknown to others. For the variables unknown to you but

FIGURE 27-1

The blind spot matrix

	Known to others	Unknown to others
Unknown to me	**Unknown-knowns** • The knowledge is out there, but you don't have it or aren't aware of it. • Talk to as many people as possible, particularly experts.	**Unknown-unknowns** • Neither you nor others are aware of these variables. • Be aware that there are things you may not know. Experimentation can help you uncover the unknown-unknowns.
Known to me	**Known-knowns** • These are known risks with a reasonable probability distribution. • Take informed risks or set yourself up for multiple "rolls of the dice."	**Known-unknowns** • You understand the variables involved, but no one knows how they may turn out (unknown probability distribution). • A good analogy can help you make sense of it.

known to others (upper left quadrant), search out the experts who have the information. For the variables you are aware of but whose outcomes can't be known (lower right quadrant), a good analogy can help you make sense of the situation. Lastly, be aware that there may be things off everyone's radar (the upper right quadrant) that will only be discovered through experimentation.

For example, when the Covid-19 pandemic erased most of our income just after we finally took the leap to buy an apartment, Nathan started freaking out, his brain running away with imagined bankruptcy and failure. Susannah challenged him to apply the matrix to our future. (More accurately, she said, "If you can't apply these tools to help yourself, you don't get to write this book!") Since money was a major worry, he pulled out a spreadsheet and started calculating our runway under different scenarios. Just putting numbers on the page helped transform a mess of anxiety into something manageable. He also had to draw on analogies to make sense of the things he didn't know. Someone had compared the Covid-19 job losses to the Great Depression, which made Nathan feel frantic. But as he thought about it, he realized the faultiness of the analogy (e.g., underlying economic shock mismanaged by government versus health shock with stimulus) and found a better analogy (work stoppages during holidays) that helped him see alternative outcomes. Then he talked to experts about their view of how things might evolve. Taking the time to figure out what he did know significantly eased his anxiety about this massive, unplanned uncertainty. Nathan continues to use this tool whenever his anxiety rears its head about the ongoing financial and career uncertainty.

Reflection and Practice

For any uncertainty you are facing right now, try to find some solid ground in what you do know. If helpful, use the blind spot matrix to get more knowns you can lean on. Be specific: it will create a reality check of the situation by revealing the comforting certainty about how much you do know (known knowns), any areas where you can learn more (unknown knowns), and outcomes that you, and everyone else, have no way of knowing (unknown unknowns). Revisit the Prime section and your risk-o-meter to get a better handle on how these risks will affect you— whether they trigger zones of aversions or affinity. Let this good, hard look at things provide some relief. Take deep breaths. You've got this!

Alternatives and Probabilities

Sometimes when facing uncertainty, we get so narrowly focused on the current situation that we lose the bigger picture and start thinking in binary outcomes like failure/success, stupid/smart, disaster/salvation. This is a normal human tendency and has been given various names like threat rigidity, status quo bias, the little pond effect, and relative deprivation. As an illustration of these effects, writer Malcolm Gladwell observed that at Hayward College, half of the students with top SAT scores chose challenging STEM degrees, while those in the lower third of SAT scores must have concluded they were not as smart as their peers and so chose easier majors. But when Gladwell looked at Harvard, he found the exact same distribution. Even though students in the bottom third of SAT scores at Harvard have better SAT scores than the top students at Hayward, they tend to compare themselves locally to their peers, not globally to their real situation, and end up concluding they aren't smart enough to pursue a STEM degree.[23]

We make this same local-versus-global mistake when facing uncertainty, blind to the many alternative possibilities we have now (*lateral options*) and will have in the future (*longitudinal options*). For example, when Nathan lost his marbles at the start of the pandemic, he got stuck seeing only looming expenses and lost income. When we sat down and brainstormed, we realized we had many lateral options. For example, we could rent the apartment and live somewhere cheaper in the countryside, we could homeschool the kids instead of sending them to private school, we could ask our children in university to take that gap year they are always talking about. We also had longitudinal options, in both the near term (take an early retirement withdrawal) and long term (find a new place to live if we lost the apartment).

A second helpful technique, in addition to expanding your options and alternatives, is to think in terms of probabilities rather than binary terms. Framing things as dichotomies has a long history that has infiltrated our thinking, but while this black-and-white approach may be helpful in making an argument, it does not describe the world in which we actually live. One of the major intellectual thrusts of the late twentieth century has been the dismantling of binary thinking, revealing the world in terms of its many shades of gray. Even the binary nature of matter has been challenged by the emergence of quantum theory, introducing the idea that particles exist as probabilities rather than as absolutes.

Unfortunately, in the face of uncertainty, and especially during times of panic, the human brain instinctively defaults to thinking in binary terms. Former tech entrepreneur Brian Blum says that "seeing ourselves and the world around us as being either one thing or the other is not only untrue, it doesn't serve us well psychologically."[24] We imagine our project being a total failure or an immense success. We see no faults in our new romantic interest and then fall into despair when they turn out to be a normal, flawed human being. We think we are dying when we read about symptoms online, but really we are just sick.

One of the things that helps innovators tackle big unknowns is thinking in terms of probabilities rather than binaries, and in terms of multiple outcomes, some more likely than others. For example, Elon Musk talks about his ventures in terms of probabilities where he took increasingly larger risks over time. When it came to SpaceX and Tesla, the risks represented huge uncertainties with a high chance of failure. "I actually thought both companies would fail," Musk told us. "It wasn't until [later] that we felt that the probability of the company succeeding was decent," at which time he took on investors.[25] But at every stage you see probabilistic thinking in action. This framework helps decrease stress and increase your ability to move forward under uncertainty.

Most importantly, thinking in terms of probabilities can give you courage to sustain yourself. Rather than thinking of your novel, composition, startup, or adventure as a success or failure, you could see it as a whole range of outcomes, all with different probabilities. As famed biologist and physician Lewis Thomas said,

> We are not like the social insects. They have only the one way of doing things and they will do it forever, coded for that way. We are coded differently, not just for binary choices, *go* or *no go*. We can go four ways at once, depending on how the air feels: go, no go, but also *maybe*, plus *what the hell, let's give it a try*. We are in for one surprise after another if we keep at it and keep alive. We can build structures for human society never seen before, thoughts never thought before, music never heard before.[26]

Reflection and Practice

1. When the possibilities you have been seeking feel threatened or seem to have failed, revisit the applications in chapter 3 (Frontiers), chapter 4 (Adjacent Possible), chapter 5 (Infinite Game), chapter 10 (Know Your Risks), chapter 11 (Personal Real Options), and chapter 16 (Fait Sur Mesure), but this time with a more nonbinary lens, one that takes in the complexity of reality. Map out different outcomes and assign them probabilities, realizing that a blend of outcomes is the most likely. As Blum says, "We can—and we must—embody both hot and cold, happy and despondent, in the same person. It's entirely OK to feel sad or depressed at times, as long as you remember that's not all you are. . . . For me, having a chronic cancer means that I'm sick but not dying—that's nonbinary thinking."[27]

2. When thinking through alternatives and options, let yourself think big, really big. There are other ways to expand possibilities by imagining, dreaming, and living them into reality. Trend forecasters consider the deeply psychological needs and the social and political contexts of their clients (and their clients' customers—meaning all of us), then translate that into colors, textures, new sorts of products, layouts, and working styles that people will want next. What is interesting is how they work to push the boundaries of what we will accept. For example, Laura Guido-Clark often includes a wild color, such as bright orange, when designing a range for Flor carpet tiles. She knows the orange will hardly sell but including it alongside the other choices encourages customers to dare a little more than they would have otherwise. Include some orange in your thinking and you will be bolder about what options you see and choose.

3. Where might you be getting stuck in binary thinking? (Hint: if you mapped out only two to three outcomes in the first practice above, you may still be thinking in binary terms.) Ask someone you trust to brainstorm with you to see where there might be other possibilities and their probabilities you haven't considered.

Creative Competition

Competition can create a great deal of anxiety and uncertainty. One healthy way to face competition, which we discussed in chapter 19, is to focus on following your values, which relieves you from obsessing about winning or losing because you win no matter what. Another way is to realize that winning, or success, doesn't always yield the best outcome. Sometimes it is better not to get the job we thought we wanted; working with our second or seventh choice gives us more opportunities for change and growth than our first choice would have. Yet another approach is to embrace competition as an opportunity to push ourselves to do our personal best, which will lead us to be more creative.

A famous race from the Tour de France illustrates the power of creative competition. "Two Frenchmen rode up a mountain in a way unseen before or since," according to a reporter for the *Independent*.[28] "They literally went shoulder to shoulder, riding side by side, leaning into each other, neither yielding, in a tumultuous battle for supremacy that would decide the outcome of the 51st Tour de France."[29] Journalists described Jacques Anquetil, the holder of four previous titles and the race leader, as a machine for his impassive, calculating approach. His challenger, Raymond Poulidor, the passionate, "whole-hearted son-of-the-soil," lagged by fifty seconds going into the grueling Puy de Dôme leg of the race, a tortuous segment resembling "an upturned saw."[30]

Unexpectedly, Poulidor let out a sudden burst of energy and caught up with Anquetil. But then, instead of drafting off Poulidor to save energy, as was normal, Anquetil "rode directly alongside Poulidor, imposing his presence on him."[31] Shoulder to shoulder, they battled up the punishing hills. "Half a million spectators lined the road leading to the top of the Puy. None had seen anything like it. The showdown continued like this—two men locked in mortal combat—for an astonishing 10km, on gradients that hit 13 per cent." Only in the last nine hundred meters did Poulidor finally break free. Anquetil's face, "until then purple, lost all its colour; the sweat ran down in drops through the creases of his cheeks."[32] Poulidor pulled farther ahead and crossed into the final leg of the race well ahead, reducing his opponent's lead to a mere fourteen seconds. Decades later, when Anquetil was dying of cancer, he confided to his old opponent Poulidor that the pain was "like racing up the Puy de Dôme."

In an ironic twist, although Anquetil won the race that year anyway, what people remember is Poulidor's spirited victory at the Puy de Dôme. In fact, Poulidor never won the Tour de France, despite racing fourteen times. Never once did he wear the yellow jersey reserved for the leader, but he became the beloved "Eternal Second." When another rider criticized him, saying, "Raymond, you're always in a daydream!" Poulidor reflected, "It was true. I thought what was happening to me was already marvelous enough. I never thought of winning. Never, ever, did I get up in the morning with the idea of winning!"[33] Poulidor got up because he loved to ride. Today, wherever you are in the world, if you walk into a bicycle shop or sports bar, there is a good chance you will find a black-and-white photo of Poulidor shoulder to shoulder with Anquetil, climbing the Puy de Dôme.

What Poulidor's attitude teaches us is that if we focus on the joy of doing something well, we can shed some of that anxiety. There is always room for unique methods, ideas, ways of thinking, and values beyond being number one. Instead of seeing competition as a threat, we can see it as something that helps us do our best work, and maybe even reinvent how the game is played. Poulidor never won the race, but he still loved it enough to compete fourteen times! And people adored him because he raced for the thrill of the sport and his love of riding. We get to choose how we face competition, whether it beats us down with anxiety or we allow it to fuel our best attempt.

Although we often fear competition, consider that having no competition means you have to forge ahead when everyone doubts you. Shuji Nakamura became convinced he had a method to create LED lights bright enough to be used as replacements for inefficient incandescent bulbs, based on his work in semiconductors. But no one believed him. At big conferences he presented to empty rooms, and while colleagues received millions in funding, he had to scavenge to build his own equipment. The criticism he heard was "you are crazy. All the big companies and universities haven't been able to do that. Why do you think you can do it at a small company?"[34] At one point his boss, who had tolerated the experiments, ordered him to stop, but Nakamura pressed on until "one winter's day, the clouds finally lifted."[35] In a hacked-together lab known for explosions and billowing smoke, Nakamura discovered the breakthrough to make LED lights one thousand times brighter than before, enabling the LED lighting revolution and winning a Nobel Prize in 2014.

Reflection and Practice

1. Do an audit about any competition you face and the stories you tell yourself about it. Is the competition showing up with colleagues at work? Friends? Enemies? At the gym or during other hobbies? With your partner? Your kids? Your parents? Others in the same industry? Instagram accounts? Strangers?

2. Get curious about using competition to your advantage. Given the negative feelings that come with competition—stress, shame, jealousy, and so on—turning it into creative fuel can be challenging. But reframing competition as an opportunity to learn and

reinvent can enable more productive energy. It may help to realize that there are many voices in any conversation; what makes yours interesting is its unique contribution, not that it was first.

3. Although we have tried to help you reframe competition as a source of learning and inspiration, this may not always be true. If there is a case where the competition is destructive (e.g., distancing you from close familial relationships), maybe it's time to recognize that fact and ask yourself what is most important to you. It's probably time to stop worrying about the competition.

4. Keep in mind that competing with yourself can go two ways. Sometimes people describe competing with themselves as productive and helpful because it pushes them to be their best. But if competing with yourself is filled with demeaning and negative self-talk, think about how to turn it into a more productive, creative competition. You can refer back to the Learned Optimism tool to effectively dispute with negative beliefs.

5. Collaborate! Creative competition can motivate but collaboration can be more creative and powerful. Hanif Abdurraqib is a poet, essayist, and cultural critic who celebrates the genius of collaboration. When telling of his experience at the Eau Claire music festival, he recounts how invigorating it was to be included in the festival's intentionally spontaneous atmosphere designed to bring performers together to collaborate. "That was so new to me—and also so freeing to me—this idea of 'we will figure it out as we go along' actually can present a type of gentleness and a type of clarity and a type of rigorousness that perhaps writing alone or making music alone doesn't always afford itself."[36] Aaron Dressner, cofounder of the music festival Abdurraqib attended, describes collaboration as "the easiest way to grow."

Worst-Case Scenario

Each of the Reality Check tools we have discussed focuses on fact-checking, sense making, or possibility expanding, all of which help to untangle the knot of anxiety that attends uncertainty. But it is often the worst-case scenario, the one at the back of our brains that we are afraid to really look at, that causes us the most anxiety. One practice, validated by psychology research, is to directly examine the worst case, unpacking what it would really mean and walking it through to the ultimate outcome.[37] What we often realize is that the worst case might not be as frightening as we imagined.

As we described earlier, the financial uncertainty created by the Covid-19 pandemic created a great deal of anxiety for Nathan, and always at the back of his mind was the worry that we would go bankrupt or the university might fold. Finally, he talked to a life coach who helped him unpack the worst-case scenario. So what would happen if the university failed and he went bankrupt? Would there still be some demand for speeches and training in the future, however modest? Could our family relocate somewhere less expensive—the countryside or even a small coastal town where there might be more time for research, writing, and the occasional speech? And if demand for his skills evaporated entirely, what other things might he enjoy? Planting a garden? Suddenly the worst-case scenario transformed from terrifying to manageable and even slightly interesting.

In discussing this technique, it is important to acknowledge the role of privilege, and how the lack of it for many people creates a different kind of worst-case scenario, which we are not addressing here. Likewise, illness, accidents, natural disasters, and cruelty inflict tragedies and are a different kind of worst-case scenario. This tool isn't meant to address these situations, although it is inspiring to read accounts of resilience, forgiveness, and transformation that often reveal the power of the human spirit to overcome such tragedies. Just two days after the November 2015 terrorist attacks in Paris, Antoine Leiris posted an open letter on Facebook to the men who killed his wife at the Bataclan: "On Friday night, you stole the life of an exceptional being, the love of my life, the mother of my son, but you will not have my hate. I don't know who you are and I don't want to know."[38]

When we talk about the worst-case scenario, we are talking about the phantom fears that haunt our minds, causing undue anxiety or keeping us from doing the things we want to do—or from doing them in the way we wish we would. Looking directly at the worst-case scenario can help decrease that anxiety and empower us to take that step forward. Isabelle Huppert, ranked in 2020 by the *New York Times* as the best actress in the world, describes using this technique to overcome the anxiety of a performance going poorly: "Even if the danger, the possibility of falling is still there . . . to reassure yourself, you say to yourself, 'If something went wrong, what would be the worst punishment?'"[39] Fortunately, the probability that the worst-case scenario occurs is usually fairly low. Speaking about this exact point, enlightenment philosopher Michel de Montaigne admitted in his 1595 *Essais* that "my life has been full of terrible misfortunes, most of which never happened."

Reflection and Practice

1. Dismantle a worst-case scenario by really looking at the reality underneath the fear. If you feel you cannot do so alone, get the help of a therapist. To walk yourself through worst-case scenario(s) to probable conclusion(s), you can ask yourself: "If _____ happened . . . "

   – *Would the worst-case scenario really ruin you?* Use Reality Check tools to interrogate all the implications. Apply the frames discussed earlier (e.g., game, hero, evolution, and timing) to imagine how you could face the adversity and still have so much possibility to live for. For example, it wasn't enough for Nathan to say he would go bankrupt. He needed to walk through his response to bankruptcy to see the many ways that life post-bankruptcy would be OK.

   – *What broader alternatives or options might prove interesting?* Often there are aspects of the worst-case scenario that start to seem intriguing and maybe even worthwhile.

   Remember to walk through worst-case scenarios with a nonbinary mindset, exploring potential outcomes while holding on to the fact that often we spend immense energy on a binary scenario with a fairly low probability of taking place.

2. Sometimes we can diminish the sting of a worst-case scenario by thinking about the regret we would have had to live with had we not tried at all. Remember Steve Blank, the engineer who never went back to his position in the Midwest after seeing the opportunities in Silicon Valley? He was willing to court a worst-case

scenario (being jobless) to eradicate a regret of not having tried. Regrets are often much worse than worst-case scenarios, which are usually temporary and always surmountable.

The Optimization Myth

When navigating the unknown feels like it's headed toward "worst case" or "failure," it's easy to bemoan how the story was "supposed" to go and see anything less as an unhappily-ever-after ending. This is an easy trap to fall into because so much of our lives is informed by trying to optimize, trying to get the best, be the best, and make it on our first try. But what if, in a world of uncertainty, there isn't a "best"? What if there are really just different paths that are impossible to compare?

Silicon Valley entrepreneur and venture capitalist Randy Komisar argues that "we live in a world of risk, and we live in a world of failure, and the real issue is how do we deal with that failure. . . . What distinguishes Silicon Valley is not its successes, but the way in which it deals with failure."[40] Komisar is one of Silicon Valley's entrepreneurial veterans, working at or with companies like Pixar, Apple, LucasArts, and Kleiner Perkins.

When looking at the broader world, he argues that "what generally is lacking is a culture of constructive failure . . . the ability to tolerate failure, proceed with your career, and do it again and take your experience and cash in on it as an asset."[41] Although GO Corporation, where Komisar was CFO, turned into a $75 million crater in the 1980s—one of the largest failures of the decade—he notes that the "management team of that company turned out to be the pioneers of the internet."[42] Veterans of that failure went on to found Netscape, Verisign, and Autodesk; lead companies like Intuit and LucasArts; and play roles in Apple's turnaround under Steve Jobs and the founding of Google. "If you look at what came from the seeds of that failure, it was success after success. And not only that, it would create a new industry."[43]

By contrast, although Komisar led Crystal Dynamics to a very positive financial outcome, he sees the experience as a failure "because the quality of what I did was not good, because I didn't have the passion to persevere and do what that company needed to do in terms of rightsizing it and redirecting it." Looking back on a long career among great innovators, Komisar says "constructive failure has left me with a very different view of what failure and what success is, and also gave me a different view of my failures."[44]

Likewise, when Nathan works with big companies and hears about "that big failure" years ago, inevitably when they trot out their current successful innovation projects, the new ones have roots in those past failures! Even at a personal level, often failures are the path to a more interesting life. Recall that when Jos and Alison Skeates almost lost everything, they found their way to a more meaningful, impactful path, leading the way in sustainable jewelry and setting an industry standard.

Likewise, when David and Clare Hieatt sold Howies when it was a financial success, it caused an immense sense of failure when the acquirer dropped the values on which the Hieatts had built their company. They were devastated. But David reflects that "if everything you do succeeds, you always do what you have done. Uncertainty is about developing new formulas for the future. . . . I'm not afraid to fail because it would just be a chance to learn." David and Clare took that opportunity to develop a new formula, and when encouraged to scale massively like they had done with Howies, David made clear he'd learned there are other ways to scale than just getting big: "We can scale in so many more ways than revenue. . . . We want to scale on impact and influence."[45]

As part of your journey into uncertainty, consider letting go of over-simplified myths of optimization. People, relationships, systems, and even nature are all built to evolve and transform on much bigger and broader terms than our imagined "best case." Put down the optimization myth and make the most with what you have now.

Reflection and Practice

1. If you still doubt the idea of optimization, take thirty seconds and do an internet search for "failure quotes" or go straight to Forbes' list of 30 powerful quotes on failure.[46] You can't help but be convinced that failure attends every new idea and that the urge to avoid it is part of the optimization myth we cling to based on our natural fear of the unknown.

2. If you can relate to the trap of optimization, do a reality check about what's going on. Consider how that skewed mindset forces a trade-off on all the other valuable and important metrics. To lessen the chokehold of an optimization myth, ask yourself some questions to ascertain whether other "optimums" might be true:

    – Does your project have multiple outcomes you could be happy with (e.g., learning, networking, perspective)? Or are you narrowly focused on one optimal outcome, and if you don't get there it's a failure?

    – What are your values? Is the metric on which you are measuring yourself and success reflecting your values, or is it one you have inherited from someone else (e.g., money is the measure of success)?

    – Do you tend to base the value of something on a twentieth-century definition of success: money, fame, speed, first, best?

    Think about your answers and how they indicate whether an optimization myth might be diminishing your ability to sustain yourself in uncertainty. Be careful, because external success metrics like money are a relentless treadmill with a constantly changing set of rules for what it will take to "make it." Using the Reframe tools to envision uncertainty as possibility and incorporating the Prime and Do tools to shift how you prepare for and navigate uncertainty, can help you break down this myth? Sustaining yourself when you lose your way requires patience and endurance, but it is so worth debunking the optimization myth and trading it in for a reality that allows you to discover what really matters to you. When we let go of fear about what we think should happen, expansive possibilities emerge that we might not have dreamed of by ourselves.

Chapter 28

Magic

The world is full of infinite possibilities appearing, hovering, evaporating, and reforming . . . on repeat. This reality can feel paralyzing until you surrender to the fact that so much of what happens is beyond your control. When we pair this with a striving for possibility, we enter the realm of magic. By "magic" we mean the sudden leaps of insight, the serendipitous encounters, the fortuitous events, and the exquisite moments that seem too good to be true. Stanford professor Tina Seelig describes these moments as luck (both good and bad), defined as success or failure apparently caused by chance. She emphasizes *apparently* as "the operative word. It looks like chance because we rarely see all the levers that come into play."[1] Seelig says that luck is like the wind— although we can't control it, we can build a sail to catch it. While it may feel magical, author and NYU professor Christian Busch believes that luck can be "learned and leveraged" and details how in *The Serendipity Mindset: The Art and Science of Creating Good Luck*, where he traces "serendipity" to the actions we take rather than unexplainable random events that we had no part in.[2]

Consider the moment when German physicist Werner Heisenberg had the breakthrough insight that laid the foundation of quantum mechanics. He had been wrestling with a puzzle that made no sense to modern science: quantum particles—the tiny packets of energy that form matter—appear to be both waves and particles, existent and non-existent at the same time. Physicist Carlo Rovelli retells the story well, describing the twenty-five-year-old Heisenberg walking about pensively in the park behind the University of Copenhagen's Institute of Theoretical Physics. It was an exceptionally dark night, the only light coming from occasional lamps along the gravel path, each casting a dim island of illumination, when "suddenly, Heisenberg sees a figure pass by. Actually, he does not see him pass: He sees him appear beneath a lamp, then disappear into the dark before reappearing beneath another lamp, and then vanishing back into the dark again. And so on, from pool of light to pool of light."[3] Because Heisenberg had been thinking and listening, the answer arrived in its own magical way. Rovelli explains that "a light flashes on in his mind," allowing Heisenberg to consider that if a "substantial, large, and heavy" object with so much mass seemed to disappear until it interacted with the island of light, maybe a quantum particle, with so little mass, could effectively disappear until it interacted with something.

We had a similar experience when a distant and foggy frontier suddenly collapsed like a telescope, and everything changed in a moment. Two years after moving to France, we felt like we faced a binary ultimatum: change our kids' school situation or move back to the United States. Concerned, we explored other options in Paris, but they were too expensive and distant (we lived in a small suburb to the south). We had barely scraped together enough to send our oldest to the American School of Paris for his senior year after the French school refused to let him stay at grade level. And while he loved the new school, the commute was two hours each way—and worse, it was a complicated route of humid, standing-room-only trains, metros, and buses. At the end of February, he said he couldn't continue like this. We looked into drivers (costly), boarding options (nonexistent), even renting an apartment that one of us would live in with him part-time (sad), and nothing felt doable. Meanwhile, the other three kids, still at the local international school, were becoming alarmingly used to traumatic incidents of bullying from both teachers and peers. Their "can do" and creative growth mindsets were shrinking by the day into a fixed and narrow view of what was possible. We decided to try to get them into the American School the following fall, but it seemed so far away.

One gloomy Saturday, after a couple weeks of discouraging brainstorming, Nathan's phone rang while he was in the canned goods aisle of the grocery store: an unrecognized number. Nathan picked up anyway. The number belonged to the director of the American School of Paris. He had been thinking about our tough situation with the commute and wondered if we would consider having the other kids join the school right away. That way our whole family could move up to Paris. "When?" Nathan asked him. "In two weeks?" the director suggested. Nathan almost dropped the phone but managed to explain the financial situation. "Let me see what we can work out, I'll be in touch."

For a week we waited on pins and needles. We came up with all the reasons it wouldn't work. We were in the middle of a rental contract in Fontainebleau, Paris was a notoriously expensive and tight rental market, our son George was set to play the Scarlet Pimpernel in the Anglophone play, and tuition wasn't cheap. On Monday the director called and worked out a plan where Nathan could do work in kind as part of the tuition. Five days later, we were racing to catch the train to Paris, suitcases in tow, their tiny wheels rattling across the cobbles. As the imminent departure buzzer sounded, and the doors slid closed with all six of us safely inside, a few of us burst into tears of relief.

Let us be blunt: Thorny situations rarely dissipate in this way. We have had telescopic moments of bad luck, tragedy and failure that felt like the gods were against us. And don't forget that magical moments still deposit you back into the reality of your life, where you have to face new uncertainties that appear as a result of the magic choice taken. Moving to Paris was extremely stressful, requiring that Nathan work harder and travel more to pay the tuition, and we left behind some fun friends that felt snubbed by our choice. But it was totally the right transition for our family, and it came together in a miraculous way. We include magic in the critical Sustain tools to leave room for the marvelous and amazing possibilities that can arise in spite of the odds.

The role we suggest you inhabit is that of the artist (poet, painter, film director, chef) who pays attention, learns to be transfigured by the ordinary materials of life, and then from that place creates beauty, meaning, or even revelations of flavor that thrill and inspire us. Author and dramatist Eden Phillpotts intuited, "the universe is full of magical things, patiently waiting for our wits to grow sharper," referring to how something as simple as a magnifying glass can reveal how "every blossom exhibits an exquisite disorder of ragged petals finer than lace."[4] Although the world may appear one way on the surface, there is more there than we may be able to see or understand right now. Seeking magic (serendipity, good luck) starts by sharpening your senses, increasing your awareness, and opening yourself up to conversations and situations where magic can happen.

Picaresque

Sometimes magic comes in the shape of what we wanted, but often it comes differently than expected—and from situations that we thought might ruin us. It's important to be alert, and open, to how it shows up. When we talked to Patrick Deedes and Isabelle Townsend, a creative couple living in a stone farmhouse at the edge of an ancient forest, it was a winter day with the fallow fields stretching out in long lines, the clouds clumped like gray and white bits of wool floating across the sky. Deedes is the estate manager for one of the region's most beautiful castles, and Townsend is an actress who puts on one-act plays and produces children's theater. (She is also the daughter of Peter Townsend, the British war hero who had a tragic love affair with Princess Margaret, the younger sister of Queen Elizabeth II.)

When we asked them about uncertainty, Deedes sat back, arms behind his head, and exhaled. "Is it something you choose?" he wondered aloud, cocking his head to one side.[5] "I'm thinking of how I began writing my own books. I had been working for years as a publisher when this woman called me up, wanting a book about the history of photography in Paris, and asked if I knew anyone who would be good. I hesitated, then I ventured, 'I could do it,' and just like that, she agreed. What if I hadn't offered?" That first book led to successive books he authored on the history of photography in London, New York, Berlin, and Venice. "Sometimes I wonder how much is our choice and how much is what we make of it. The word that comes to mind is picaresque."

Our thoughts flashed to the gray stone building dominating the quay on a corner near Pont Royal in Paris, where Voltaire died two hundred years earlier. Voltaire fought back against authoritarianism and intolerance, arguing for freedom of thought and religious tolerance. Today he is considered one of the major philosophers of the Enlightenment—one of the reasons Paris is called the City of Light. In 1791, when his remains were moved to the Panthéon, high on a hill overlooking the city, one million people followed the procession.

His magnum opus, *Candide*, describes the misadventures of a young man who believes, like many in that period, that we live in the best of all possible worlds (sounds like an optimization myth!). That is, until he finds his hopes of marrying the local baron's daughter dashed when he is exiled abroad, conscripted into a foreign army, and whipped when he deserts that army, only to be shipwrecked in Portugal, after which he flees to South America, stumbles into an unexpected fortune, loses much of the fortune to thieves, and finally returns to Europe, all while meeting and losing contact with his love numerous times until they reunite on a farm outside Constantinople. The novel took the world by storm and came to epitomize an entire literary genre: the picaresque novel, where the hero has to live by wit and will in a capricious world, making the best of what happens.

"It means," as Deedes explained, "things happen to you rather than you making it happen." Then he pushed further. "I sometimes ask myself, Are we really creating the situation or is it finding you? . . . Often when you are in your worst element, and you have pretty much thrown in the towel . . . then you get that phone call, and everything changes. This has happened to me again and again."

Such a phone call led to his fortuitous meeting with Ralph Lauren and Isabelle Townsend. At the time, Deedes had been running small fashion shoots on the side to underwrite his startup, Lighthouse Artist Management & Production, a fashion agency for budding photographers. One day, out of the blue, he got a call from a photographer at *British Vogue* who asked if Deedes could come handle a shoot for Ralph Lauren. "It was that shoot where I met Isabelle! That shoot kick-started my business in London, Paris, and New York. . . . It just makes me question the notion of going after something. . . . It seems more like you show up, dignified, and you do your best." Coming back to Voltaire's *Candide* (where, at the end, the characters conclude that their best course of action in an unpredictable world is to "cultivate the garden"), Deedes reflected that "it means the best we can do is take what comes . . . but you do have to do one thing—you have to continue on. You have to cultivate the garden. It is much more than just waiting to see what happens to you; it is cultivating!"

Deedes and Townsend ask interesting questions about uncertainty and possibility. As much as we may want to be the knight pursuing a glorious quest, we must be alert to the possibility that our real quest, the one life is offering us, might be different from the one we imagined. Famed artist Carl Larsson spent years in Paris, his oil paintings rejected by the salons repeatedly, until a friend found him despondent, living in squalor in a tiny attic apartment. The friend dragged him to the artist colony in Barbizon, just south of Paris, where he learned to watercolor and met his wife, Karin Bergöö. It was the watercolors of their life together, Larsson said in his 1992 autobiography, that "became the most immediate and lasting part of my life's work. For these pictures are, of course, a very genuine expression of my personality, of my deepest feelings, of all my limitless love for my wife and children."

For Jos and Alison Skeates, their quest was not to have a global jewelry network but to lead the way in sustainable production. For Pádraig Ó Tuama, it was not to become a priest but to work in conflict resolution with Northern Ireland's Corrymeela Community and help thousands of people deal with disappointment, grief, and conflict through poetry. Even for pure rationalists like Max Levchin and Peter Thiel, their quest was not to create encryption software libraries, as they had once imagined, but to kick-start mobile payments. As you encounter uncertainty and pursue possibilities, approach the obstacles and setbacks with curiosity, looking for and believing in the picaresque magic that can change the landscape in an instant.

Reflection and Practice

The School of Life offers a beautiful discussion of what Voltaire's advice to "cultivate the garden" could mean for people living in the twenty-first century. We capture an excerpt here:

> What did Voltaire mean with his gardening advice? . . . Because our minds are haunted and prey to anxiety and despair, we need to keep ourselves busy. We need a project. It shouldn't be too large or dependent on many. The project should send us to sleep every night weary but satisfied. It could be bringing up a child, writing a book, looking after a house, running a small shop, or managing a little business.[6]

Revisit the robust framework you have been creating while reading this book: your frontiers, infinite roles, personal real options, values, and uncertainty balancers. They all help to cultivate your garden. As you begin to put this framework into practice, remember to celebrate the projects you have envisioned, started, or finished as a result of reframing uncertainty as a portal to possibility.

As If

In his book *Letters to a Young Contrarian*, the social critic Christopher Hitchens describes the political philosophy that helped human rights advocates during the twentieth century sustain themselves through the tortuous, stagnant periods when it seemed as if nothing would change. The strategy, simply, is to live as if the change we desire has already occurred. Hitchens traces this "mild-sounding but actually deeply subversive and ironic decision" back to several key advocates, such as historian E. P. Thompson and Václav Havel. After the Warsaw Pact invasion of Czechoslovakia in 1968, Havel "realized that resistance in its original insurgent and militant sense was impossible," so instead he "proposed living 'as if' he were a citizen of a free society."[7] Havel wrote about this approach in *The Power of the Powerless*, and over time, by living this reality with so many others, succeeded in breaking down totalitarian power, later becoming the first president of the new Czech Republic.

Hitchens provides other examples of this mindset: how Irish writer Oscar Wilde decided to act as if society were not deeply hypocritical in relation to morals, how US activist Rosa Parks decided in 1955 "to act 'as if' a hard-working black could sit down on a bus at the end of the day's labor," how in the 1970s Russian novelist Aleksandr Solzhenitsyn decided to act as if a scholar could investigate the history of his own country, and how the Filipino people deposed dictator Ferdinand Marcos by acting as if they lived in a free democracy and voting against him in the snap election of 1985. Hitchens admits that living "as if" is not easy or necessarily intuitive and reminds us that "it is important to remember the many dreary years when the prospect of victory appeared quite unattainable." He stresses that "on every day of those years the 'as if' pose had to be kept up until its cumulative effect could be felt."[8]

Hitchens's proposal for creating and sustaining political change has deeper roots, including the much earlier work of German philosopher Hans Vaihinger, who wrote a dissertation in 1887 titled "The Philosophy of As If."[9] Vaihinger argued that an important part of making sense of life is the construction of useful fictions that help us understand and take action. For example, he points out that while no one has seen an atom, the fiction we create about what atoms look like helps us understand them. Vaihinger says that a fiction, even if false, can be useful because what we believe is just as important as the underlying reality.

Although Vaihinger's ideas may seem abstract, they influenced central figures in psychology like Sigmund Freud and Alfred Adler, and they have been borne out by contemporary research. Ellen Langer, a psychologist at Harvard, conducted a series of studies on the impact of living as if something were true. In one study, people suffering from diabetes were asked to complete a timed task, but a rigged clock ran at half or double speed. When researchers measured participants afterward, their blood sugar levels aligned with the time shown on the rigged clock, not the actual time. Likewise, in a study of hotel cleaners, Langer found that simply explaining to them that their work constituted vigorous exercise led to decreases in weight, waist-to-hip ratio, body mass, and blood pressure, compared with a control group. Finally, in perhaps the most unusual study of them all, Langer took eight men in their seventies to a retreat center, where for a week they lived as if it were two decades earlier. Staff wore fashions and the men watched "new releases" from twenty years prior. After only a week, Langer found that the men looked "noticeably younger" and that their vision, hearing, strength, and cognitive processes improved. While they were waiting for the bus to take them home, the men, many of whom had come to the center with canes, started a touch football game in the parking lot.[10]

Living "as if" also turns out to be an important tool for innovators creating new industries. In a study of the early mobile gaming industry before the rise of app stores, researchers at Stanford observed a dilemma: Tiny startups trying to create games had to attract the attention of industry titans like AT&T.[11] The more successful startup leaders imagined the future industry, with themselves as central actors, and then caught the attention of a big giant like Samsung by announcing they were working with AT&T on the future of gaming. Then, while they were in talks with Samsung, they popped over to Verizon, introducing themselves as working on the future of gaming with Samsung. At a tactical level, the entrepreneurs were engaging in parallel rather than sequential negotiations, but the researchers are clear that the more critical task was envisioning the future industry and then acting as if they were the entrepreneurs who would make it come true. By contrast, less successful entrepreneurs tended to stick to what they knew—their own business—making games that then struggled to find a home.

It could be easy to dismiss this research as reinforcing the old dictum "fake it till you make it." But there is more to the story than that. It is less about faking and more about believing in something so much that you willfully live as if that something is already true. Nely Galán, who immigrated to the United States from Cuba at the age of five, has become one of the most successful female *and* Latina television producers. She attributes her success to how she thinks about herself: "I've walked into many situations where I'm the only Latina, the only woman. . . . I never think they are thinking I'm the only token, because what you think and how you present yourself is how people will see you. I think of myself as the expert in something that no one in the room knows." She admits, "I will tell you, there are moments when I've been intimidated in a room." What does she do? She lives as if she were already confident. To help, she conjures up memories of her first boss, who was a very confident, demanding person: "I literally would channel him . . . when I act like, 'Of course I know what I'm talking about,' because I do . . . then things come."[12]

Living "as if" isn't easy. As Hitchens reminds us, "there must have been days when the 'as if' style was exceedingly hard to keep up. All I can recommend therefore, apart from the study of these and other good examples, is that you try to *cultivate* this attitude."[13]

Reflection and Practice

Hitchens uses the verb cultivate as Voltaire did in *Candide*, with all the repetitive effort that verb evokes. Given that it's so hard to sustain living "as if" in a world that doesn't agree yet with our view, the fact that it has enabled radical change adds to its magic. Perhaps another magical aspect is the way it works across types of need: activism and other political endeavors, winning support for ideas or work, or even personal evolution of any kind (physical, social, financial, personality). Here are some ways to encourage "as if" thinking in your life.

1. Consider where you could apply "as if" as an experiment in a tricky relationship. Do you have a "spirited" child, a bossy in-law, or a rude colleague who saps your energy because being around them requires so much effort? What would living as if look like?

2. Are you struggling to make changes to your calendar that would prioritize your well-being? If you lived as if you'd already made those changes, you might start right now and find a nonnegotiable daily slot in your calendar (it can change day to day) for alone time, creative time, an exercise class, a movie night, etc.—and if you could deliver on your promise to yourself, you would live it into reality.

3. "Be the change you wish to see in the world" has been attributed to Gandhi, but it actually comes from educator Arleen Lorrance. Lorrance, an educator at a Brooklyn high school, watched in despair as the school deteriorated. "For seven years I served my sentence and marked off institutional time; I complained, cried, accepted hopelessness, put down the rest of the faculty for all the things they didn't do, and devoted all my energies to trying to change others and the system," she says.[14] Then one day, "it came in on me loud and clear that I was the only one who could imprison—or release—me, that I was the only one who could do anything about changing. So I let go of my anger and negativism and made a decision to simply be totally loving, open, and vulnerable all the time."

    Lorrance lived as if her happiness were up to her, and it turned out that it was. She founded the Love Project, focused on giving students growing up in rough neighborhoods a safe, accepting place to retreat at school. As it turns out, Gandhi's exact words were, "If we could change ourselves, the tendencies in the world would also change. As a [hu]man changes his own nature, so does the attitude of the world change towards [them]. . . . We need not wait to see what others do."[15]

Helping Others

Each of us is more powerful than we realize if changing our nature changes the world. One obvious way this plays out is the way we engage our fellow beings. There is magic in helping others, one that has empirically verifiable foundations. When sociologist AnnaLee Saxenian conducted her groundbreaking study of why two comparable tech hubs in the 1970s—Boston and Silicon Valley—evolved so differently, she concluded that it wasn't the education, money, or government contracts that set Silicon Valley apart, but rather the collaborative spirit of sharing and helping each other. While engineers in Boston lived in a culture of secrecy, Silicon Valley engineers met up after work, talked openly about technology problems, and tried to help each other solve them. Meanwhile, in Boston, hierarchical companies focused on winning big contracts and rarely collaborated, and if you left to start your own company and failed, it was seen as a stain on your career. In Silicon Valley, an ecosystem of smaller firms actively collaborated with each other, often creating complex contracts to share development costs across a group of contributors. Moreover, if you left your firm to pursue a startup and failed, you were a hero with courage, not a failure—a spirit pervading the Valley today.[16]

Although sociologists explain such outcomes in terms of networks, reciprocality, and recombination, these words don't fully capture the magic of what happens when people help each other. Jerry Sanders, an entrepreneur in Silicon Valley whose mantra was to always help others, spent a weekend working with an acquaintance, Ascher Shmulewitz, on his business plan. Months later, Shmulewitz, a doctor and inventor, approached Sanders with the prototype for a new way to measure blood flow in the heart. He invited Sanders to join the startup as CEO. Ten months later they sold the company for two hundred times their original investment, an outcome that came from helping someone else.[17]

Helping others can also relieve the anxiety you feel, replacing a self-doubting stance with one of leadership. Ricardo dos Santos founded STEM nonprofit Scientella, an organization run by STEM-oriented teenage girls with the goal of mentoring other, like-minded teenage girls. The beauty of the organization, aside from side-stepping the adult-save-the-kid mentality, is that by mentoring other girls in STEM, the girls doing the mentoring experience reduced self-consciousness, self-absorption, and anxiety about their future. By focusing their energy on helping others, they sustain themselves.[18]

Helping others might also deliver on what you need. Heather LeFevre was working in brand strategy for a major agency when she began wondering if she should negotiate for a raise. Since she "had zero idea what to do" but had read that good negotiations start with data, she started a survey about salaries, asking acquaintances to contribute and offering to share the results anonymously. In addition to the many notes she got to thank her for the helpful information, she got a $12,000 raise and a promotion! "I've done it for ten years now, and really everything good that has happened to me career-wise has been from this act of generosity of investing my time. . . . I've just met so many amazing people, I got to move overseas, [and] work in these incredible places."[19]

Helping others becomes more relevant as uncertainty increases. We had the chance to interview some physicians working in Syria during the devastating civil war that engulfed the country starting in 2011. They shared, with heartbreak, how their normal suburban lives had turned so quickly into a nightmare of dust and rubble. One of the women, an MD working tirelessly to help her fellow Syrians, reflected, "When you face that kind of uncertainty, you narrow the window of what you worry about, but you expand the view of who you help." She did not explain further, she just pursed her lips to hold back the emotion. But at the risk of putting words in her mouth, when we help others, we receive something greater than just "something in return."[20]

Benjamin Gilmour, the paramedic and filmmaker we have mentioned several times, illustrated this recently in a miraculous story he shared with us via email. In his own words:

> Sher Alam is the man who played the father in my film *Son of a Lion* and the taxi driver in *Jirga*. . . . He lives with 12 children in a small, two-room mud dwelling in a hamlet on the edge of Kohat in Pakistan, a stone's throw from the Afghan border. Very poor in material terms, but there is a light in his eyes that I rarely see in men in my own country. . . . One day his adult son confided in him that he'd fallen in love with a woman and wanted to marry her. This is rare in the area as they mostly have arranged marriages chosen by the parents. But Sher Alam, being open-minded and loving his son, agreed to try and make it happen. Unfortunately, the family of the girl demanded a very high "bride price" . . . so high no family in the whole camp would have been able to afford it. Sher Alam had to break the news to his son that he could not marry the love of his life. On the day he would tell his son, Sher Alam's mobile phone rang (an old flip phone I left with him). It was another friend of mine who I'd sent to give Sher Alam $500. It was the bride price. The son married his true love.[21]

Helping others obviously creates possibility for others, but it helps us as well. Perhaps this is why Gilmour's films are "experiments in empathy," as he puts it, to encourage people to imagine the lives of other people and understand how we are connected.

As we encounter uncertainty, it can feel tempting to pull back, fortify, and protect yourself. Happily, as Stanford psychologist Jamil Zaki found, in the aftermath of Hurricane Katrina, while some incidents of crime took place, there were more instances of people helping one another.[22] Likewise, Sigal Samuel, author and former associate editor at the *Atlantic*, documented a remarkable outpouring of care when the Covid-19 pandemic left many elderly and vulnerable individuals in lockdown.[23] Despite age-old arguments from psychology, behavioral economics, and evolutionary biology about the existence of an innate "selfish gene" in humans, an instinct for altruism exists and has magic in it that cannot be quantified.

Reflection and Practice

It can be counterintuitive to reach out to others when you are distressed. Why would helping others render comfort to you? But acts of service provide a healthy break from ruminating on our own woes. The Greater Good Science Center at UC Berkeley, which promotes "a new scientific movement to explore the roots of happy and compassionate individuals, strong social bonds, and altruistic behavior," has done numerous studies that reveal the importance of altruism, compassion, empathy, and generosity. Individuals who participated in volunteering efforts or helped others were found to exhibit greater happiness and well-being during the Covid-19 pandemic. One study showed that trust and generosity were critical coping tools during the pandemic. Another pandemic-related study of one thousand participants revealed that "on days when participants helped others, they felt greater positive emotions and were happier with their relationships, compared to days when they didn't help anyone else." The definition of helping included formal volunteer activities as well as informal small acts of service, such as delivering groceries to a neighbor. And on days when individuals showed emotional support for others (listening rather than trying to fix the problems), they reported fewer negative emotions themselves than on days when they hadn't provided emotional support for someone else.

Here are some ways to put these ideas into practice:

1. At the Greater Good Science Center's website, you can learn about the twelve building blocks of individual and community well-being and take quizzes to find out your well-being profile for each. For more, go to https://greatergood.berkeley.edu/key.

2. Dr. Vivek Murthy has made this altruistic aspect of human interaction a major talking point during his second tenure as US Surgeon General, "The question I have found myself asking again and again is, What can we do in our lives, through the decisions we make, choices we make, about how to tip the scales in the world away from fear and toward love? How can we do that through how we treat other people, through what we say, through the issues we choose to speak up on in the public square, through the jobs we take and the purpose we seek to fulfill?"[24]

3. Follow the advice of Greek Stoic philosopher Epictetus: "Never suppress a generous impulse."[25] If you have a kind idea, act on it, since becoming aware of others' needs is the first obstacle to helping them.

Memento Mori

Memento mori is Latin for "remember, you must die." Although it may sound distressing, the idea holds incredible magic to sustain you through uncertainty. The philosophy of memento mori was practiced by the Stoics not to promote cautious living but to encourage themselves to act boldly and virtuously—immediately! Marcus Aurelius exhorted, "You could leave life right now. Let that determine what you do and say and think."[26] Similarly, many Buddhists practice the *maranasati* meditation on the impermanence of life to encourage deliberate living. We include memento mori as a Sustain tool because for many interviewees in this book it held magic to recover from setbacks and spark courage for doing new things.

Consider the case of Jonathan Herson, a startup investor and entrepreneur. Several years ago, while on a trip, his leg started swelling. At the emergency room the physician informed Herson that he had a pulmonary embolism that would have killed him by the next day. Further tests revealed that Herson has anticardiolipin syndrome, a condition that creates unnecessary blood clots. For several years Herson did well on blood thinners, until one day his other leg went completely numb. Doctors found his body had clots throughout and his heart was functioning at only 20 percent, and diagnosed catastrophic antiphospholipid syndrome, which carries a 50 percent mortality rate. For three months Herson had to wear a massive vest that could jump-start his heart automatically. If he moved suddenly, the vest started an automatic countdown to shock his heart, and he would have to hurriedly unplug it. Herson recalls that "walking around with this thing . . . was a constant reminder like, 'Hey, your heart could stop at any moment.'"[27] Several times since then, Herson has been hospitalized for related illnesses and been forced to wear the vest.

But Herson remains immensely grateful for his illness.

> This existential crisis was the most powerful thing that could happen to me, because it's given me . . . the truth that I'm gonna die. . . . If you really hold your mortality in your head at all times, and you remember that 'I'm on this earth for a very short time period,' yeah, there are gonna be things that go wrong, that are not in my control most of the time. I get up, I stand up, and I go again because life is short, and I will regret it if I don't.

Herson added that his condition has helped him "be a lot more of a risk-taker, doing things that might not work out. I take calculated risks, if you will. It doesn't mean be stupid. But you only live once; you should live like this is going to end." The trap is that "most people wait too long, until they get sick or they're too old. . . . They act like they're going to live forever. They do not go and do things. If you look at a lot of entrepreneurs, specifically, the vast majority of them, the one thing that they did was go and take that chance."

Trying and failing is also part of the journey. When Herson tries something and it fails, he doesn't let it bother him. "Just because you failed one thing, it doesn't define you. And just because you succeed at one thing, it doesn't define you." In short, when teaching others how to practice memento mori, Herson explains, "I try to frame it from a sense of gratitude. . . . I encourage people to drive by graveyards, [and] really look. Be grateful. Go out there, and remember how good you have it." From that perspective, he explains, "Effectively, everyone's got everything going for them, but they don't know it. And even when bad stuff happens, they still have stuff going for them. It's just how you look at it."

We can invoke this tool to invoke magic in almost every ordinary day when we focus on even the simplest things that we would sorely miss if we didn't get to, or even *have to*, do them again. Death doula Alua Arthur supports terminal patients and their families at the end of life. She explains,

> Looking at a body that life has just left, you see the incredible stillness of it with the understanding that that person will not speak any more words. . . . They'll never get to look at their niece or listen to her laugh. They won't eat another orange. When I'm in my own life, doing those things, I bring so much more presence to it and a lot more gratitude. . . . It's very life-affirming. Because I think, "Ah, I'm actually still living." It also is a nice reminder that we don't know how much time we have left. So it's like, "I'm here now. Let me do it now. Let me break up with that guy. Let me go to Fiji."[28]

Reflection and Practice

1. *Practice memento mori.* Wake up and savor that you are alive, even if you feel sick or have a stressful or depressing day—after all, it could always be worse. On your next commute, which likely has become both boring and so familiar that you don't even notice what's going on around you, imagine if it was the last time you would ever take that trip. Notice the small details, the smells, the sounds, the people you pass, the frustrations (traffic, noise, construction, etc.) and see if there is anything you would miss. Is there something about it that you didn't realize you kind of like?

2. *Adopt a Memento Mori tool.* You might find it useful to have a symbol to remind you of this perspective. Throughout the ages,

people have used objects like skulls. Today there are tools like the memento mori calendar, which has a box for every week of your life to push you to make the most of them, and even apps that send you daily messages to remind you of the urgency of life.

3. *Practice gratitude.* If memento mori doesn't work for you, try plain gratitude. Research underscores that practicing gratitude leads to more and better relationships; improved physical, psychological, and mental health; better sleep; better self-esteem; increased empathy; and reduced aggression.[29] Have you started the gratitude journal we talked about in chapter 27? It is so easy to do. The journal can be a digital list in an app on your phone or something you scribble down in a notepad you carry with you. It doesn't matter how or when or where you make your list, but the idea is that you take a few moments to write down five things you are grateful for every single day. Let someone know you are grateful for them!

Techs You Live By

We are citizens of the twenty-first century, so technology plays a role in almost every aspect of our lives. And while we agree that much technology is essential (vaccines, clean energy, etc.), it is a worrisome reality that technology also creates addiction, isolation, and misinformation. Consider that the average American spends 5.4 hours on their mobile phone each day.[30] If it takes 10,000 hours to master a subject, 5.4 hours a day could help the average American learn the violin, data analytics, or anything else in a mere five years. As writer Annie Dillard observed, "How we spend our days is, of course, how we spend our lives."[31]

Since technologies play an ever-greater role in our lives, it's important to pause and ask which ones you are choosing to live by and how they are affecting you. Tech scholar W. Brian Arthur defines technology as any "phenomenon put to use."[32] By this definition, technology can include your phone, but also coffee (caffeine harnessed to provide energy) as well as art (stylistic devices to evoke an experience). But these technologies differ in how they operate, a division we could label as "low tech" versus "high tech." By low and high, we don't mean basic versus cutting-edge, but instead the clarity of the input-output relationship. Low techs, like coffee, have a very clear, repeatable input-output relationship (drink it and get energy). By contrast, high techs, like art and philosophy, have a more opaque input-output relationship, which means you could read ten poems and feel nothing until the eleventh transforms your worldview!

The challenge for each of us is that low techs are so easy to use that they can easily colonize our lives like an invasive species, and then without recognizing it we are bingeing on coffee, email, Instagram, and Netflix. While these might provide a short-term hit, we run the risk of being stimulated but ultimately unsatisfied; low techs might help us live, but high techs remind us why and how to live. Art, music, literature, and philosophy may feel daunting compared with the next meme in your feed, but high techs have the power to inspire and enlarge the boundaries of who we are and what we are capable of. Tinder may help you find love, but *Anna Karenina* will teach you what it means to love well. So make a conscious choice to invest in high techs that lead you to live a life you choose, not just one overgrown with low techs.

Once you have reflected on the mix of low and high techs you live by, consider the ways you are choosing to use each one. The same technology can be used in different ways, but most of the time we simply adopt an inherited, rather than thoughtful, view of how or what it's for. For example, the different ways we are taught to think about the technology of money—one of the most pervasive and homogenous technologies— are illustrated by a long-running conflict between venture capitalist David Hornik and one of his partners. As Hornik tells it, every time one of their investments had an exit, paying out a proportion of the gains to the partners, Hornik would donate his money to a charity or fund some project that he believed in. Often, Hornik's partner shook his head, chiding him for making unwise investments, until one day they realized they use the same technology in different ways. Hornik explained,

> My partner's view was that the purpose of earning money is to stack it up and earn more money with it. My view was that the purpose of earning money is to give it away. Sure, I invested in a Broadway show for the hearing impaired that I knew would lose ninety-nine cents of every dollar. But at the end of that show when the audience, many of whom had never had the chance to fully experience a theater production, all shook their hands in

unison in sign language for 'thank you,' I knew it was one of the best investments I had ever made![33]

Putting the techs we use to better use can start with small tweaks. Rather than posting that envy-creating picture or leaving that nasty comment on Instagram, commit to an online presence that encourages others. When internet trolls attacked Scott Hutchinson, the singer for the band Frightened Rabbit, calling the band members ugly, fat, and "furry brick built men" that are "built like a cruise ship," Hutchinson responded by flipping the script. He worked with friends to produce a T-shirt that read "Furry Brick Built Men: Ugly, Hairy, and Built Like a Cruise Ship Since 2004," donating the proceeds to an anti-bullying group.[34] Sadly, Hutchinson died by suicide a mere three years later, tweeting just beforehand, "Be so good to everyone you love. It's not a given."[35]

Using both low and high techs in the best ways (read: the kindest, noblest, most generous, most helpful, least addictive ways) will create more chances for magic. But if you really want to have more fun with magic, add more high techs (music, art, poetry, and philosophy). Entrepreneur David Hieatt argues that CEOs should be reading poetry because it will help them think differently about the world: "Science has shown that consuming poetry has a long-term positive effect on augmented thinking and the decision-making process. . . . Poetry is a can opener. It puts us into a state where we can quieten our cleverness and make room for new ideas. The status quo doesn't stand a chance against a poet-reading CEO."[36] But there are less obvious, and equally important, reasons to pursue high techs. As Anne Pasternak, director of the Brooklyn Museum, explains, art "ignites radical imagination" because museums are "places of inspiration and learning, and we help expand empathy and moral thinking. We are places for difficult and courageous conversations."[37]

Most importantly, high techs help us become our best selves. As the actor Ethan Hawke said, "Most people don't spend a lot of time thinking about poetry. They have a life to live, and they're not really that concerned with Allen Ginsberg's poems or anybody's poems . . . until their father dies, they go to a funeral, you lose a child, somebody breaks your heart, they don't love you anymore, and all of a sudden you're desperate for making sense out of this life and [asking] 'Has anybody ever felt this bad before? How did they come out of this cloud?' . . . That's when art's not a luxury, it's actually sustenance. We need it."[38]

If one high tech has been ruined for you (i.e., by a teacher who treated poetry like a complex one-solution puzzle rather than letting you read what you love) try another high tech. Writer Priya Parker, who we mentioned earlier, describes how we can transform a common gathering like a birthday or dinner party into an enlightening, enriching experience based on our intention that it be meaningful and serve a purpose. Make conscious, thoughtful choices about technology so you can have an extraordinary life, a magical life—even better, a life you can look back on and feel proud of. As Hawke admonishes us, "We know this: the time of our life is so short. . . . Are we spending it doing what's important to us? Most of us not. I mean, it's hard. The pull of habit is so huge. . . . So don't read the book that you should read, read the book you want to read. Don't listen to the music that you used to like. Take some time to listen to some new music. Take some time to talk to somebody that you don't normally talk to." Just as the magnifying lens enabled Philpotts to behold the magic of the ordinary buckbean, invest in the empowering "technologies" that can bring peace, innovation, and healing. If we do this, magic does await us all.

Reflection and Practice

1. Take an inventory of the technologies in your life. Where do you spend the most time? Most smartphones have a way to analyze your behavior in the last week. Look at which apps you used and add up the time spent on the top five apps. Now multiply that by a year. How many hours does it represent?

2. How are you putting to use the technologies in your life? Could you use them in a more healthy or generous or kind way?

3. Are you using "high" technologies? How many books have you read in the last month not tied to your profession—just because you wanted to? When did you last go to a museum and let yourself wander to what inspires you?

4. Feeling lost about where to start? There are resources to help: Subscribe to Poetry Unbound, a weekly reading of amazing poems from around the world by Pádraig Ó Tuama. Look at a

few lists of "books that will change your life" and pick out a few titles that call to you. Make some time to do something new.

5. There is artistry and high technology in many things. We may consume things like cheese or bread every day like a low tech, but have you ever seen a master maker, baker, or creator at work? Go visit an artisan bread maker, cheesemaker, winemaker, boat maker, or whatever strikes your curiosity, and be prepared for magic.

Conclusion

Uncertainty, Courage, and Magic

"I remembered that the real world was wide, and that a varied field of hopes and fears, of sensations and excitements, awaited those who had the courage to go forth into its expanse, to seek real knowledge of life amidst its perils."

—Charlotte Brontë

Notice in the quote above how Brontë uses the word "real" twice: once to describe the world and once to describe knowledge. She understood that there was an artificial version of both and that we could hide in a tiny world of our own choosing, protected by artificial buffers against change, but in so doing, we would miss the real beauty of a world full of possibility.

Although reality brings challenge, discomfort, and heartache, it is the only place where innovation, solution, and evolution happen. Essayist Nassim Taleb's work has explored the world of risk, volatility, and uncertainty in an effort to demonstrate that, like weightlifting, in which tearing muscles ultimately builds them, *sometimes* these challenges actually make things stronger and better. Taleb's empowering idea—that we can strive to be more "anti-fragile"—definitely shaped our thoughts about the upside of uncertainty. But his survival-of-the-fittest, stay-in-the-ring-the-longest, resilience-oriented view doesn't thrill us like the notion of transilience does.

Transilience is something *beyond* resilience. Resilience is being able to withstand shocks and recover. But transilience is about transformation, leaping from one state to another. It is the moment when hardened steel turns to molten metal, ordinary stone becomes smooth sculpture, and terrifying uncertainty becomes insight, wisdom, and opportunity. The framework we have shared with you is meant to encourage you to meet every uncertainty with hope, creativity, and a belief in an upside you may not yet see.

The upside of uncertainty is just as real as the downsides, but like an underdog, it just needs a fair chance to show what it can do. The upside at first can feel flimsy and tenuous: possibility? hope? transformation? Really? The downsides feel more real because they trigger fundamental warning alarms: danger, scarcity, shame, and so forth. Indeed, as venture capitalist Jerry Neumann argues, for entrepreneurs, everyone else's fear of uncertainty is a competitive advantage, the "moat" that protects them from competition while they create something new.[1] But uncertainty is much greater than just a deterrent. For all of us, regardless of career or circumstance, uncertainty is arguably the portal to every growth, change, and courageous act we will ever undertake. It attends every invitation to cultivate a more meaningful, inspired, and authentic life.

So friends, remember that uncertainty will bring peril that can't be easily swept away (illness, debt, injury, trauma) and ambiguous loss that may never find complete closure. There will be mistakes, regrets, injustices, and unfairness as we navigate it. *But* if we try to avoid uncertainty or give up too soon—or if we mistakenly decide it's safest to do nothing—the downsides of uncertainty will find us anyway. Because the truest downside to uncertainty is living a life smaller than what you are capable of.

So how do we keep leaping for possibility? We suggest four critical things to remember:

1. *Reframe uncertainty as an essential portal to opportunity* and consider *all* the possibilities you can imagine. Acknowledge self-doubt as a normal part of every hero's journey.

2. *Prime yourself and the uncertainty you face* with self-knowledge, research, balancers and supporters, and a collection of real options and potential exit strategies.

3. *Face every uncertainty based on values, cognitive flexibility, and curiosity* to reveal the essence waiting to be activated and

unlocked. Be prepared to take ten thousand shots, experiment, and use bricolage to bring it to life. Those aren't weaknesses—that's how the brightest possibilities are born.

4. *Sustain yourself and your projects with emotional hygiene, reality checks, and magic.*

Stay curious and believe in your personal story and your ability to make it happen, even as it shifts under your feet. Ask for help and continue this light-switch leap, from downside to upside, for as long as you are alive.

We share these beliefs, not just from the comfort of the interviewer's chair, but from living and applying these tools, always asking: how can we transform this uncertainty into possibility? It has not always been easy. While revising a draft of this book (our marching orders: cut it in half!), we were also neck-deep in uncertainty about how best to help one of our young adult children in the grip of severe depression. In early spring, he had confided that his Covid-related malaise had turned a corner into more debilitating feelings. While we acted quickly to find medical help and secure an official leave from art school for him, he spiraled into a psychic break while visiting our oldest child, whom he hadn't seen for eighteen months due to travel restrictions.

The harrowing journey of retrieving him in that altered and terrified manic state and bringing him back to France left us vulnerable and unprepared for things to get worse. Upon our return, his psychiatrist prescribed a battery of pills (all without our knowledge, since he is a legal adult) after which he slid into a state of excruciating numbness and despair. Riddled with a double dose of antipsychotics, a mood stabilizer, lithium, an antidepressant, and antianxiety pills, his brain was both turned off and turned on in complicated and unbearable ways. He was like a disappearing figment of himself, fading more each day, curling into the fetal position, staring at the wall. We couldn't find a local psychiatrist willing to offer a second opinion given the complexity of the prescriptions, our calls to in-patient facilities went unanswered, and a last-ditch, daylong wait in the ER ended with the physician handing Susannah a form letter announcing a yearlong wait-list. It was bleak.

We canceled our much-needed summer vacation and embarked on a very different summer: to find help for our son. That part was obvious. But managing the uncertainty would have been less obvious without the tools described here. We started by reframing the situation: we are lucky we have enough wellness ourselves to focus on this, and we have resources and a psychiatrist friend in the United States who agreed to work with us if we could get our son there. Still, the downsides of uncertainty invaded our well-being and frayed our nerves. It felt bigger than us and it made us question living abroad. We spent much of our prized "runway," carefully meted out because of our decreased earnings during the Covid-19 pandemic, on a last-minute trip back to the United States.

The family friend/psychiatrist saw our son and immediately started titrating him off the medications one by one, but due to the trailing effects of that toxic cocktail, our son actually became worse. We had to remember our story, invoke our uncertainty manifesto, do a reality check on our dwindling finances, all while keeping a constant vigil to keep him alive. Even as we rewrote this book, frantically pulling together our favorite examples and quotes, the downsides of the present uncertainty were gnawing at us. We returned to France, jetlagged and grouchy; it felt like such a waste, and we were mad at ourselves for not demanding information earlier about what medications he was on. We wanted to blame each other.

The romantic couples trip that we couldn't cancel became a "whale love" trip—a term we coined after learning about how parent whales often swim on either side of a new whale pup to protect it and make it feel safe. While we pounded on our computers to meet the deadline for this book, our son lay next to us, fully clothed in the heat of summer. Our shared hope became seeing if we could get him to smile once a day. We took him for ice cream, burgers, and nice meals and encouraged him to listen to music. He ate in silence, turned his back to the sea, and never listened to the music that has always been his constant companion.

Each day he refused to swim—until one day, without saying a word, he pulled off his T-shirt and followed Nathan down to the dock, where he jumped in. He slowly started swimming deeper and deeper. Susannah watched anxiously, and Nathan, already in the water, followed him, fearing that he meant to swim too far. But then, he touched the buoy and turned back, smiling.

The next day he swam again, this time to two buoys, and flipped through a magazine. On the third day, he ate "the best" chicken and eggplant he had ever tasted. Finally, he could taste the care of the Provençal chef who had prepared it. The picture Nathan snapped holds all of the bittersweet tenderness of this summer with our son: eyes tinged with happiness and pain, an ever-so-slight smile assuring us that he was going to be okay. He was alive. And he wanted to be.

We now call it the reframe of the century. Because a really exhausting, disastrously expensive summer, under circumstances we would have never chosen, is what we now refer to as our "triumphant" summer. Who needs a happy summer when you can be triumphant? Happy is so much easier. It's comforting, yes, but there is no "Look what we did." We are still moving. We are figuring this out. Possibilities are coming.

If it is the challenging nature of life's perils that enables the wider world with hopes and yes, fears, we can all learn to be more eager about uncertainty. All it takes is an earnest longing to find the upside. If you can do that, you will find one.

Notes

Introduction

1. Berry Liberman, "Jostein Solheim: CEO, Futurist, All 'Round Champ," October 17, 2017, in *Dumbo Feather Podcast*, produced by Beth Gibson, MP3 audio, 28:29, https://soundcloud.com/dumbo-feather/16-jostein-solheim-ceo-futurist-all-round-champ.

2. Till Alexander Leopold, Vesselina Ratcheva, Saadia Zahidi, "The Future of Jobs," World Economic Forum Report, 2016, https://www3.weforum.org/docs/WEF_Future_of _Jobs.pdf.

3. Melissa Healy, "About 110,000 Californians Have Bought a Gun since the Coronavirus Arrived, Study Says," *Los Angeles Times*, October 17, 2020.

4. Dean Essner, "Study: CEO Turnover Rate in 2018 Was the Highest in 10 Years," PRsay, 2018, https://prsay.prsa.org/2019/01/17/study-ceo-turnover-rate-in-2018-was-the -highest-in-10-years.

5. Morten Karlsen Sørby, interview by author, February 28, 2017.

6. Sam Yagan, interview by author, May 21, 2020.

7. Gemma D'Auria and Aaron De Smet, "Leadership in Crisis: Responding to the Coronavirus Outbreak and Future Challenges," March 16, 2020, https://www.mckinsey .com/business-functions/people-and-organizational-performance/our-insights/leadership-in -a-crisis-responding-to-the-coronavirus-outbreak-and-future-challenges.

8. Thomas Z. Ramsøy and Martin Skov, "How Genes Make Up Your Mind: Individual Biological Differences and Value-Based Decisions," *Journal of Economic Psychology* 31, no. 5 (2010): 818–831.

9. Martin van den Brink, interview by author, May 4, 2020.

Chapter 1

1. These elaborate systems were demonstrated by neuroscientists at the California Institute of Technology (Caltech) in an experiment where participants were given the chance to win $10 by drawing a red card from one of two decks. Deck one contained ten red and ten blue cards. It was called the "risk deck" because the probability of drawing a red card was known. The second deck had an unknown number of red and blue cards. It was called the "uncertainty deck" because the probability was unknown: the deck could be all red, all blue, or any other possible combination. When given the choice between the two decks, almost everyone chose the risk deck, because the probability of winning felt more certain. The Caltech neuroscientists found that multiple neural systems ring alarm bells in our heads when we confront the unknown. When facing risk, the loss-averse, calculating part of our brain kicks in, but when we face uncertainty, we feel a flash of instinctual fear in another part of the brain. Because we have these dual warning systems, many people make the mistake of trying to avoid uncertainty entirely.

2. Mark A. Griffin and Gudela Grote, "When Is More Uncertainty Better? A Model of Uncertainty Regulation and Effectiveness," *Academy of Management Review* 45, no. 4

(2020): 745–765; Vaughn Tan, *The Uncertainty Mindset: Innovation Insights from the Frontiers of Food* (New York: Columbia University Press, 2020).

3. Amos Tversky and Daniel Kahneman, "The Framing of Decisions and the Psychology of Choice," *Science* 211, no. 4481 (1981): 453–458.

4. Simon Schindler and Stefan Pfattheicher, "The Frame of the Game: Loss-Framing Increases Dishonest Behavior," *Journal of Experimental Social Psychology* 69 (2017): 172–177.

5. Ellen C. Garbarino and Julie A. Edell, "Cognitive Effort, Affect, and Choice," *Journal of Consumer Research* 24, no. 2 (1997): 147–158.

6. Schindler and Pfattheicher, "The Frame of the Game."

7. Byron Katie, "The Work of Byron Katie," https://thework.com/instruction -the-work-byron-katie.

8. David Whyte, *The Three Marriages: Reimagining Work, Self, and Relationship* (New York: Penguin, 2009).

Chapter 2

1. Interview by author, March 11, 2020.

2. Anne Fisher, "This Is the Top Reason People Quit Their Jobs—It's Not Money," *Fortune*, September 27, 2018.

3. Esther Perel, *Mating in Captivity: Unlocking Erotic Intelligence* (New York: Harper, 2007).

4. Mary J. Benner and Michael L. Tushman, "Exploitation, Exploration, and Process Management: The Productivity Dilemma Revisited," *Academy of Management Review* 28, no. 2 (2003): 238–256.

5. Chris Sullivan, "Grenson Shoes," *The Chap*, issue 108 (2021): 60–65.

6. Vaughn Tan, *The Uncertainty Mindset: Innovation Insights from the Frontiers of Food* (New York: Columbia University Press, 2020).

7. Hamilton Mann, interview by author, September 15, 2021.

8. Jamie Rosen, interview by author, April 6, 2021.

9. Kelly Schmutte and Seamus Yu Harte, "How Do We Push the Boundaries of the Learning Zone without Dipping in the Panic Zone?" Learning Zone Reflection Tool, May 2019, https://dlibrary.stanford.edu/ambiguity/learning-zone-reflection-tool.

10. Srini Pillay, "Living Life Fully: The Possibility Quotient (PQ)," *Psychology Today*, February 20, 2011, https://www.psychologytoday.com/us/blog/debunking-myths-the -mind/201102/living-life-fully-the-possibility-quotient-pq.

Chapter 3

1. Denis O'Brien, interview by author, October 9, 2019.

2. Benjamin Gilmour, interview by author, February 20, 2020.

3. Brad Aaron Modlin, interview by author, September 20, 2019.

Chapter 4

1. Steven Johnson, "The Genius of the Tinkerer," *Wall Street Journal*, September 25, 2010, https://www.wsj.com/articles/SB10001424052748703989304575503730101860838.

2. John Brockman, "The Adjacent Possible: A Talk with Stuart A. Kauffman," Edge. org, November 9, 2003, https://www.edge.org/conversation/stuart_a_kauffman -the-adjacent-possible.

3. "Lord Lister, 'Father of Antiseptic Surgery,'" King's College, London, March 16, 2017, https://www.kcl.ac.uk/lord-lister-father-of-antiseptic-surgery-2; Pierpaolo Andriani and Gino Cattani, "Exaptation as Source of Creativity, Innovation, and Diversity: Introduction to the Special Section," *Industrial and Corporate Change* 25, no. 1 (2016): 115–131.

4. Alinker Inventions Ltd., "The Alinker IndieGoGo Campaign April 2016," April 22, 2016, YouTube video, 3:27, https://youtu.be/zy5xyLw7P88.

5. Alinker Inventions Ltd., "Alinker—In Depth," August 2, 2018, YouTube video, 3:34, https://www.youtube.com/watch?v=qhPChBdvNTk.

6. Vicki Saunders, "It's Possible to Make Money and Do Good," Do Lectures, August 15, 2018, video, 19:40, https://vimeo.com/285060016.

7. Vicki Saunders, "How It Works: With SheEO Founder Vicki Saunders," SheEO, November 11, 2017, YouTube video, 5:35, https://youtu.be/_W7uU9Ch9xQ.

8. Adrian Gardère, interview by author, February 2015.

9. Steve Blank, interview by author, March 2009.

10. Martin Erlic, "What Is the Adjacent Possible?" Medium, November 26, 2016, https://medium.com/@SeloSlav/what-is-the-adjacent-possible-17680e4d1198.

11. Buckminster Fuller, *Guinea Pig B: The 56 Year Experiment* (Clayton, CA: Critical Path Publishing, 2004).

12. L. Steven Sieden, *A Fuller View: Buckminster Fuller's Vision of Hope and Abundance for All* (Studio City, CA: Divine Arts, 2012).

Chapter 5

1. James Carse, *Finite and Infinite Games: A Vision of Life as Play and Possibility* (New York: Free Press, 2013).

2. Joan Gould, *Spinning Straw into Gold: What Fairy Tales Reveal about the Transformations in a Woman's Life* (New York: Random House, 2006), 278.

3. "Mrs. Roosevelt, First Lady 12 Years, Often Called 'World's Most Admired Woman,'" *The New York Times*, November 8, 1962.

4. "Mrs. Roosevelt," *The New York Times*.

5. Sterling Anderson, interview by author, 2014.

6. Elon Musk, interview by author, 2014.

7. Elon Musk, "The First Principles Method Explained by Elon Musk," Innomind, December 4, 2013, YouTube video, 2:48, https://www.youtube.com/watch?v=NV3sBlRgzTI.

8. Matthew Herper, "How Two Guys from Queens Are Changing Drug Discovery," *Forbes*, September 2, 2013, http://www.forbes.com/sites/matthewherper/2013/08/14/how-two-guys-from-queens-are-changing-drug-discovery/.

9. George Yancopoulos, interview by author.

10. Nathan Furr, Kate O'Keeffe, and Jeffrey H. Dyer, "Managing Multiparty Innovation," *Harvard Business Review*, November 2016, 76–83.

11. Kate O'Keeffe, interview by author, 2015.

12. Zach Klein, "Build the Company That You Wouldn't Sell," Do Lectures, September 30, 2013, YouTube video, 16:41, https://www.youtube.com/watch?v=3_GBmRENbEs&ab_channel=DOLectures.

13. Yvon Chouinard, *Let My People Go Surfing: The Education of a Reluctant Businessman* (New York: Penguin, 2016).

14. Santa Clara Valley Historical Association, "An Interview with Steve Jobs," October 6, 2011, 1:39, https://www.youtube.com/watch?v=kYfNvmF0Bqw.

15. Christer Windeløv-Lidzélius, interview by author, April 2020.

16. David Hornik, interview by author, January 2020.

17. Kathryn Dill, "This Is Why Class Valedictorians Don't Become Millionaires," CNBC, May 25, 2017, https://www.cnbc.com/2017/05/24/what-happened-to-your-class-valedictorian-probably-not-much.html.

18. Saj-nicole Joni, interview by author, November 2017.

19. *In Search of Greatness*, directed by Gabe Polsky, IMG Films, 2018.

Chapter 6

1. Thomas More, *Utopia*, supplement by Ursula K. Le Guin (New York: Verso, 2016).

2. David Hieatt, interview by author, July 11, 2019.

3. David Hieatt, "Local Heroes #8 Hiut Denim," Sol Beer, August 10, 2015, YouTube video, 2:04, https://www.youtube.com/watch?v=a4Qk2U0gigk&ab_channel=SolBeer.

4. David Hieatt, "Local Heroes #8."

5. Tali Sharot, *The Influential Mind: What the Brain Reveals about Our Power to Change Others* (New York: Henry Holt and Company, 2017).

6. Søren Kierkegaard, *Søren Kierkegaard's Journals and Papers*, vol. 6, 1848–1855 (Bloomington, IN: Indiana University Press, 1978), 440.

7. Søren Kierkegaard, *Either/Or: A Fragment of Life* (Penguin UK, 2004).

8. Esha Chhabra, "How This Nebraskan Entrepreneur Built 'the Bay,' a Startup That Helps Youth across the United States," *Forbes*, August 31, 2017, https://www.forbes.com/sites/eshachhabra/2017/08/31/how-this-nebraskan-entrepreneur-built-a-career-out-of-helping-youth-across-the-united-states.

9. Melinda Thomas, "The Courage to Begin," Stanford eCorner, January 29, 2020, video, 41:39, https://ecorner.stanford.edu/videos/the-courage-to-begin.

10. Elizabeth Gilbert, "What to Do If You *Can't* Find Your Passion," *O, the Oprah Magazine*, November 2010.

11. Gilbert, "What to Do."

12. Stafford Cliff, *Home: What Our Homes Really Mean to Us* (New York: Artisan, 2006), 34–36.

13. Benjamin Gilmour, interview by author, February 20, 2020.

Chapter 7

1. Jeff Bezos, interview by author, April 2010.

2. Ibid.

3. Daniel Kahneman, *Thinking, Fast and Slow* (New York: Macmillan, 2013).

4. Daniel Kahneman and Amos Tversky, "Prospect Theory: An Analysis of Decision under Risk," in *Handbook of the Fundamentals of Financial Decision Making*, Part I, eds. Leonard C. MacLean and William T. Ziemba (University of British Columbia, 2013), 99–127.

5. John S. Hammond, Ralph L. Keeney, and Howard Raiffa, *Smart Choices: A Practical Guide to Making Better Decisions* (Boston: Harvard Business Review Press, 2015).

Chapter 8

1. Richard P. Feynman, *"Surely You're Joking, Mr. Feynman!": Adventures of a Curious Character* (W. W. Norton & Company, 2018).

2. John Steinbeck, *Working Days: The Journals of the Grapes of Wrath*, ed. Robert DeMott (New York: Penguin, 1990).

3. Ibid.

4. Ibid.

5. Adam Grant, "The Surprising Habits of Original Thinkers," filmed February 2016, TED video, 15:15, https://www.ted.com/talks/adam_grant_the_surprising_habits_of _original_thinkers.

Chapter 9

1. John Winsor, "John Winsor Explains How to Ride the Avalanche of Disruption," HBS Online, March 13, 2017, YouTube video, 2:17, https://www.youtube.com /watch?v=U_U3rY5GdNA&ab_channel=HBSOnline.

2. Ibid.

3. Ibid.

4. David Heinemeier Hansson, interview by author, October 26, 2020.

5. Irvin D. Yalom, *Love's Executioner: And Other Tales of Psychotherapy* (London: Hachette UK, 2012).

Chapter 10

1. Tina Seelig, interview by author, March 2009.

2. Robert Sutton, interview by author, February 2005.

3. Melinda Thomas, "The Courage to Begin," Stanford eCorner, January 29, 2020, video, 41:39, https://ecorner.stanford.edu/videos/the-courage-to-begin.

4. Tina Seelig, "The Little Risks You Can Take to Increase Your Luck," filmed June 2018, TED Salon video, 11:30, https://www.ted.com/talks/tina_seelig_the_little_risks _you_can_take_to_increase_your_luck.

5. Piet Coelewij, interview by author, December 2, 2021.

Chapter 11

1. Ben Feringa, interview by author, October 18, 2016.

2. George Crawford and Bidyut Sen, *Derivatives for Decision Makers: Strategic Management Issues* (New York: John Wiley & Sons, 1996); Nassim Nicholas Taleb, *Antifragile: How to Live in a World We Don't Understand* (London: Allen Lane, 2012).

3. Ricardo dos Santos, interview by author, March 2013.

4. Ricardo dos Santos, interview by author, September 2021.

5. Timothy B. Folta, Frédéric Delmar, and Karl Wennberg, "Hybrid Entrepreneurship," *Management Science* 56, no. 2 (2010): 253–269; Joseph Raffiee and Jie Feng, "Should I Quit My Day Job?: A Hybrid Path to Entrepreneurship," *Academy of Management Journal* 57, no. 4 (2014): 936–963.

6. LaToya M. Smith, "What Is Hybrid Entrepreneurship? (And Why You Should Consider It)," *Black Enterprise*, May 2, 2011, https://www.blackenterprise.com/what-is-hybrid -entrepreneurship-and-why-you-should-consider-it.

7. Nathan R. Furr and Daniel C. Snow, "Intergenerational Hybrids: Spillbacks, Spillforwards, and Adapting to Technology Discontinuities," *Organization Science* 26, no. 2 (2015): 475–493.

8. Barry M. Staw, "Knee-deep in the Big Muddy: A Study of Escalating Commitment to a Chosen Course of Action," *Organizational Behavior and Human Performance* 16, no. 1 (1976): 27–44.

9. Barry M. Staw and Ha Hoang, "Sunk Costs in the NBA: Why Draft Order Affects Playing Time and Survival in Professional Basketball," *Administrative Science Quarterly* 40, no. 3 (1995): 474–494. "Poor performers" was operationalized as a control for on-court performance, injuries, trade status, and position played; from George W. Ball, "A Compromise Solution in South Vietnam," in Neil Sheehan et al., comp., *The Pentagon Papers* (Boston: Beacon Press, 1971), 2:615–617.

10. "Blocked," *The New Yorker*, June 14, 2004.

11. Rhys Newman, "Omata: At a Steady 18 Km," *The Side Project Report: Observation and Enquiry* (Wales: Do Lectures, 2017), 30–33.

12. David Hieatt, "Observation and Enquiry," *The Side Project Report: Observation and Enquiry* (Wales: Do Lectures, 2017), 145.

13. *The Outsiders: New Outdoor Creativity*, eds. Jeffrey Bowman, Sven Ehmann, and Robert Klanten (Berlin: Gestalten, 2014), 6.

14. Håkan Nordkvist, interview by author, April 16, 2020.

Chapter 12

1. Sam Yagan, interview by author, May 21, 2020.

2. Ibid.

3. Andrew B. Hargadon and Yellowlees Douglas, "When Innovations Meet Institutions: Edison and the Design of the Electric Light," *Administrative Science Quarterly* 46, no. 3 (2001): 476–501.

4. Lindsay Tauber, interview by author, June 23, 2016.

5. Stafford Cliff, *Home: What Our Homes Really Mean to Us* (New York: Artisan, 2006), 34.

6. Christina Ohly Evans, "Tadao Ando: 'We Need Unbreakable Passion to Survive the Unknown Future,'" *Financial Times*, May 24, 2021.

7. Bronisław Malinowski, *Argonauts of the Western Pacific: An Account of Native Enterprise and Adventure in the Archipelagoes of Melanesian New Guinea (1922/1994)* (London: Routledge, 2013).

8. Timothy J. Gallagher and Jerry M. Lewis, "Rationalists, Fatalists, and the Modern Superstitious: Test-Taking in Introductory Sociology," *Sociological Inquiry* 71, no. 1, (2001): 1–12; J. L. Bleak and Christina Frederick, "Superstitious Behavior in Sport: Levels of Effectiveness and Determinants of Use in Three Collegiate Sports," *Journal of Sport Behavior* 21 (1998): 1–15.

9. Cristine H. Legare and André L. Souza, "Searching for Control: Priming Randomness Increases the Evaluation of Ritual Efficacy," *Cognitive Science* 38, no. 1 (2014): 152–161; Markus C. Becker and Thorbjørn Knudsen, "The Role of Routines in Reducing Pervasive Uncertainty," *Journal of Business Research* 58, no. 6 (2005): 746–757.

10. Nichole Force, "Humor as a Weapon, Shield, and Psychological Salve," PsychCentral, May 17, 2016, https://psychcentral.com/lib/humor-as-weapon-shield-and -psychological-salve.

11. Ibid.

12. Benjamin Gilmour, interview by author, February 20, 2020.

13. Antonin J. Obrdlik, "'Gallows Humor'—A Sociological Phenomenon," *American Journal of Sociology* 47, no. 5 (1942): 709–716.

14. Catherine Ingram, "Facing Extinction," catherineingram.com, 2019, https://www .catherineingram.com/facingextinction.

15. Mike Rhodin, interview by author, December 1, 2016.

16. Morten Karlsen Sørby, interview by author, February 28, 2017.

17. Dallas Roberts, interview by author, December 29, 2018.

18. Cole Feix, "Churchill's Character: A Rigid Daily Schedule," The Churchill Project, February 6, 2019, https://winstonchurchill.hillsdale.edu/churchill-character-daily-schedule.

19. Zachary Palmer, "A Curious Education: Winston Churchill and the Teaching of a Statesman," the Imaginative Conservative, June 17, 2020, https://theimaginativeconservative.org/2020/06/curious-education-winston-churchill-zachary-palmer.html.

20. Feix, "Churchill's Character."

21. Barry Schwartz, *The Paradox of Choice: Why More Is Less* (New York: Ecco, 2004).

Chapter 13

1. Kate Bezar, "Dumbo Feather Conversations Presents Kate Bezar," Dumbo Feather, July 9, 2013, YouTube video, 47:55, https://www.youtube.com/watch?v=VkJYuFrCyP8&t=371s.

2. Kuroyi, interview by author, December 29, 2017.

3. Sarah Mouchot and Nico Alary, interview by author, July 10, 2020.

4. Sarah Mouchot and Nico Alary, interview by author, September 29, 2021.

5. David Whyte, *The Three Marriages: Reimagining Work, Self, and Relationship* (New York: Penguin, 2009).

6. Elizabeth Gilbert, *Big Magic: Creative Living beyond Fear* (New York: Penguin, 2016).

Chapter 14

1. Warren Packard, interview by author, September 2007.

2. Thomas Zoëga Ramsøy, interview by author, September 1, 2017.

3. Sarah Mouchot and Nico Alary, interview by author, July 10, 2020.

4. Interview by author, November 2009.

5. Cristina Mittermeier, "Enoughness," TEDxVailWomen, January 6, 2014, YouTube video, 10:15, https://www.youtube.com/watch?v=Xw8U5LxaItM&ab_channel=TEDxTalks.

6. Philip Brickman, Dan Coates, and Ronnie Janoff-Bulman, "Lottery Winners and Accident Victims: Is Happiness Relative?" *Journal of Personality and Social Psychology* 36, no. 8 (1978): 917–927.

7. Interview by author, July 2016.

8. "The Emergence of 'Enoughness,'" workshop at the Australian Strategic Planning Institute, February 14, 2007, http://www.taspi.com.au/events/6/the-emergence-of-enoughness.

9. Kyle Nel, interview by author, March 2017.

10. Nathan Furr, Kyle Nel, and Thomas Zoëga Ramsøy, *Leading Transformation: How to Take Charge of Your Company's Future* (Boston: Harvard Business Review Press, 2018).

11. Jeffrey H. Dyer, Hal B. Gregersen, and Clayton Christensen, "Entrepreneur Behaviors, Opportunity Recognition, and the Origins of Innovative Ventures," *Strategic Entrepreneurship Journal* 2, no. 4 (2008): 317–338.

Chapter 15

1. "Dark Energy, Dark Matter," NASA Science, https://science.nasa.gov/astrophysics/focus-areas/what-is-dark-energy.

2. Rob Adams, interview by author, February 8, 2020.

3. Adrienne LaFrance, "When You Give a Tree an Email Address," Positive News, September 2015, https://www.positivenewsus.org/when-you-give-a-tree-an-email-address.html.

4. Adams, interview.

5. James M. Utterback, *Mastering the Dynamics of Innovation*, 2nd ed. (Boston: Harvard Business Review Press, 1996).

6. Kyle Nel, interview by author, March 2017.

7. Marissa Mayer, "Creativity Loves Constraint," Stanford eCorner, May 17, 2006, video, 1:41, https://ecorner.stanford.edu/videos/creativity-loves-constraint.

8. Matthew E. May, "How Intelligent Constraints Drive Creativity," hbr.org, January 30, 2013, https://hbr.org/2013/01/how-intelligent-constraints-dr.

9. David Heinemeier Hansson, "Constraints Are Your Friends," Stanford eCorner, January 20, 2010, video, 1:57, https://ecorner.stanford.edu/in-brief/constraints-are-your-friends.

10. Ibid.

Chapter 16

1. Khoi Vinh, "The Sagmeister Phenomenon," subtraction.com, February 21, 2008, https://www.subtraction.com/2008/02/21/the-sagmeist.

2. Stefan Sagmeister, "The Power of Time Off," filmed July 2007, TED video, 17:24, https://www.ted.com/talks/stefan_sagmeister_the_power_of_time_off.

3. For more information on Lynne Curran and David Swift, see their Instagram page: https://www.instagram.com/stuffandnonsensestudios.

4. David Swift, email message to author, September 2020.

5. Rachel Burgess, Jason A. Colquitt, and Erin Long, "Longing for the Road Not Taken: The Affective and Behavioral Consequences of Forgone Identity Dwelling," *Academy of Management Journal* (2020).

Chapter 17

1. Siegfried Streufert and Susan C. Streufert, "Risk Taking in Military and Economic Decision Making: An Analysis via an Experimental Simulation," Office of Naval Research, technical report no. 16, November 1968, https://apps.dtic.mil/sti/pdfs/AD0678951.pdf.

2. David Hieatt, interview by author, July 11, 2019.

3. Elizabeth Gilbert, *Big Magic: Creative Living beyond Fear* (New York: Penguin, 2016).

4. Jakob Wolman, "Creative Leadership—A Course at Kaospilot," Medium, May 2, 2016, https://jakobwolman.medium.com/creative-leadership-a-course-at-kaospilot-a80f1b97c112.

5. André Leon Talley, *The Chiffon Trenches: A Memoir* (New York: Ballantine Books, 2021), 14.

6. Talley, *The Chiffon Trenches*, 15.

7. Talley, *The Chiffon Trenches*, 17.

8. Kate O'Keeffe, interview by author, November 19, 2020.

9. Rainer Maria Rilke, *Letters to a Young Poet*, trans. Charlie Louth (New York: Penguin, 2014).

10. Gilbert, *Big Magic*.

Section Three

1. John O'Donohue, *Walking in Wonder: Eternal Wisdom for a Modern World* (New York: Convergent, 2018), 22.

2. "Max Richter Recomposes 'The Four Seasons,'" NPR, November 21, 2012, https://www.npr.org/sections/deceptivecadence/2012/11/21/165659291/max-richter -recomposes-the-four-seasons.

Chapter 18

1. "Biography of Maria Montessori," Association Montessori Internationale, https:// montessori-ami.org/resource-library/facts/biography-maria-montessori.

2. Valve Corporation, "Valve Handbook for New Employees," 2012; Nathan Furr and Jeff Dyer, *The Innovator's Method: Bringing the Lean Startup into Your Organization* (Boston: Harvard Business Review Press, 2014).

3. Mary J. Benner and Michael L. Tushman, "Exploitation, Exploration, and Process Management: The Productivity Dilemma Revisited," *Academy of Management Review* 28, no. 2 (2003): 238–256.

4. Sourobh Ghosh and Andy Wu, "Iterative Coordination and Innovation," HBS Working Knowledge, June 22, 2020, https://hbswk.hbs.edu/item/iterative-coordination -and-innovation.

5. Vaughn Tan, *The Uncertainty Mindset: Innovation Insights from the Frontiers of Food* (New York: Columbia University Press, 2020).

6. Mark A. Griffin and Gudela Grote, "When Is More Uncertainty Better? A Model of Uncertainty Regulation and Effectiveness," *Academy of Management Review* 45, no. 4 (2020): 745–765; Nathan R. Furr and Kathleen M. Eisenhardt, "Strategy and Uncertainty: Resource-Based View, Strategy-Creation View, and the Hybrid between Them," *Journal of Management* 47, no. 7 (2021): 1915–1935.

7. Adrien Gardère, interview by author, October 13, 2020.

8. Ralph Hamers, interview by author, April 4, 2018.

9. David Whyte, *The Three Marriages: Reimagining Work, Self, and Relationship* (New York: Penguin, 2009).

10. Ibid.

11. Tyler Mitchell, *I Can Make You Feel Good* (Munich: Prestel, 2020).

12. Ibid.

13. Whyte, *The Three Marriages*.

14. Olivier Blum, interview by author, May 18, 2017.

15. Shefali Tsabary, *The Awakened Family: How to Raise Empowered, Resilient, and Conscious Children* (New York: Penguin, 2016), 26.

16. Pádraig Ó Tuama, *The Pause*, October 3, 2020, https://onbeing.org/newsletter.

Chapter 19

1. Robert Waldinger, "What Makes a Good Life? Lessons from the Longest Study on Happiness," filmed November 2015, TEDxBeaconStreet video, 12:38, https://www.ted .com/talks/robert_waldinger_what_makes_a_good_life_lessons_from_the_longest_study _on_happiness.

2. Steve Sivak, "Live a Better Life in Just One, Really Hard Step," Innovate Wealth, August 27, 2017, https://www.innovate-wealth.com/article/live-a-better-life-in-just-one-really-hard-step.

3. Alain de Botton, "The Materialistic World: An Ordinary Life Is No Longer Good Enough," London Real, February 19, 2020, YouTube video, 7:49, https://www.youtube.com/watch?v=wLt24P8-cCs&ab_channel=LondonReal.

4. David Heinemeier Hansson, interview by author, October 26, 2020.

5. Adam M. Grant et al., "Impact and the Art of Motivation Maintenance: The Effects of Contact with Beneficiaries on Persistence Behavior," *Organizational Behavior and Human Decision Processes* 103, no. 1 (2007): 53–67.

6. Adam M. Grant, "The Significance of Task Significance: Job Performance Effects, Relational Mechanisms, and Boundary Conditions," *Journal of Applied Psychology* 93, no. 1 (2008): 108–124.

7. David Hieatt, *Do Lectures Newsletter*, October 23, 2020, https://thedolectures.com/newsletter.

8. Naomi Shihab Nye, *Words under the Words: Selected Poems by Naomi Shihab Nye* (Portland, OR: Far Corner Books, 1995).

9. Elle Luna, *The Crossroads of Should and Must: Find and Follow Your Passion* (New York: Workman Publishing Company, 2015).

Chapter 20

1. Karl E. Weick, "The Collapse of Sensemaking in Organizations: The Mann Gulch Disaster," *Administrative Science Quarterly* 38, no. 4 (1993): 628–652.

2. Weick, "The Collapse of Sensemaking," 633.

3. Weick, "The Collapse of Sensemaking," 641.

4. Mike Cassidy, interview by author, October 2006.

5. Nathan R. Furr, Fabrice Cavarretta, and Sam Garg, "Who Changes Course? The Role of Domain Knowledge and Novel Framing in Making Technology Changes," *Strategic Entrepreneurship Journal* 6, no. 3 (2012): 236–256; Nathan R. Furr, "Cognitive Flexibility: The Adaptive Reality of Concrete Organization Change" (PhD diss., Stanford University, 2009), https://www.proquest.com/openview/ea91a4de772a302ab296a11b18b61926/1.

6. Sen Chai, "Near Misses in the Breakthrough Discovery Process," *Organization Science* 28, no. 3 (2017): 411–428.

7. Jean Lenihan, "Centralia-Born Dancemaker Merce Cunningham Dies," *The Seattle Times*, July 27, 2009.

8. Martin van den Brink, interview by author, May 4, 2020.

9. Jerry Neumann, interview by author, September 30, 2021.

10. Krista Tippett, "Derek Black and Matthew Stevenson: Befriending Radical Disagreement," May 17, 2018, in *On Being with Krista Tippett*, podcast, MP3 audio, 51:15, https://onbeing.org/programs/derek-black-and-matthew-stevenson-befriending-radical-disagreement.

Chapter 21

1. Martin van den Brink, interview by author, May 4, 2020.

2. Susan L. Cohen, Christopher B. Bingham, and Benjamin L. Hallen, "The Role of Accelerator Designs in Mitigating Bounded Rationality in New Ventures," *Administrative Science Quarterly* 64, no. 4 (2019): 810–854.

3. Debbie Sterling, "Disrupting the Pink Aisle," Stanford eCorner, April 25, 2017, video, 56:50, https://ecorner.stanford.edu/videos/disrupting-the-pink-aisle-entire-talk; Rebecca J. Rosen, "Can a Kids' Toy Bring More Women into Engineering?" *The Atlantic*, September 18, 2012, https://www.theatlantic.com/technology/archive/2012/09/can-a-kids -toy-bring-more-women-into-engineering/262373.

4. Cohen, Bingham, and Hallen, "The Role of Accelerator Designs."

5. David Hieatt, email message to author, October 15, 2020.

6. Mark W. Moffett et al., "Ant Colonies: Building Complex Organizations with Miniscule Brains and No Leaders," *Journal of Organization Design* 10 (2021): 55–74.

7. Robert A. Burgelman, "Fading Memories: A Process Theory of Strategic Business Exit in Dynamic Environments," *Administrative Science Quarterly* 39, no. 1 (1994): 24–56.

8. Piet Coelewij, interview by author, September 2019.

9. Kathleen M. Eisenhardt, Nathan R. Furr, and Christopher B. Bingham. "Microfoundations of Performance: Balancing Efficiency and Flexibility in Dynamic Environments," *Organization Science* 21, no. 6 (2010): 1263–1273; Christopher B. Bingham, Kathleen M. Eisenhardt, and Nathan R. Furr, "What Makes a Process a Capability? Heuristics, Strategy, and Effective Capture of Opportunities," *Strategic Entrepreneurship Journal* 1, no. 1–2 (2007): 27–47.

10. David Hornik, interview by author, January 25, 2020.

11. Robert P. Bremner and Kathleen M. Eisenhardt, "Organizing Form, Experimentation, and Performance: Innovation Lessons from the Nascent Civilian Drone Industry," *Organization Science*, published ahead of print, December 8, 2021.

12. Robin Chase, interview by author, June 27, 2018.

13. Gertrude Stein, *Paris France* (New York: Liveright, 2013), 65.

Chapter 22

1. Sam Yagan, interview by author, May 21, 2020.

2. Dallas Roberts, interview by author, December 29, 2018.

3. Adam Grant, "The Surprising Habits of Original Thinkers," filmed February 2016, TED video, 15:16, https://www.ted.com/talks/adam_grant_the_surprising_habits_of_ original_thinkers.

4. Ibid.

5. Elon Musk, interview by author, July 15, 2015.

6. Samuel Gibbs, "Jeff Bezos: I've Made Billions of Dollars of Failures at Amazon," *The Guardian*, December 3, 2014.

7. Christopher Klein, "10 Things You May Not Know about Dr. Seuss," history .com, March 1, 2012, https://www.history.com/news/9-things-you-may-not-know-about -dr-seuss.

8. Alp Mimaroglu, "How Jack Ma Overcame His 7 Biggest Failures," *Entrepreneur*, September 9, 2016, https://www.entrepreneur.com/article/275969.

9. Erica R. Hendry, "7 Epic Fails Brought to You by the Genius Mind of Thomas Edison," *Smithsonian*, November 20, 2013, https://www.smithsonianmag.com/innovation /7-epic-fails-brought-to-you-by-the-genius-mind-of-thomas-edison-180947786.

10. Ibid.

11. Angela Duckworth, *Grit: The Power of Passion and Perseverance* (New York: Scribner, 2016).

12. Malcolm Gladwell, *Outliers: The Story of Success* (New York: Little, Brown, 2008).

13. Guy Winch, *Emotional First Aid: Healing Rejection, Guilt, Failure, and Other Everyday Hurts* (New York: Penguin, 2013).

14. Carol S. Dweck, *Mindset: The New Psychology of Success* (New York: Random House Digital, 2008).

Chapter 23

1. Saras D. Sarasvathy, *Effectuation: Elements of Entrepreneurial Expertise* (Edward Elgar Publishing, 2009).

2. Raghu Garud and Peter Karnøe, "Bricolage versus Breakthrough: Distributed and Embedded Agency in Technology Entrepreneurship," *Research Policy* 32, no. 2 (2003): 277–300.

3. Ibid.

4. Clayton M. Christensen, *The Innovator's Dilemma: When New Technologies Cause Great Firms to Fail* (Boston: Harvard Business Review Press, 2013).

5. Ted Baker and Reed E. Nelson, "Creating Something from Nothing: Resource Construction through Entrepreneurial Bricolage," *Administrative Science Quarterly* 50, no. 3 (2005): 329–366.

6. Julienne M. Senyard, Ted Baker, and Per Davidsson, "Entrepreneurial Bricolage: towards Systematic Empirical Testing," *Frontiers of Entrepreneurship Research* 29, no. 5 (2009): 5.

7. Christian Busch and Harry Barkema, "From Necessity to Opportunity: Scaling Bricolage across Resource Constrained Environments," *Strategic Management Journal* 42, no. 4 (2021): 741–773.

8. Ibid.

9. Ibid.

10. Charlotte Cory, *Charlotte Brontë at the Soane*, pamphlet from the exhibit of the same name, Sir John Soane's Museum London, 2016.

11. Ibid.

Chapter 24

1. Alex Hern, "Pokémon Go: How the Overnight Sensation Was 20 Years in the Making," *The Guardian*, July 15, 2016.

2. Timothy E. Ott and Kathleen M. Eisenhardt, "Decision Weaving: Forming Novel, Complex Strategy in Entrepreneurial Settings," *Strategic Management Journal* 41, no. 12 (2020): 2275–2314. The section describing Zaarly, Paintzen, and Traveling Spoon draws heavily on the research study by Ott and Eisenhardt, including much of the quotes and chronology, though it is supplemented by additional secondary research. But full credit for the quotes and findings should be given to these authors.

3. Ibid.

4. "Founders," travelingspoon.com, https://www.travelingspoon.com/founders.

5. Ibid.

6. Ibid.

7. Ken Moore, interview by author, July 9, 2020.

8. Kurt Workman, interview by author, September 2, 2020.

9. Timothy Ferriss, "Aim for the Impossible," Do Lectures, June 24, 2012, video, 26:52, https://vimeo.com/2396001.

10. Andrew Gelman, "'Any Old Map Will Do' Meets 'God Is in Every Leaf of Every Tree,'" Statistical Modeling, Causal Inference, and Social Science, April 23, 2012, http://andrewgelman.com/2012/04/23/any-old-map-will-do-meets-god-is-in-every-leaf-of-every-tree.

11. Charles Gorintin, interview by author, December 15, 2021.

12. Scott Adams, *How to Fail at Almost Everything and Still Win Big: Kind of the Story of My Life* (New York: Penguin, 2013).

13. Brad Aaron Modlin, interview by author, September 26, 2019.

14. Jessica Abel, "Interview," *The Side Project Report* (Wales: Do Lectures, 2017), 53.

15. Annemarie O'Sullivan, interview by author, July 9, 2019.

16. Matt Zoller Seitz, *The Wes Anderson Collection* (New York: Abrams, 2013), 58.

17. Wes Anderson, *Spitzmaus Mummy in a Coffin and Other Treasures*, Kunsthistorisches Museum, Vienna, 2018.

18. Nathan Furr and Jeff Dyer, *The Innovator's Method: Bringing the Lean Startup into Your Organization* (Boston: Harvard Business Review Press, 2014).

Chapter 25

1. Jessica Livingston, *Founders at Work* (New York: Apress, 2008).

2. Peter Thiel, interview by author, March 16, 2004.

3. Alexander Jarvis, "Startup Pivots: Nokia and PayPal," alexanderjarvis.com, https://www.alexanderjarvis.com/before-they-were-famous-15-startup-pivot-to-fame-3-nokia-and-paypal.

4. Gajus Worthington, interview by author, March 7, 2006.

5. Eric Ries, "Eric Ries Explains the Pivot," Interloper Films, October 19, 2012, YouTube video, 3:35, https://www.youtube.com/watch?v=1hTI4z2ijc4.

6. Christophe Vasseur, *Le Pain: De la Terre a la Table* (France, Manufacture d'Histoire Deux Ponts, 2016); Christophe Vassuer, interview by author, May 21, 2021.

7. Krista Tippett, "What the Berlin Wall and 'The Handmaid's Tale' Taught Me about Time," *On Being*, November 8, 2019, https://onbeing.org/blog/what-the-berlin-wall-and-the-handmaids-tale-taught-me-about-time.

Section Four

1. Alexandre Thumerelle and Marie Thumerelle, *Life in Paris: The First 171 Publications of Ofr, 1996–2021* (Paris: Ofr, 2021), 3.

Chapter 26

1. As quoted in Ari Wallach, "Why We Need to Be More Emotional to Save the World," BBC Future, March 2, 2020, https://www.bbc.com/future/article/20200228-how-our-emotions-could-help-save-the-world.

2. Kevin Randall, "Inner Peace? The Dalai Lama Made a Website for That," *New York Times*, May 6, 2016; Atlas of Emotions, http://atlasofemotions.org.

3. Guy Winch, "Why We All Need to Practice Emotional First Aid," filmed November 2014, TEDx Linnaeus University video, 17:15, https://www.ted.com/talks/guy_winch_why_we_all_need_to_practice_emotional_first_aid.

4. Ibid.

5. Petronellah Lunda, Catharina Susanna Minnie, and Petronella Benadé, "Women's Experiences of Continuous Support during Childbirth: A Meta-Synthesis," *BMC Pregnancy and Childbirth* 18, no. 167 (2018).

6. David Heinemeier Hansson, interview by author, October 26, 2020.

7. Luca Belpietro, interview by author, December 27, 2018.

8. "Luca Belpietro," Earth Changers, https://www.earth-changers.com/sustainable-development/luca-belpietro-kenya-cyk-mwct.

9. Elisabeth Kübler-Ross and David Kessler, *On Grief and Grieving: Finding the Meaning of Grief through the Five Stages of Loss* (New York: Simon and Schuster, 2005).

10. Martha Beck, "The Gathering Room: Getting through the Damn Day," March 22, 2020, Facebook video, 29:32, https://www.facebook.com/themarthabeck/videos/213044560009364.

11. Martha Beck, "Growing Wings: The Power of Change," marthabeck.com, January 2003, https://marthabeck.com/2003/01/growing-wings-the-power-of-change.

12. Kate O'Keeffe, interview by author, November 19, 2020.

13. Krista Tippett, "On Hope," *Orion*, March 2, 2020, https://orionmagazine.org/article/on-hope.

14. Jos Skeates and Alison Skeates, interview by author, April 2019.

15. Wisdom app, On Being, https://onbeing.org/wisdom.

16. Dallas Roberts, interview by author, December 29, 2018.

17. Christer Windeløv-Lidzélius, interview by author, April 14, 2020.

18. Constantijn Van Oranje, interview by author, January 25, 2021.

19. Damian Le Bas writes about his journey to visit these hallowed places remembered by his family in his memoir, *The Stopping Places: A Journey through Gypsy Britain*. An Oxford University–trained Romany writer, Le Bas wrestles with belonging and notions of home.

20. Stafford Cliff, *Home: What Our Homes Really Mean to Us* (New York: Artisan, 2008), 38.

21. Ibid.

22. Mary Frances Kennedy Fisher, *The Gastronomical Me* (New York: Macmillan, 1989).

23. Krista Tippett, "Christine Runyan: What's Happening in Our Nervous Systems?" March 18, 2021, in *On Being with Krista Tippett*, podcast, MP3 audio, 50:47, https://onbeing.org/programs/christine-runyan-whats-happening-in-our-nervous-systems.

Chapter 27

1. Amy Blankson, *The Future of Happiness: 5 Modern Strategies for Balancing Productivity and Well-Being in the Digital Era* (Dallas: BenBella Books, 2017); Amy Blankson, "4 Ways to Embrace Fearless Positivity in the Midst of Uncertainty," *Forbes*, Mar 19, 2020, https://www.forbes.com/sites/amyblankson/2020/03/19/4-ways-to-embrace-fearless-positivity-in-the-midst-of-uncertainty/?sh=542ef6b33535.

2. Ibid.

3. Ming Hsu et al., "Neural Systems Responding to Degrees of Uncertainty in Human Decision-Making," *Science* 310, no. 5754 (2005): 1680–1683; Peter P. Wakker, *Prospect Theory: For Risk and Ambiguity* (Cambridge University Press, 2010); Katrin Starcke and Matthias Brand, "Decision Making under Stress: A Selective Review," *Neuroscience and Biobehavioral Reviews* 36, no. 4 (2012): 1228–1248.

4. David Heinemeier Hansson, interview by author, October 26, 2020.

5. Zadie Smith, interview with author, March 17, 2021.

6. Martin E. P. Seligman, *Learned Optimism: How to Change Your Mind and Your Life* (New York: Vintage, 2006).

7. Martin E. P. Seligman, "Learned Helplessness," *Annual Review of Medicine* 23 (1972): 407–412.

8. Seligman, *Learned Optimism.*

9. Gregory McClellan Buchanan, Cara A. Rubenstein Gardenswartz, and Martin E. P. Seligman, "Physical Health Following a Cognitive–Behavioral Intervention," *Prevention & Treatment* 2, no. 1 (1999); Gregory McClell Buchanan, Martin E. P. Seligman, and Martin Seligman, eds., *Explanatory Style* (London: Routledge, 2013); Mark Ylvisaker and Timothy Feeney, "Executive Functions, Self-Regulation, and Learned Optimism in Paediatric Rehabilitation: A Review and Implications for Intervention," *Pediatric Rehabilitation* 5, no. 2 (2002): 51–70; Wikipedia, s.v. "Learned Optimism," accessed March 10, 2021, https://en.wikipedia.org/wiki/Learned_optimism.

10. Seligman, *Learned Optimism.*

11. Ben Feringa, interview by author, October 18, 2016.

12. This section is adapted from Nathan Furr, "You're Not Powerless in the Face of Uncertainty," hbr.org, March 27, 2020, https://hbr.org/2020/03/youre-not-powerless-in-the-face-of-uncertainty.

13. Peter Fenton, interview by author, April 2007.

14. Elon Musk, interview by author, July 15, 2015.

15. Notably, this specific example is drawn from *The Stoic Challenge*, by William B. Irvine, with which many of these frames have some overlap, even though they were developed independently. However, in no way do we want to diminish the originality of the work done in *The Stoic Challenge.*

16. David Heinemeier Hansson, interview by author, October 26, 2020.

17. Ibid.

18. Birgitta de Vos, interview by author, March 21, 2019.

19. Håkan Nordkvist, interview by author, 16 April 2020.

20. Benjamin Gilmour, interview by author, February 20, 2020.

21. Oprah Winfrey, "Oprah's Gratitude Journal," Oprah's Lifeclass, April 30, 2012, video, 3:38, https://www.oprah.com/oprahs-lifeclass/oprah-on-the-importance-of-her-gratitude-journal-video.

22. David Hornik, interview by author, January 25, 2020.

23. Malcolm Gladwell, "Why You Shouldn't Go to Harvard," Google Zeitgeist, October 20, 2019, https://www.youtube.com/watch?v=7J-wCHDJYmo.

24. Brian Blum, "Blunder of Binary Thinking: How Can Humans Be Both Happy and Despondent?" *The Jerusalem Post*, July 3, 2020, https://www.jpost.com/health-science/the-blunder-of-binary-thinking-how-can-humans-be-happy-and-despondent-633557.

25. Elon Musk, interview by author, July 15, 2015.

26. Richard Dawkins, ed. *The Oxford Book of Modern Science Writing* (Oxford: Oxford University Press, 2009), 225.

27. Blum, "Blunder of Binary Thinking."

28. "Great Sporting Moments: Jacques Anquetil v Raymond Poulidor, Tour de France, Stage 22, Brive to Puy de Dôme, 10 July, 1964," Independent, July 16, 2009, https://www.independent.co.uk/sport/general/others/great-sporting-moments-jacques-anquetil-v-raymond-poulidor-tour-de-france-stage-22-brive-puy-de-d-ocirc-me-10-july-1964-1746647.html

29. Ibid.

30. Richard Allchin, *Golden Stages of the Tour de France* (Norwich, UK: Mousehold Press, 2003).

31. Ibid.

32. Wikipedia, s.v. "Raymond Poulidor," last modified November 13, 2021, https://en .wikipedia.org/wiki/Raymond_Poulidor.

33. Ibid.

34. Glenn Zorpette, "Blue Chip," *Scientific American*, July 5, 2000, https://www .scientificamerican.com/article/blue-chip-2000-07-05.

35. "Shuji Nakamura—Facts," nobelprize.org, https://www.nobelprize.org/prizes /physics/2014/nakamura/facts.

36. Hanif Abdurraqib, "Harvest Together (feat. Aaron Dessner)," October 1, 2021, in *Object of Sound*, podcast, MP3, audio, 22:07, https://object-of-sound.simplecast.com /episodes/harvest-together-feat-aaron-dessner.

37. David A. Clark, "Cognitive Restructuring," in *The Wiley Handbook of Cognitive Behavioral Therapy*, ed. Stefan. G. Hofmann (John Wiley & Sons, 2013); Melina M. Ovanessian et al., "A Preliminary Test of the Therapeutic Potential of Written Exposure with Rescripting for Generalized Anxiety Disorder," *Journal of Experimental Psychopathology* (April 2019); Chelsea Moran et al., "An Exploratory Study of the Worst-Case Scenario Exercise as an Exposure Treatment for Fear of Cancer Recurrence," *Supportive Care in Cancer* 25, no. 5 (2017): 1373–1375.

38. Kate Kellaway, "'You Will Not Have My Hate': Antoine Leiris on Losing His Wife in the Paris Attacks,'" *The Guardian*, October 16, 2016, https://www.theguardian.com /books/2016/oct/16/antoine-leiris-you-will-not-have-my-hate-interview-paris-attacks-helene -bataclan.

39. Florian Zeller, "The Exquisite Nonchalance of Isabelle Huppert," *Financial Times*, September 22, 2021, https://www.ft.com/content/3fa000ce-918e-4b1a-8bf1-d90ef6ed580c.

40. Randy Komisar, "Randy Komisar: The Biggest Successes Are Often Bred from Failures," Stanford, August 13, 2008, YouTube video, 8:27, https://www.youtube.com /watch?v=0RP1sS8rMsQ.

41. Ibid

42. Randy Komisar, "Lessons Learned from Failures," CosmoLearning, December 31, 2009, video, https://cosmolearning.org/video-lectures/lessons-learned-from-failures-7638.

43. Ibid.

44. Komisar, "Randy Komisar: The Biggest Successes Are Often Bred from Failures."

45. David Hieatt, interview by author, July 11, 2019.

46. Ekaterina Walter, "30 Powerful Quotes on Failure," *Forbes*, December 30, 2013, https://www.forbes.com/sites/ekaterinawalter/2013/12/30/30-powerful-quotes-on -failure/?sh=37b595a024bd.

Chapter 28

1. Tina Seelig, "How to Catch the Winds of Luck," Stanford eCorner, July 27, 2018, https://ecorner.stanford.edu/articles/catch-winds-luck.

2. Christian Busch, *The Serendipity Mindset: The Art and Science of Creating Good Luck* (New York: Riverhead Books, 2020).

3. Carlo Rovelli, *Reality Is Not What It Seems* (New York: Riverhead, 2017).

4. Eden Phillpotts, *A Shadow Passes* (London: Forgotten Books, 2012).

5. Patrick Deedes and Isabelle Townsend, interview by author, September 8, 2019.

6. "What Voltaire Meant by 'One Must Cultivate One's Own Garden,'" The School of Life, https://www.theschooloflife.com/thebookoflife/cultivate-own-garden-voltaire.

7. Christopher Hitchens, *Letters to a Young Contrarian* (New York: Basic Books, 2009).

8. Ibid.

9. Hans Vaihinger, *The Philosophy of "As If"* (Routledge, 2021).

10. Ellen J. Langer, *Counterclockwise: Mindful Health and the Power of Possibility* (New York: Ballantine Books, 2009).

11. Pinar Ozcan and Kathleen M. Eisenhardt, "Origin of Alliance Portfolios: Entrepreneurs, Network Strategies, and Firm Performance," *The Academy of Management Journal* 52, no. 2 (2009): 246–279.

12. Nely Galán, *Self Made: Becoming Empowered, Self-Reliant, and Rich in Every Way* (Spiegel & Grau, 2016).

13. Hitchens, *Letters*.

14. Quote Investigator, "Be the Change You Wish to See in the World," n.d., https://quoteinvestigator.com/2017/10/23/be-change/.

15. Hitchens, *Letters*.

16. AnnaLee Saxenian, "The Origins and Dynamics of Production Networks in Silicon Valley," *Research Policy* 20, no. 5 (1991): 423–437.

17. M. Diane Burton and Katherine Lawrence, "Jerry Sanders," Case 9-498-021 (Boston: Harvard Business School, 1998).

18. Ricardo dos Santos, interview by author, September 2021.

19. Heather LeFevre, "Heather LeFevre: Applying Strategies to Life," Do Lectures, July 12, 2017, video, 18:47, https://www.youtube.com/watch?v=GD3Gp7CHJ0Y.

20. Interview by author, October 2017.

21. Benjamin Gilmour, email message to author, 2020.

22. Jamil Zaki, "Catastrophe Compassion: Understanding and Extending Prosociality under Crisis," PsyArXiv, May 12, 2020, doi:10.31234/osf.io/ubdz7.

23. Sigal Samuel, "How to Help People during the Pandemic, One Google Spreadsheet at a Time," Vox, updated April 16, 2020, https://www.vox.com/future-perfect/2020/3/24/21188779/mutual-aid-coronavirus-covid-19-volunteering.

24. Krista Tippett, "Vivek Murthy and Richard Davidson: The Future of Well-Being," December 2, 2021, in *On Being with Krista Tippett*, podcast, MP3, audio, 75:53, https://onbeing.org/programs/vivek-murthy-and-richard-davidson-the-future-of-well-being/#transcript.

25. Thich Nhat Hanh, *The Art of Living* (New York: Random House, 2017).

26. Marcus Aurelius, *Marcus Aurelius: Meditations, Books 1–6* (Oxford University Press, 2013).

27. Jonathan Herson, interview by author, September 30, 2021.

28. Alua Arthur, interview by Kyla Marshell, *Kinfolk*, no. 38 (December 2020).

29. Amy Morin, "7 Scientifically Proven Benefits of Gratitude," *Psychology Today*, April 3, 2015, https://www.psychologytoday.com/us/blog/what-mentally-strong-people-dont-do/201504/7-scientifically-proven-benefits-gratitude.

30. Deyan G., "How Much Time Does the Average American Spend on Their Phone in 2021?" *TechJury*, updated December 7, 2021, https://techjury.net/blog/how-much-time-does-the-average-american-spend-on-their-phone.

31. Annie Dillard, *The Writing Life* (Harper Perennial, 2013).

32. W. Brian Arthur, *The Nature of Technology: What It Is and How It Evolves* (New York: Simon and Schuster, 2009).

33. David Hornik, interview by author, January 2020.

34. Andrew Trendell, "Frightened Rabbit Fight Back at Trolls with Brilliant T-shirt," Gigwise, July 28, 2015, https://www.gigwise.com/news/101899/frightened-rabbit-hit-back-at-trolls-with-furry-brick-built-men-tshirt.

35. "Concern for Missing Frightened Rabbit Singer," BBC, May 9, 2018, https://www
.bbc.com/news/uk-scotland-44055054.

36. David Hieatt, Do Lectures newsletter, October 15, 2020.

37. Anne Pasternak, "The Transformative Role of Art during the Pandemic," recorded
June 2020, TED2020 video, 21:09, https://www.ted.com/talks/anne_pasternak_the
_transformative_role_of_art_during_the_pandemic.

38. Ethan Hawke, "Give Yourself Permission to Be Creative," recorded June 2020,
TED2020 video, 9:07, https://www.ted.com/talks/ethan_hawke_give_yourself_permission
_to_be_creative.

Conclusion

1. Jerry Neumann, "Productive Uncertainty," *Reaction Wheel* (blog), November 23,
2020, https://reactionwheel.net/2020/11/productive-uncertainty.html.

Index

About the Authors

As best friends for more than thirty years, **Nathan Furr** and **Susannah Harmon Furr** have shared a journey filled with many uncertainties. Sometimes chosen and other times not, these uncertainties have often been disorientating and filled with trepidation. Whether parenting four young kids while Nathan earned his PhD at Stanford and Susannah started a clothing line from their on-campus student housing, navigating expat life in France while simultaneously undergoing an existential faith crisis, or dealing with the stress of buying an apartment at the start of the pandemic when the majority of Nathan's work suddenly disappeared, the Furrs have learned that the uncertainty implicit in each challenge has an upside. It is always a portal to possibility. Their goal is to encourage individuals to avoid backing away from uncertainty and instead to meet it boldly, with curiosity and a belief that they can navigate it well. Nathan is a professor at INSEAD, where he studies innovation and technology. He is the author of four books on innovation: *Innovation Capital*; *Leading Transformation*; *The Innovator's Method*; and *Nail It Then Scale It*. Susannah is an entrepreneur and designer currently creating a "hope accelerator" in Normandy, France.